# Out of the Darkness
# Into the Light

A Memoir: Of Suicide Survival,

Strength and Love

By Kerri Gardner

June 18, 2017

Nana,
Thankyou for
being such a
lovely friend
and neighbor!
Will miss you!

Love, Trevor, Kerri
Britain, Sky
& Luke
xxoo

Printed in the United States of America, 2015
Editing and Marketing: Susie Bencen - www.bestbookbuzz.com
Cover & Book design: Jennifer FitzGerald - www.MotherSpider.com
Photographer for Cover: Gray O'Neal – www.imagerybygray.com
ISBN 978-1-942728-19-1

# Dedication

For the loves of my life:

Trevor Gardner,

And our three amazing children,

Sky, Britain and Luke

'No way!' my mom shrieked, on the verge of hysteria. 'You got to be kidding me. You cannot put my daughter in a padded cell. There's got to be another room for Kerri!'

'No, ma'am, we are full this month,' the nurse said. 'We've tried to make the room as comfortable as possible. As soon as another room comes available, we will move her.' Somehow, that wasn't very reassuring.

I took another look. The room was about 8 feet by 12 and covered with row after row of brown faux leather with thick padding behind it. In the middle of the room, toward the left outside wall of the building, was a tiny window made of unbreakable glass. The ceiling was covered in the same faux brown leather material with the only break in the pattern being a ceiling light in the center of the room. There was a bed in the corner that looked like it had been borrowed from Alcatraz and a battered old bureau against the wall. A thin white robe with a zipper lay folded on the bed, and a pair of slippers lay on top.

Over a week ago, I probably wouldn't have cared; I was suicidal after all. Now I felt different as I hadn't had drugs in my system for more than a week, and the thick fog in my mind was starting to clear. Here I was in this awful place against my will. I had to earn the trust of not only my mother, but also the staff, doctors and anyone else who had the authority to sign the papers saying I was 'OK.'

One of the nurses stayed in the room while my mom helped me unpack. Everything had to be inspected before I could put it away in the battered old bureau. The power cord for my portable cassette player was confiscated since it could be used for strangulation. My BIC disposable razors were confiscated as well so I couldn't slit my wrists. The nurse explained they would keep the razors and provide them for use during shower time only. Anything that could potentially be used to harm myself or others was taken from me, even my belt. These items which I used every day and which I had no idea could be so dangerous, were put in a plastic box labelled with my name.

A staff member inventorying my confiscated items with yellow stickers marked 'inspected' said, 'Your items are still yours, Kerri, but you do not have the privilege to use them as freely as you did before. Once you prove you can be trusted and are well enough to leave this hospital, your items will be returned to you.'

The whole process was demoralizing. I felt like I was truly in prison. The only things missing were the metal bars, a disgruntled roommate, and a disgusting rotting toilet. It was time for my mom to leave. I looked at her with tears running down my face, and my hands balled into fists. 'Mom, please don't leave me here,' I pleaded. 'I promise I won't ever do it again!'

She gave me the biggest hug; it reminded me of the times when I was little and upset. All I needed was a hug from her that fixed everything. I could feel her tears running down the side of my cheek as she held onto me as tightly as she could. Then, she backed away. 'Kerri, believe me, I don't want you to be here at all, but you need to understand, I don't trust you anymore. I don't know why you did this to yourself, and I don't know if you'll try again. Dr. Green said that you were a danger to yourself. I have to take the doctor's advice and keep you here until they say otherwise, or until we see a change in you.'

She kissed me and said, 'I love you. I am only a phone call away. I'll be back to visit each week.' More tears streamed down her face as the nurse ushered her out.

I felt completely alone and terrified knowing I had to sleep in this horrible room. The padded door with a small index-sized window closed behind them. I sat down on the creepy old bed and cried.

They call these places loony bins for a good reason. Strangely enough, I felt like I was the only sane one. This place was full of kids who wanted to kill themselves and had been stopped from doing so. Not a day would go by without one of them trying to finish off what they had started, often with gruesome results.

One day, I was playing solitaire with Jerry, a staff member there. Jerry was such a sweet man, who smelled like sour milk. Being friends with him was my only fond memory of the place. He must have been 400-pounds and wore clothes from Big and Tall. His job was to have extra eyes on us kids, a guard, so to speak. It was really hard to inhale his stench as we'd sit every day for several hours playing solitaire, checkers, and other games while discussing everyday stuff like, how did I sleep, what were my favorite foods, was there anything new to tell from the last visit I had with my family? He was the only one who accepted me as I was and didn't pester me with questions about what I did and how I ended up here.

Suddenly, a teenage boy sitting at a long craft table on the other side of the room caught my eye. He had been busy drawing and coloring when he sat abruptly back in his chair. Placing a pencil in each hand, he proceeded to jam a pencil into each of his eyes. He screamed as blood spurted everywhere. Jerry flew out of his chair and hit the emergency alarm…

# Author Note with Disclaimer

To write my book, I relied on my personal journals, researched facts when necessary, and consulted with several of the people who appear in the book. I also called upon my own memory of these events during that time in my life from ages 13 to 22 and age 42.

I have changed the names of most but not all the individuals in this book. To preserve anonymity, I also modified identifying details. When needed, I omitted people and events that had no impact on the substance of the story.

Disclaimer:

Writing this book has been, by no means, easy. It includes my true confessions of attempting suicide, the years that led up to that attempt, and the years of rebuilding that followed. I describe various personalities and their interaction with me, and my perceptions of them from my, admittedly, depressed state. While I have taken pains to ensure that the information included in my memoir is, to the best of my recollection, as accurate as possible, I acknowledge that different people develop different perspectives on the same sets of facts and circumstances. I recognize that words are powerful. While I have no wish to hurt anyone, because I believe my confessions may resonate with others facing emotional challenges, and may help to show them that hope is always around the corner, I have persisted in publishing this memoir. It is my deepest hope that it will provide perspective for those who are contemplating suicide, and that it can serve as a resource for others who want to know why people commit or attempt to commit suicide, and how best to help those contemplating this irrevocable act.

# Contents

# OUT OF THE DARKNESS INTO THE LIGHT

# Foreword by Dr. Nicole Swiner

As a family doctor, I am very aware of how impactful depression and suicidal thoughts and attempts are on our lives. I try my best to listen and help patients who are going through tumultuous times and are crying out for help. It's incredibly important to hear their cries and bring them out of their darkness.

This book tells the story of how my friend, Kerri, has been able to come out of her darkness into the light with strength and an enormous amount of courage. You see her when she's at her worst and as she grows into an amazing, beautiful person. I'm incredibly proud of her and her accomplishments. What makes this book great is its raw honesty and truth. It's also a real page turner. As the story goes from start to finish, it has the reader on their toes, and then allows them to leave with a happy ending. It's a very important book to pay attention to.

C. Nicole Swiner, M.D.

## Why I Wrote This Book

In the fall of 2012, I received an email from our daughter's seventh-grade school. I knew it wasn't going to be good, but I had no idea that opening this email would reopen old wounds and secrets. These secrets I had kept hidden from my neighbors, co-workers, friends and our children for the last 25 years. Only my husband, Trevor, knew of my scars. What I read shocked me. I felt as if I had been punched in the gut, and I burst into tears. This email would undo everything I had tried to keep buried for so long.

I read that a girl named Mary, our daughter's classmate whom I had never met, had killed herself. She was 13 years old. They described in detail Mary's suicide. Mary went home and took medications out of her parents' bathroom. Pills in hand, she made a cocktail and swallowed. The email informed us about how the school was going to take immediate measures to break the news to the students. They'd also give them the opportunity to speak to a psychiatrist. I knew Mary's death would not only affect the students and staff at school, but also affect our daughter deeply. She would be devastated. She had mentioned on several occasions her friend Mary, how many classes they shared, and how much she liked her. For me it hit home; it felt raw, like déjà vu, because, in that moment, I was Mary all over again. I was the 13-year-old girl who planned her own suicide and survived. This secret, the one I had been ashamed of, the one our kids, neighbors, co-workers, and friends didn't know about, was bound to come out. It tore at my heart that I might have had the opportunity to save Mary. That I could have talked to her and explained how I had experienced those same feelings, and to let her know it's okay. I wished I had had the opportunity to show her how happy I was coming out of it, how I found the love of my life who saved me all those 25 years ago. My daughter and I talked about her day in school, how she witnessed other kids' reactions to Mary's death and how some kids were making fun of Mary's suicide. It was a very emotional and stressful day for her and the entire school. She then told me how the psychiatrist suggested journaling as a way to express her feelings about the tragedy. Listening to our daughter talk about her feelings, all I could hear was pain, anger and confusion. She was so mad at Mary. Sky didn't understand why she lost her friend so suddenly. I kept thinking how I completely understood how Sky felt, as I felt this way trying to rebuild my life after my attempted suicide. There wasn't a day I hadn't felt many emotions and the struggle to deal with each of them. I was also witness to my family's pain. It took a long time for all of us to heal. I felt so sad for Mary's family, the pain that led her to leave this world, she also left for her parents to endure. So many people were hurting. I wanted to stop our daughter's pain and help answer any questions she had. I knew it was a poor replacement for Mary, but maybe it would be enough to help her through the stages of healing. I decided it was time to share my story. I needed to use my story to help in some way. I just knew I couldn't be silent anymore; I had to help.

I made the decision right there and then to tell our kids. I wanted to express my feelings and relate my own experience and why I tried to commit suicide. I wanted to explain to them what I learned after my attempted suicide, that life doesn't have to continue to be painful and horrible. I wanted to share my conviction that it helps to talk with people who love and unconditionally support us about however we are feeling. I decided I would write my story. I needed to make a difference and thought that maybe, just maybe, telling my story will encourage those who read it to never take that final step of committing suicide.

Thus began my newly found mission: to write my book, to get my story told, and to help kids from elementary school age to college age.

I didn't know how this was all going to happen, but I knew the first step would be writing this book to help others.

# OUT OF THE DARKNESS INTO THE LIGHT

# PREFACE

I watched the last few passengers boarding the plane, rushing to stow their carry-ons in the overhead bins, and thought about how even though everyone had their own separate journeys, we all ended up here on this flight together tonight. I thought a lot about my past and how those events led me to be on this plane. I was extremely excited and looking forward to planning a life with Trevor.

I also wondered if I would have met him and fallen in love with him so quickly and completely, if I hadn't made the decision to kill myself. Would we have ever been in the same place at the same time? Would we have even met? Would I be on this plane right now?

I felt the panic surge through me as the plane began to roll away from the terminal. This was it. There was no turning back. It was finally happening. I was starting a new chapter in my life. I was overjoyed, enthusiastic, and a little scared at the same time. I thought of all I was leaving behind; my family, my friends, my job, the past 21 years of my life – left behind like luggage I couldn't carry. I didn't know when or even if I would return, but I chose to believe with the love in my heart that it would all work out.

Opening the window shade, I looked out towards the Boston night sky on the Fourth of July. I thought about how ironic it was for me to leave, of all days, on Independence Day. Fireworks were still being lit and exploding beautifully in the night sky. Not only was the entire country still celebrating Independence Day, I too was celebrating my own independence from my old life and was looking forward to a new life with Trevor. I whispered a final goodbye to the United States.

# OUT OF THE DARKNESS INTO THE LIGHT

# CHAPTER 1 – THE LAST DAY

*Tonight was the night.* I doodled idly on my math folder waiting for the bell to ring. I was finally going to end it, once and for all. I had it all planned out. My mom and George, my stepdad, were off for their usual Friday night bingo, followed by the habitual greasy Chinese takeout in front of the TV. I would have plenty of time to take care of things while they were gone. Seventh-grade had been the toughest school year so far, and it showed no signs of getting better. The last two years had been an inferno of never-ending persecution, anguish, and misery. Compared to the friendly, easy-going tempo of fifth grade, everyone seemed to have changed between graduating elementary and starting middle school. Even the teachers' attitudes were different.

I looked up from my doodling and glanced around the classroom, doubting anyone here would notice I was gone. I would just be an empty chair. The Brainiacs at the front would still be the studious teacher's pets that they were, and the boys would still be the same immature idiots, snapping bra straps and making obnoxious noises during class, while the small clique of popular girls at the back would still be the meanest people around. They took pleasure acting like they owned the school—looking down on you, commenting on your choice of clothes or accessories that were not their particular brand. I swear that those girls went to some secret bitch camp last summer and graduated with honors.

All four of them, suddenly aware of my existence, glared at me.

'What are you staring at, freak?' snapped top #1 bitch, the ringleader.

'What did you say to me?' I snapped back. Most kids didn't stand up for themselves, but I did.

Throughout my years in school, I made sure no one tried to bully me. My brother was a little chubby and smaller than most of the boys in his elementary class, and the mean boys enjoyed picking on him for these reasons. I wasn't able to protect him from the verbal abuse at school because I was in middle school. However, after school, if they tried to hurt him physically, he would always find me to help protect him. It was known if you tried to pick on my brother you'd have me to deal with, and you'd better finish it, or I would. I could hold my own, though I wasn't about to start now. I simply didn't have the time for a distraction.

She turned down her nose to me like I was a piece of shit, turned back to her friends, whispered something, and they all started to laugh in unison.

Returning to my doodle, I violently scribbled through it. I wasn't going to miss this hellhole, that was for sure. Every day, for as long as I could remember, I felt like an ALIEN compared to everyone in my household and the kids at school; I took medication twice a day, saw doctors every three months like a lab rat, and to make matters worse, I couldn't seem to find any happiness in my miserable life. I was suffering all the time, trying to fit in and trying to keep up appearances ... It was incredibly difficult when I felt consumed with depression, and all I ever thought about was how much I hated my life—it couldn't keep going on like this with no hope in sight. For the last seven years, I lived in a black hole of emptiness ... I don't think I was always like this, and yet I couldn't remember a time when I was truly happy. I kept wondering: what does happiness mean anyway? I saw people smiling, laughing and engaging with one another. I felt so completely ostracized by it all.

It probably didn't help that, at thirteen, I was a year older and a foot taller than everyone else in class, because I had to repeat second grade. I stood out in the crowd and not in a good way. This only increased the feeling of being an alien. Just another checkmark on the list of differences compared to the rest of my classmates. From the age of six, I had always found my schoolwork difficult and confusing. I had a harder time processing the information being taught in class. Unfortunately, this was one of the many side effects of taking my medication.

When I was little, my mother wanted me to feel more involved with other kids, and around the age of seven or eight, she enrolled me in a tap dance class. I remember one incident to this day. I was given instructions, along with the other girls in class, on a new tap step. We were then asked to perform it. I couldn't do it; I looked around at the other girls who were smiling and performing this new step with ease. I felt frustrated and completely stupid. Sitting down in the middle of class, I started to cry hysterically. My mother had warned me if I threw another tantrum she would take me out of the class. Well, I did, and she pulled me out. That was the last time she enrolled me in anything until I was in middle school. Since then the tantrums stopped. But, the schoolwork became increasingly difficult as the years progressed, as each year, my medication dosage increased. The higher dosage made my brain feel heavy, like a thick layer of fog had settled into my skull. That sensation only increased my confusion, making it harder for me to understand certain subjects like advanced math.

I know when this all happened to me. I've been told the story many times. The summer of 1975. I was two years old when my father took my baby brother and me to visit his family who lived in the country, about six hours away to the north. My mother couldn't come since she had to work. My grandfather owned a large home with a barn that he graciously filled with horses and small ponies. As you can expect, a two-year-old would be itching to get out of the car to run around and play. Once my father's family greeted us with hugs and kisses, we hurried over to the barn. I was in awe of these animals. I had never seen one close up before. Without anyone noticing, I wandered off into the corral for a closer look. One pony, in particular, was hot-tempered. He took one look my way before charging full force at me. The pony's metallic horse-shoe made contact with my head as he trampled me down. My father and family heard the commotion and came running. They found me on the ground unconscious, my face and shirt covered in blood. Everyone thought I was dead. I had a nasty head injury, but thankfully it wasn't as serious as it first appeared. I just needed stitches on my right eyebrow. The doctor did a full physical and informed my father I was fine and could go home.

Four years later at age six, my parents were divorced. It was my father's scheduled time to take my brother and me for our annual visit to his family, a place where accidents tended to happen. During our journey, my father stopped at a friend's house to rest a bit before continuing to our grandfather's home.

I remember the day vividly. The start of our journey, I felt fine. The three of us had our snacks and drinks, and we sang along to songs on the radio from some of my favorite singers - Carly Simon, Simon & Garfunkel, and Joni Mitchell. The time passed by quite quickly in the car, without incident. As soon as we arrived at the home of my dad's friend from high school, my head started to ache, and I began to feel nauseous. Those symptoms gradually became worse, and then I began to sweat. I asked my dad's friend if I could rest. He said, 'Sure,' and led me into the living room to his brown leather couch. As I lay down, I placed my head on the armrest. I remember feeling thankful I could rest my hot head against the cool leather. Lying there, my head began to pound with pain, sweat beaded on my forehead and down my neck, my stomach felt tight, and the slightest movement increased the nausea.

After several minutes, the leather armrest started to heat up. I didn't know why until I opened my eyes and noticed the sun pouring in through the window. I needed to move. I got up, switched to the other side of the couch, closed my eyes and that's all I remember. I am not sure how long afterward, but I could hear screaming, and I understood the screaming was coming from my brother. Then I heard our father's voice, and he was demanding to know what my brother did to me. Joe said he didn't do anything. My poor four-year-old brother was beside himself, watching me convulsing on the floor, choking on my tongue and seeing the whites of my eyes as they rolled back into my skull. I was having a full epileptic seizure. My father gathered me up on his lap and held my head in one hand while using the other to stop me choking on my tongue. I finally came to and was out of breath, drenched in sweat and terrified. My body ached from head to toe. I had no idea how I ended up on the floor. I could only remember the screaming.

My father called my mother who took the first flight out from Boston and met us at the hospital. It was the same hospital I had been rushed to four years earlier after the pony accident. An MRI, CAT scan, EEG and blood work revealed that as I was growing up, a substantial amount of scar tissue had developed as a result of my head injury. The scarring eventually obstructed my normal brain activity and induced a seizure. I like to compare it to a stroke when the brain sends a signal to the heart to pump, and the blocked artery doesn't allow that to happen. With my body still steadily developing, the doctors knew I would start to have regular 'episodes.' To control them, I needed to be put on drugs. The drug of choice was phenobarbital, a barbiturate. Along with the promise of controlling my seizures, my parents were also warned of the drug's side effects in children my age. Depression, agitation, mood swings, dizziness, confusion and many others I'd soon learn about for myself. I was sent home with a prescription and a game plan to have me re-evaluated every three months with blood work, CAT Scans, EEGs, and MRIs. The drug did, in fact, stop the seizures, but it also crippled me mentally.

From the age of six to the age of thirteen, I lived in a black hole. I felt imprisoned in my mind. I knew there was something really wrong with me, but I didn't know how to explain this to my mom. My head felt heavy with depression. I was frequently confused and thinking, *why do I always feel this way?* Why can't I smile like the other kids do all the time? Why do I have to be different? In school, I would feel anxious because I found it hard to grasp new teaching points. It took me twice as long to learn something new, than the other kids. This infuriated me, because I could see the other kids coping comfortably with the same assignment. My schoolwork began to suffer. I was confused all the time. This constant depression and anger continued to build. I was on edge; at any moment, I could burst out crying for no apparent reason. On many occasions, I did.

Due to my difficulty in learning and retaining information, my mother was advised to hold me back in second grade. Not knowing what else to do, she reluctantly agreed with my teachers. To get left behind was one thing, to feel left out at the same time crushed my self-esteem entirely. Staying back in second grade was when I started to refer to myself as an ALIEN.

At this point in my life, I hated each and every day. While repeating second grade was what I needed, I also found myself being bullied by the kids, especially the ones I thought were my friends from my previous class. They started to make fun of me because I had been kept back.

On top of that, my mom met our soon-to-be stepfather, George, and had him move in sometime after her divorce. I remember at the time feeling safe knowing we had a new dad who would love and take care of us, unlike our 'real' dad. Unfortunately, several years revealed the harsh reality that he never wanted kids. He only wanted my mother. My brother and I were an unwanted part of the whole package. Even so, my mother loved him and tried to make the relationship work between the three of us. Sadly, she was always caught in the middle, defending us to him and defending him to us. It was the Bermuda Triangle. Nothing good came of it. The same string of problems that never got solved were swept under the rug for us to stumble across, again and again.

The last bell of the day buzzed loudly through the overhead speakers, distracting me from my thoughts. The classroom instantly became a bustling inferno of energy as everyone gathered their belongings. I gathered my things and followed the herd into the corridor, dodging others as I scrambled towards my locker. My locker had once been decked out with pictures of TV heartthrobs, doodles and brightly colored locker accessories, much like everyone else's. I cleaned it out over the last few weeks, trashing mostly everything inside and giving away whatever else I had to whoever wanted it. All that was left was a few books on the shelf and a lone picture of Davy Jones lining the inside of the door. I stuffed it all into my bag. Seeing there was nothing left, I closed the locker and headed for the bus.

'Hey, Kerri,' Teresa greeted me as I sat next to her.

'Hey, TT,' I answered. Everyone called her that.

'You wanna hang out on Sunday?' she asked.

'Uhh, sure.' I shrugged, not that I had plans beyond today.

Teresa was a year older than me, but that didn't stop her from becoming my best friend. She was one of the first few people I had met when we moved three years ago. I remember the day we met. My family and I were unpacking and moving boxes into the house. She was riding her bike around the neighborhood and stopped by to introduce herself. That was pretty much it. We clicked and became fast friends. I was excited she lived so close, just down the street. We hung out practically every day after school at her home and swam in her pool during the summer months. It was a welcome break from school and home to be with TT. While most people saw me as a nobody, and my family, I felt, saw me as a burden, TT accepted me for who I was. I knew she would be devastated - I would have been as well if she made the decision to end her life as I had. I was truly sorry for that, but I had made up my mind.

The decision to kill myself wasn't something I reached in a day. These thoughts had been around since the beginning of seventh grade, even though I had hoped a new school year would usher in a new beginning that would save me from the black hole I was living in. That same year, however, I hit puberty and got my period. Sure enough, I needed a heavier dose of medication to control my seizures on top of my ever-changing body and additional hormones. My depression spiraled as a result. I thought my decision through, and a month before the attempt, I chose to give my belongings away. By doing this, it solidified wanting to end my life as I was no longer going to be here to use them. I made sure I didn't completely empty my room, which might have tipped my parents off that something unusual was afoot.

The bus stopped at the corner of my road, and I fought the urge to give TT a big hug. I had to keep up appearances, so I meekly said goodbye and got off the bus. I headed straight for my house and let myself in through the front door.

'Joe!' I called out to my younger brother.

There was no reply, which I took as a good sign. That and the lack of vehicles in the driveway meant that nobody was home. I went into the kitchen and dragged a chair over to the refrigerator. Standing on the chair, I opened the door to the cabinet above the fridge, finding the bottle of phenobarbital in its usual spot. Emptying the bottle on the kitchen counter, I counted the small white round tablets. There were 64 left. Would it be enough? I decided it would have to be, and carefully put the pills back. These pills were the cause of so much of my suffering. Surely, they could be used to put an end to it?

I made myself a ham and cheese sandwich, poured myself a Pepsi, and retired to my room, ignoring the dirty dishes in the sink and the basket of laundry waiting for me on the couch. I had been slacking on my chores for the last week or so, but I'd be gone soon, and it wasn't like my mother would be able to ground me. I sat on my bed with a pad of paper and a pen and wondered whether I should leave a note. If so, what should I write?

*Goodbye, I hope you all enjoy life better without me?*

No, people usually gave some indication as to why.

*I hate my life, and I can't stand to live a minute longer.*

I stared at the blank paper for a while. I finally decided that I wouldn't leave a note. I didn't see the point.

'Kerri!' I heard my brother calling as he entered the house.

'I'm in my room,' I shouted.

I heard him coming down the hallway. He found me still staring at the blank paper.

'Whatcha doin'?' he asked.

Joe was so beautiful to me. He still had a baby face with wavy dirty blond hair, striking blue eyes, small rounded nose with rosy red cheeks and full lips. Short for his age and a little chubby, he was surprisingly strong, and would always win when we had an arm wrestling match.

'Nothing.' I tossed the pad of paper and pen on the floor and looked up to see him making the weirdest and most disturbing faces at me; scrunching up his face while sticking out his tongue. The grossest one was when he took his fingers and pulled his eyelids back.

Joe was exactly like how a baby brother should be – annoying. I did my best to ignore him. Not getting any reaction, he gave up and turned around, tossed his school bag into his pigsty of a bedroom across the hall.

'Joe, can you please close my door?'

He slammed it shut, and I heard him stomp down the hall, back towards the living room.

'Thank you,' I yelled.

'Whatever,' he yelled back. Then I heard the TV come on.

That was the gist of our typical conversations, on a good day.

George came storming into my room as soon as he got home and saw the undone dishes and laundry.

'What have you been doing?' he shouted, raising his voice and emphasizing the last word of each sentence. 'I'm fed up with you not pulling your weight around here. You know your mother is at work all day, and the last thing she should be doing when she gets home is housework. You need to help out.'

'Well, what about Joe? He doesn't do anything. He doesn't even keep his room clean. I don't see you shouting at him.'

'You watch your mouth, young lady,' he yelled, leaning so far forward I thought he might lose his balance. 'Who the hell do you think you are, talking to me like that? If I tell you to do something, you do it. You're grounded for a week!'

'What? That's not fair,' I protested.

For half a second, I was furious and almost forgot my plans. What did I care if I was grounded anyway? It wasn't like it was going to last for long. After tonight, I was FREE.

'That means no going out, no friends, no TV, and no phone. You will come home from school and go straight to your room. '

Breathing heavily and red in the face, he turned and left, his weighted footsteps receding to the living room where I heard Joe protest as George changed the TV channel.

George was not one for back-chatting to. When he gave an order, he expected you to listen. I never felt George really loved us. I felt he put up with us - the baggage that came with my mother. I felt we both deserved better. I saw him for who he was. He thought dishes, housework, and laundry were women's work. He was a man, and men did stuff like yard work or fixing the car. That was probably why Joe never had any real chores to do. The few chores he did have, he still ignored, and I did them so my mom wouldn't have to. It was a never-ending cycle.

When my mom came home from work at the office, I heard her arguing about me with George in the kitchen. Moments later, she came into my room to talk.

'I understand you haven't done your chores for the last few days,' she said. 'George and I have discussed your behavior, and I have to support him in grounding you. I'm sorry, Kerri, you need to stay in your room for the evening. You can't come out, even after we're gone.'

'Fine,' I said, indifferent. This wasn't a big surprise; she sided with him most of the time.

'We'll discuss this in the morning, okay? I love you,' she leaned over and kissed me, and then slowly got up, closing the door behind her.

After they left, I waited ten minutes, and then went to find Joe. He was lying on the floor watching TV.

'Have they gone?' I asked him.

'Yeah,' he answered, not bothering to look up.

I proceeded to the kitchen and took down my pills from the cabinet above the fridge. Pouring them out onto the countertop, I divided them roughly into sets of four and five. I poured myself a large glass of orange juice and started swallowing the pills, one set at a time. I thought about my life since my first seizure and when I had to start taking these pills. I was done with being constantly pinched and prodded at by doctors every three months, never knowing if the tests would ever stop. Hating school, the continuous problems with my father, the arguments I overheard concerning Joe and me between George and my mother, and my father and his new wife. I swallowed the last pill with a big gulp of orange juice and felt as if a huge weight was rising from me. I washed out my glass, dried it and put it away in the cupboard, thinking George would be so proud that I had cleaned up after myself. I put the empty tablet bottle back in its place in the cabinet and returned to the living room.

Standing behind the coffee table so Joe wouldn't notice, I took a last long look at my baby brother. He was twelve and still in that awkward stage of pre-puberty; his chubby frame was dressed in matching gray sweatpants and sweatshirt. I watched him pat his wavy dirty blond hair with the permanent cowlick in the middle of his forehead. Seeing Joe's innocent, sweet round face, full lips, and cleft chin, reminded me of our childhood days when I wanted to be his little mother and take care of him. I felt so much love for him at that moment. When he wasn't pissing me off, he could make me laugh. Joe loved all his heroes: Batman, The Hulk, and Superman, to name a few. On many occasions, Joe was our comedian, coming up with something crazy to say to Mom and me. He would do this by imitating his heroes' voices while telling a joke. It would catch you off guard, and we would always burst out laughing. He and I had been through so much together with our parents' divorce and the addition of our stepparents. We were a team once upon a time, getting along and protecting one another. Because we had to share a bedroom for almost seven years in the apartment, we used to spend a lot of time together; playing with our toys, games, and creating forts in our closets. When we moved to our new house, we had our own bedrooms, and as time went on, we hardly spoke to each other. If by some miracle we did, it was simply to argue about trivial things. I loved him and would miss him, but I needed to go. There was nothing left for me here.

I kneeled down next to him.

'I love you,' I said and reached out for a hug.

'Yeah,' he murmured, eyes still glued to the TV.

I returned to my bedroom and shut the door. Closing the blinds, I got into bed, turned off the lights and lay myself to rest. Lying there, I wondered how this would work. Would I fall asleep? Would it hurt? I had read in a newspaper how the effects of an overdose would affect the body. I didn't know how long it took, and would I be aware of the moment just before my heart stopped beating? Soon enough, I started to feel drowsy. I was having trouble keeping my eyes open, and I eventually dozed off.

'Kerri … Kerri.'

'Kerri!'

I struggled to open my eyes. My brother was leaning over me, hands clasped on my shoulders, shaking me awake.

'Get off me,' I muttered, trying to get my eyes to focus.

'TT's on the phone, and she says it's urgent.'

I didn't know how long I had been asleep, and I was in no mood to talk to anyone.

'Tell her I'm asleep,' I snapped at him.

'She won't get off the phone until she talks to you,' he insisted. 'She says it's urgent!'

'I want to be left alone! How hard is that for you to understand?' I hissed back at my brother. He winced.

I threw the covers off and got up. My head felt too heavy to hold up on its own, like I had several cement blocks stacked on top of it. Within seconds of standing, my body tingled. It felt as if I had put on a full-bodied sumo wrestler's costume, and I was sliding around in it, rather than it belonging to me. I was practically tripping over myself trying to walk my way to the phone.

''Ello,' I slurred.

'Oh, my God, Kerri, I almost got abducted!' she screamed at me. 'I was walking home from the corner store and out of nowhere this white van pulls up, the door opens and this man tried to grab me. I ran as fast as I could to get home. Kerri, I'm freaking out, I'm so scared.'

There had been reports of a white van with two men cruising through our neighborhoods for months trying to pick up kids late at night. You would think the local police would dispatch several cars to patrol the neighborhood every night, pulling over all white vans on the road until these guys were caught and put away. Instead, the police sent a notice to all residents, assuring everyone they were doing everything they could to apprehend these men and to ensure all children were off the roads and safely in their homes by sunset.

My mind was fuzzy and I was finding it hard to concentrate.

'TT that's awful, are you okay?' I asked, my voice lacking any conviction.

'Ah, yeah, I'm okay,' she calmed down a little. I think she noticed. 'Kerri, you don't sound right. Are you okay?'

'Err ... hmm, yeah, I'm fine, just tired.'

My legs were suddenly very shaky, and I knew they were going to give way any minute. I couldn't stand here much longer.

'You don't sound like yourself. What's going on?' she pressed.

'I'm fine; I gotta go.' I really needed to lie down now.

'I'm coming over!'

'No, TT, don't!' I snapped.

By then, I was fed up with her questions. This was an intrusion I hadn't planned on, and I didn't want to waste any more time on the phone. I could feel the pills really kicking into full gear. I didn't have the strength to stand; every muscle in my body was becoming numb. I needed to end the conversation.

'If you must know, I took the rest of my seizure pills,' I snapped at her, loud enough for only her to hear me, 'so leave me alone to die in peace!'

After that, I hung up. I dragged myself back to the bedroom and shut the door, this time locking it. I made it to my bed just as my legs gave out. Mustering whatever strength I had left, I wiggled myself beneath the covers. I was suddenly cold. My head continued to feel weighed down, and it seemed to sink right into the pillow. Once again, I started to pass out, hopefully for the last time.

BANG, BANG, BANG!

The knocking resounded in my head like a bad dream. It seemed close yet so far.

BANG, BANG, BANG!

'KERRI! KERRI! It's Teresa's mom. Open the door, sweetie.'

I could hear my brother crying hysterically in the distance. He sounded so scared. I didn't think about that. Not once did I consider how people would feel about me killing myself. I felt terrible for him. These thoughts were so unexpected and came charging at me like the pony did all those years ago, leaving me feeling trampled and paralyzed.

'Joe, listen to me,' TT's mom said to my brother. 'Call your mom and tell her we're taking your sister to the hospital, okay?'

BANG, BANG, BANG!

'Kerri, please open the door, honey.'

'No, I can't, go away.'

My voice didn't even sound like me. It seemed to come from somewhere outside, almost a whisper. I was telling the truth. I couldn't have opened that door even if I wanted to. I could hardly move. It took every bit of energy I had just to move my head to look at the door. I felt a sudden surge of panic as I listened to my brother and TT crying, along with TT's mother shouting through the door. It was never my intention to hurt anyone, just me.

I imagined my mom answering the phone call at the bingo, my brother screaming for help, telling her what I had done.

The banging continued. Soon, everything grew fainter and fainter. I caught a fleeting glimpse of the door bursting open as the world faded away.

## CHAPTER 2 – DO YOU KNOW WHAT YOU HAVE DONE?

I could hear voices, voices of people I didn't recognize. They were surrounding me, touching me, prodding me. I was being moved around and arranged like a puppet. I felt the steel blade of the scissors as they clumsily cut their way up my clothing and the cold blast of air as the fabric was peeled away. I felt chilled and vulnerable. I was aware of everything that was being done to me, but, I couldn't open my eyes to see what was going on. The frigid air, the sterilized smell and the sounds of monitoring machines all told me where I was. I was in the Emergency Room. I just couldn't remember how I got there.

I was told later by my mother that TT, her mom, and sister, kicked in our front door, breaking the deadbolt and scaring Joe half to death. They quickly informed my brother that I had taken my pills to kill myself. Teresa's mom and sister broke my bedroom door. The three of them half dragged, half carried me to the car, and then raced to the hospital.

I felt the wristband being slapped and clamped hard onto my wrist.

'Are you cold, honey?' said a woman's voice. 'Here, let's get this gown on you, and you'll feel a little better.'

I felt her hands lift my arms as she slipped the Johnny on me. She pulled me onto my side to slide the gown underneath and tie the strings at the back. I was left alone for a few moments before the nurses returned in full force.

My mouth was forced open, and as hard as I tried to close it, something or someone kept aggressively reopening it. I struggled in desperation as a thick, disgusting liquid was poured down my throat. I began to choke and spat it out.

'Help me, somebody help me!' I screamed, but, no one came to my rescue.

I desperately fought back, my arms and legs flailing in the darkness as I tried to shove the hands away, all the while attempting to muster up the strength to open my eyes. It was no use. There were too many of them. They held my mouth open and kept on pouring.

'KERRI!'

The voice sent shivers running through me. My blood turned cold. I recognized that voice. This can't be happening. He can't be here.

'Kerri! You listen to me!' My dad shouted an order as if I was one of his perps he just arrested.

I could picture his disdain, his stern face looking down on me.

'You will do exactly as you are told, do you hear me? You will not scream. You will not put up a fight. Do you understand?'

I had somehow lost the ability to talk, so I nodded in agreement. I knew that tone only too well. I knew right then and there I had to stop fighting and obey, or I would have to deal with much worse. Just a look from him or the tone of his voice always sent shivers down my spine because I knew the violence he could inflict. In the short years I lived with my father, I witnessed his outbursts of anger, which were easily set off from the pressure of being a young husband and father. That anger would then be directed toward my brother and I, but mostly our mother.

I was too little to be able to recall the exact images. However, the shouting, the punched holes in our apartment walls, watching a lamp fly across the room and smash into pieces; these are all vivid memories.

I found out later that my mom had called my dad's police station from the bingo hall. He had been on patrol in Boston, 45 minutes away when he got a call from dispatch that his daughter had tried to commit suicide. He put his sirens on and sped all the way to the hospital ahead of my mother.

It wasn't long before my stomach responded to the nasty cocktail, and I started to vomit. I was finally able to open my eyes as I choked on the thick black tar and pills being expelled from my stomach. The violent spasm of regurgitation sent globs of tar splattering all over my hospital gown. The nurses tried to have me purge into a bucket, only it was impossible for me to keep still. It just kept coming. Every violent retch sent waves of pain crashing through me. And when I thought I was done, it started over and over again. It seemed like hours before I slumped back on the hospital bed, sweaty and exhausted. Every bone and muscle in my body were in agony. I was finally able to collapse against my pillow after the nurses cleaned me up yet again, thankfully for the last time. Finally left alone, I fell into a deep sleep.

\* \* \*

I awoke the next morning and my entire body ached. I felt as if a bunch of big strong men tagged-teamed one another and they ALL jumped in the ring to beat the living shit out of me. Shifting in my bed sent shooting pain through me, especially in my chest and stomach. I wasn't sure where I was, and I was confused by the sound of loud swishing noises around me. Slowly opening my eyes, I saw my mom leaning over the bedrail to my left, hovering over me. Her hazel eyes were red and swollen, still wet with fresh tears. Her brown hair was a mess, and some of it was stuck to her damp cheeks. She was four inches shorter than George's 5'11 who was also there. He didn't look so good either. His light brown hair was disheveled, and his face was pale sporting new stubble. It surprised me to see that he had been crying too. I had never in my life seen her look so awful. I quickly sobered up to the reality of where I was and what I had done the night before.

Looking over the room, I could see rows upon rows of kids hooked up to life support. I was in the Children's Intensive Care Unit. How ironic to find myself in a place where kids were fighting for their lives when I deliberately tried to end mine. Apparently, there had been no other beds available, and they had to stick me in here until another bed opened up. The realization of knowing I was very much alive and what I had to deal with next felt unbearable. I was torn with still feeling I wanted to die and now had to deal with the fact my parents knew. I was also confused; I didn't understand why they cared so much.

'Are you okay? Are you thirsty? Are you uncomfortable?'

The mention of comfort made me shift in my bed, followed by a sharp surge of pain down below. I looked down and yanked on the tube protruding from the blankets and then hollered in pain as I realized I was attached to it.

'It's okay, honey.' My mom took my hand off the tube and explained what the catheter was and what it was doing there.

Trying to relax, my entire body still ached from last night's ordeal. I wondered if I had broken any of my ribs.

A nurse, who was checking in on another patient, saw that I was awake and came by to introduce herself. 'My name is Nurse Molly. How are you feeling this morning?' she said with a comforting voice.

She didn't wait for an answer and continued talking, more to my parents than to me.

'You had quite a rough night last night!' she said while rearranging my pillows and blankets. 'Your ribs, stomach and throat are most likely going to be very sore for a few days. When you feel up to going to the bathroom on your own, give me a shout, and I'll come and remove the catheter and help you, okay?'

'Okay,' I whispered, my throat still sore.

'You'll probably notice that your urine and poop are a different color,' she went on. 'Jet black is to be expected, and it will take a few days to return to normal.'

'Black?' I managed to say.

'Your body still needs to filter out the tar that you drank last night,' she explained. 'Make sure you drink lots of water. That'll help flush it all out.'

When the nurse left, my mom handed me a card with a wooden heart that read 'I LOVE YOU.' Sitting there staring at the words, I felt uncertain as to why she would love me after what I tried to do.

There was uncomfortable silence for 10 or 15 minutes. During that time, my mother pulled up a chair and stared at me. George kept glancing between my mother and me. It was obvious we all didn't know what next to say. I knew I had just been through a violent detoxification ordeal and would have to answer some awkward questions, but I wasn't sure when my mother would ask. I was about to break the silence when my mother did that for us.

'Why did you do it, Kerri? Why did you try to kill yourself?' she asked.

I guess I should have expected this question, only I wasn't prepared for it. When I had planned on taking my life, it ended there. There was no continuation, no judgment. I didn't plan this part at all. Now I had to deal with the realization of what I did and how my decision affected everyone else.

'Because,' I began and stopped there.

I could see my mother was doing her best to stay calm and not lose control. It was obvious she had been up all night crying; her hair looked like she had run her fingers through it all night. They both looked exhausted with black circles under their eyes and were still wearing their clothes from the night before. My mother kept looking at me, pleading with her eyes to tell her why, but I wasn't ready to talk about why I wanted to kill myself. I needed time to deal with all that had happened. Thankfully, she took mercy on me and decided not to press any further. The next day, a ward bed opened up, and I was moved. A few days later, I was relocated to a private room.

My mother had taken medical leave from work. She thought it was best to keep Joe home while I was at the hospital. However, she mentioned that my dad was likely to come and see me today. Surprisingly, I was excited to see him; I hadn't seen him in such a long time. Hearing him four nights ago didn't exactly count, and I was hoping we could start over.

There was a knock on the door, and my mother opened the door to my father. I could see the furious glint in his eyes. At that moment, I saw my mother change from the broken woman to my protector once again.

She stood between us and warned him, 'Do not upset her. You can talk to her for a few minutes, but remember it's only been four days, and she is still fragile … do not upset her,' my mom repeated.

'Yes, I understand,' my dad said, leaning into my mother as he answered her.

'I'll be right outside the door if you need me, okay, sweetie,' she said, leaving the room.

He pulled up a chair beside my bed. We exchanged awkward 'Hello's.

I stared at him; he always appeared taller to me than his 5'7" frame. Being a cop, he took pride in his appearance. He made his health and fitness a priority, worked out regularly, and had earned his black belt in Karate. When I was little, I always enjoyed how his short wavy brown hair fell into place perfectly no matter how many times I ran my hands through it.

He looked back at me; we shared the same brown eyes. My dad was handsome, although I never liked his mustache, I preferred him clean shaven.

Then, my father fell onto his knees, raised his hands in the air in prayer, and laid his head down on my bed, sobbing. He nearly ran out of breath thanking the heavens that I was alive.

NO, WAIT, that only happens in movies. It doesn't happen in real life and most certainly you would NEVER, and I mean NEVER, see this kind of reaction from my father. *Rewind* ...

'Do you know what you've done?' he thinned his lips grimly at me, giving me the 'death stare' meaning you were in serious trouble and required punishing.

I stared blankly at him, confused by what was happening. I could see this was making him even more furious.

'Do you know how you've made me look, back at the station? Everyone knows!' His unflinching eyes bored into me. 'I'm the cop whose kid tried to kill herself! How do you think it looks, being a police officer, getting a call from my own dispatch unit telling me that my daughter tried to kill herself? Do you realize that you have a permanent record against you now, a file with your name on it? Do you understand how bad this makes me look? Answer me!'

He was blaming me. I realized then that he didn't care if I lived or died. My attempted suicide was, quite simply, an inconvenience to his work life. Being selfish to the core didn't change just because he almost lost his only daughter four days ago. I was right all along. My dad didn't love me. I burst into tears, hysterically crying. My mom ran in.

'I told you not to upset her,' she raised her voice at him. 'You need to leave now. Get out!'

'Fine!' He turned, giving me one last venomous glare before storming out and slamming the door behind him.

My mom climbed into bed with me, pulling me close.

'It's going to be okay, Kerri. Your father doesn't know how to react to everything that has happened,' she whispered.

I appreciated her trying to protect my brother and me from our dad. She was our savior when we were very little. She would always intervene at the right moment, when my father's belt was coming off. Thankfully, Joe and I never took a beating. Unfortunately, that left my poor mother to suffer his wrath.

Another day or two passed, and I began to feel a little better. I was eating properly, and the pain had subsided. The color had returned to my face, and as my system had been phenobarbital-free for the past five days, my mood had improved considerably. My family and I discussed the prospect of me going home. The only problem was, I had to be evaluated by a qualified psychiatrist before I could be discharged.

# CHAPTER 3 – THE EVALUATION

One week had passed since I tried to kill myself. The last several days my head began to clear, and the constant weight of confusion had disappeared. The weight of the depression was finally lifting off of my shoulders, and I could breathe again. I felt more in control than I ever had. Yet as I sat in my hospital bed, hour after hour, all I could think was, 'What now?' I wanted to go home, but what would my home life be like now? What would my family think of me?

As normal, my mother stopped by after breakfast and I knew she would stay with me until dinnertime. Conversation was typically light chit chat about what my brother was getting up to during his summer vacation, a new take-out they had tried, not wanting to cook, and what her activities were outside of seeing me now that she took an extended leave of absence from work. She was still very vulnerable from what I had done. She wasn't sleeping, circles shadowed her eyes, and from the way her clothes hung on her, you could tell she wasn't eating and had lost quite a bit of weight. I didn't want to say anything that would upset her. I just wanted to go home. I asked when that was going to happen.

'Kerri, I'd love to take you home, only it's not as if you came to the hospital with the flu or a broken leg. You tried to kill yourself, and we cannot take that lightly. There are rules and procedures. First of all, you need to be evaluated by the hospital's psychiatrists, and after that session with the psychiatrist, we'll be able to find out what the next step is.'

'When do I have to see the psychiatrist?'

'Actually, before I came in this morning, I stopped by the front desk, and they said they made an appointment for you today after lunch.'

'What do you think will happen?'

My mother took a deep breath. 'To be honest, Kerri, I hope she's able to get into that head of yours and let us all know why you tried to kill yourself. You haven't said anything that would explain your actions since that night except for 'because' and that's not a reason, Kerri. It's not enough for me to feel you are whole. Something is terribly wrong. I wish you'd let me in and tell me why.'

I couldn't answer that. The truth, I knew, would hurt her. It hurt me still. At least I felt one big part of my horrible life was over; the phenobarbital. Not having it in my system over the last few days, I started to feel like a different person. The depression seemed to be lifting, and for the first time in my life, I felt hopeful.

However, I was not looking forward to meeting the psychiatrist.

After lunch, a very young woman in her twenties with long brown hair, bangs, dark blue eyes that made me think of the Caribbean ocean, and a calming smile came to visit me. The minute she entered my room dressed in her black pantsuit with a bright pink collared shirt and black high heels, I knew exactly who she was before she introduced herself. She stood out like a sore thumb compared to the doctors and nurses and the rest of the staff that milled around like white and blue wallpaper.

Feeling intimidated, my stomach started to tighten, and I thought I might be sick. Her presence seemed to fill the room, and I felt her eyes on me immediately. I didn't like the idea of her judging me. What if I answered her questions wrong or not at all? She held all the control and would make the final decision to release me or not.

'Hi, I am Dr. Jennifer Green. I'm the hospital psychiatrist, and I've come to escort you to my office for our appointment.' With her cheerful introduction, it felt as though she was taking me to a party. A party I didn't want to go to. I immediately didn't trust her.

My mother and I stared at her. We'd been expecting this, just not her. She was the complete opposite of the stereotype associated with psychiatrists. I was expecting a tightly wound bun, thin gold-rimmed spectacles, polyester clothes adorned with a large white doctor's jacket and a stern look that emphasized every word I shared would be scrutinized.

I got out of bed and gave my mom a hug. I wasn't sure when I'd be back. I followed Dr. Green to her office two floors up, passing by several offices before we finally came to hers. She opened the door and told me to take a seat. I had expected a sofa and comfortable pillow, but that wasn't the case. Dr. Green's office was not spacious by any means, but it was extremely well-organized. I was surprised by how the light-colored green walls instantly made me feel calmer. There was a row of shelves filled with so many books that it reminded me of my town library. The back wall held several framed diplomas, licenses, and certifications. In the center of her office were two padded chairs and a small round table with a box of tissues that I presumed were for me. I took my seat as instructed, knowing the minute I was comfortable we'd have to begin.

'So, Kerri, how are you feeling today?'

'A lot better these last couple of days,' I replied. 'I like your office.'

'That is very nice of you to say. I want to make the most out of the time we have today. I'd like to start by asking you some questions about yourself.'

'Okay.'

'Great. So how many people are in your family, Kerri?'

I was sure she had all this information on file. I also knew I would not get out of here if I remained silent.

'Well, there's me and my brother Joe, my mom and George. He's my mother's boyfriend, not my dad. My mom and dad have been divorced for almost nine years now, and my dad married his second wife four years ago.'

'So you have two sets of parents, your mom and George, and your dad, and your stepmother?'

'I would say I have my mother and George, a father who doesn't love me … And I would never call her my stepmother.'

'Oh, you don't like her?'

'No.'

'Hmm, okay, that's a good start. How are your relationships with each of them?' she asked.

What relationships? I only had one with my mother. I didn't know how to answer this question. I froze for a moment, thinking about how I should answer.

She decided for me. 'Let's start with your father.'

I had so much to say, but where to begin? I recalled the last time we saw each other before my attempted suicide. To say that our relationship had been a constant battle for as long as I could remember would be an understatement. As I had grown older, I had come to the realization of all that had happened between us over the years: those times my brother and I had waited for hours on our apartment front steps with our bags packed, excitedly waiting for him to pick us up for our weekend with him, and him never showing, the continuous bickering over child support, and the year he moved out and left us and didn't bother to contact us, not once whilst he was gone. That relationship was irreparable. I didn't think there was any point in talking about it, especially after the way he treated me during his visit two days ago.

'I don't see my father anymore, except of course, him turning up last Friday night and a couple of days ago,' I said.

'Can you please give me more detail about that?' she pressed.

'No.'

'Maybe we should move on to your stepfather, George. When did he become your stepfather and what is it like living with him?'

I never had a father figure in my life. I couldn't count on my real father and as for George, he wasn't much of a replacement either.

He only wanted my mother, not the baggage that came with her. As a result, we had never seen eye to eye since George had moved in. We were a dysfunctional family. The division showed itself in many ways, but 'especially at dinner'. Before George, my mom had always made us a nice meal, and the three of us would sit down as a family and discuss our days. That all changed when George moved in. Every day, as soon as he got home from his laboring job on the construction site about four in the afternoon, he would kick off his steel-tipped boots outside, shower, dress into jeans and a T-shirt, then rule the TV remote control. When my mom got home, he would cook dinner for us all, grab a plate for himself and head into the living room, plopping down in front of the TV again. Reluctantly, my brother and I would follow. He would be sprawled out on the couch with his feet up, and my mom would perch herself on the far end, jamming herself into the small space between his feet and the armrest while Joe and I settled on the floor. We watched whatever George wanted, the channels flicking by with the click of the remote whenever he got bored. I grew up believing this was what everyone else did until I started to have sleepovers at my friend's house and realized it wasn't.

It didn't feel much like a family. Not sitting at our dinner table like other families did, meant never making the effort to connect with each other by asking about each other's day. We lost that connection. The weekends weren't much different. There was George on one side, and Joe and I on the other. My mom was torn between the two. We were competing for her attention. More often than not, Joe and I lost. As the years passed, I never lost that feeling that we were an inconvenience. We were in the way. Nothing more, nothing less. I guess I learned to accept that.

How could I tell Dr. Green what it was truly like living with George? What would the result be? Me hurting my mother more? I'd hurt her so much this past week that I couldn't bear to cause her any more pain.

'I think I was five when George moved in with us,' I said. 'Living with him is different, I guess.'

'What do you mean by different?'

'Just different.' I shrugged.

Pursing her lips, she paused to look at her notes.

'Kerri, for me to write up your evaluation, you have to be more forthcoming with how you've felt and how you're feeling now.'

Her tone changed from friendly to stern. 'I need this information to make the best judgment on your behalf and where we proceed from here.'

Seeing I wasn't going to elaborate, she moved on and asked more questions.

'I see that you have been taking phenobarbital since you were six. Can you tell me why you had to start taking the phenobarbital and how that made you feel?'

This was probably the easiest of all the questions. This, at least, I felt comfortable to talk about.

'When I was two, my dad took me to visit his family. My grandfather owned horses. Anyway, I wandered into one of the enclosures, and one of the ponies charged at me, knocking me to the ground and trampling my head. They found me lying on the ground, unconscious with blood everywhere. He hit me above my right eye, here.'

I showed her the light scar running through my right eyebrow.

'Oooh,' she winced, leaning forward to see the scar. 'How many stitches did you have?'

'Seven stitches I think, not sure really. The doctor said I could have been blinded, paralyzed or even killed if the pony had kicked any lower.'

'Wow, you were lucky. Now, your parents were still married at that time, weren't they? Was your mom there?'

'No, I believe she had to work.'

'I see, so what happened next?'

'Well, four years later when I was six, my dad took us again to visit his family.'

I paused, thinking about all the incidents that had happened when my dad had taken us to visit his family; the pony incident, Joe being attacked by our grandfather's Doberman Pinscher, the dog biting into his neck like a vampire and shaking him around like a rag doll. I had almost fallen out of my aunt's car on the highway when the door opened. Thankfully, she grabbed me before I fell.

'Kerri,' Dr. Green said. I didn't realize I had drifted off.

'Oh … yeah … sorry. Anyway, we stopped for a break at my dad's friend's house. All I remember was that I was lying on his couch when I had a seizure.' I told her the whole story in detail about the seizure and how my dad held me until I came to—hot, sweaty and crying.

'That sounds very scary. I imagine you must have been very frightened?'

'I guess.'

In truth, I was scared to death. My dad had called my mom, and she flew out immediately to meet us at the hospital. An X-ray showed scar tissue from the pony accident had grown along with my developing brain. It produced a surge in brain activity, inducing a seizure.

'So the doctor prescribed the phenobarbital to control the seizures?'

'Yes.'

'How did the drug make you feel?'

'I don't know. Not great.'

Actually they made me feel terrible. One of the many side effects of phenobarbital is depression, and the minute I started taking it, my life was completed altered. At age six, my little life turned into a full-time nightmare. I found it impossible to smile. I had forgotten how to, and I had no idea why. I didn't have patience for anything. I felt anxious and cried all the time. I'd cry if I didn't get something I wanted, and I'd cry if I did get it. You couldn't win with me. I watched all the other kids in school engrossed in conversations and having fun during recess. To me, it seemed so easy for them to enjoy their days. I envied them. I felt like an outcast.

To make matters worse, every three months like clockwork I was scheduled for a day full of tests. I'd have to stay up as late as possible the night before to guarantee that I would sleep through the EEGs and CAT Scans. My mother knew how much I hated going and how it made me feel like a lab rat surrounded by several doctors who always asked the same questions and pricked and prodded at me. She would try to make the night before fun, taking me to the video store. Sometimes, I chose a late-night show that I wasn't usually allowed to stay up and watch. After the EEGs and CAT Scans, the nurse would take several vials of blood to test for hormone levels and then the doctor would adjust my phenobarbital dosage accordingly.

'You haven't had any since you arrived here at the hospital,' Dr. Green said, checking her notes. 'How are you feeling without it?'

'Okay, I guess.'

'Good. You've had no seizures or difficulties without it?'

'No.'

'That's great. I think this is a good start, Kerri. Do you feel okay talking about this?'

'Sure.'

'I think we're starting to make some progress.'

She looked down at her notes again. When she looked up at me, she adjusted her position in her chair, crossed her legs and leaned forward. Once in this more intimidating position, she commenced with the tough questions; the ones we were really here for. 'What were you feeling last week when you tried to take your life?'

I fidgeted in my seat and folded my arms. 'I wanted to die,' I said blankly. 'I think that's quite obvious.'

She sighed, 'But *why* did you want to kill yourself?'

'Because I wanted to.'

'There must have been a reason?' she implored.

'Because I wanted to die.'

My answer didn't go down too well with her. She continued to interrogate me, rewording that question in different ways with increasingly heavy sighs in between. My answer stayed the same. I thought it was pretty obvious why I did what I did. I might've given her a little more insight had I fully understood what my life was supposed to be like and why it wasn't. My life seemed completely out of control for so long that I had forgotten what being normal was like. My days consisted of being strung out and depressed on drugs, arguing with family who obviously found me a burden, ostracized from friends, and dealing with schoolwork that I couldn't quite get half the time. I didn't want my life to be this way anymore, and I saw no other way out, no future for myself. I couldn't take it any longer, so I wanted to die. It was that simple. Why does anyone do anything? Because they want to! I'd put my mother through so much this week I wasn't willing to be truthful and hurt her any further. I stuck with my answer.

Eventually, she gave up asking. 'Well, Kerri, our time is up. Let me walk you back down to your room where I can have a talk with your mother.'

'Okay.'

I felt our time was a complete waste. Dr. Green apparently was annoyed that I wouldn't answer her questions. I felt torn myself. I wanted to tell Dr. Green *exactly* how I felt, yet I wasn't willing to be honest and cause more pain for my family. I started to feel sick to my stomach again thinking I might have thrown away the only opportunity to get out of this place. I got up, and she escorted me down the corridor to the elevator and then to my waiting mom.

'How did it go, Dr. Green?' my mom asked.

'Can I have a word with you please, outside?'

'Yes, of course,' my mom said.

'Kerri, please sit down and put on the TV. This should only take a few minutes.'

I slowly walked over to my bed as they exited the room. Once the door closed, I tiptoed back and pressed my ear to it.

'I'm afraid I don't have good news,' I heard Dr. Green say quietly. 'Unfortunately, Kerri was not as forthcoming as I expected. She did answer a few questions somewhat satisfactorily. However, I was hoping to gain some insight on why she tried to take her life, and sadly, she would not elaborate on the subject.'

'Oh.' My mother sounded disappointed. 'What does that mean?'

'I feel Kerri is still in a fragile state of mind and would most likely attempt to take her life again. In my opinion, she is a danger to herself and should be supervised around the clock. I recommend that Kerri is placed in the nearest mental health hospital for at least 30 days of observation and counseling. After 30 days, I will re-evaluate her and see if there has been any improvement. I've compiled this information in my session with Kerri and will make copies for her doctor as well. I know this is not what you wanted to hear, but I think this is what's best for Kerri.'

'I understand. I am terrified she will try again. I can't lose her. If you feel this is the direction we need to take, then I agree with you,' I heard my mother say sounding like she was on the verge of tears.

'I will finish my report and send you a copy to sign off on,' Dr. Green said.

I couldn't believe Dr. Green said that. *Why* would she say I wanted to *kill* myself again? I didn't. I was full of anger with her assuming I was a danger to myself. I kept quiet for the sake of my mother. I didn't want to hurt her any more than I already had. Because of this, I was going to be sent off to a mental hospital. This had better be a joke and a cruel one at that. I heard them wrapping up their conversation.

I tiptoed my way back to bed and attempted to look like I was reading the magazines my mother had bought me, but it was no use when my mother entered the room with tears in her eyes.

I couldn't help myself. I began to cry too.

'I'm so sorry, Kerri. We have to send you away.'

## CHAPTER 4 – THE LOONY BIN

I arrived at the Mental Health Hospital in an ambulance. I was not allowed to be discharged to the care of my parents who were more than capable of transporting me to the hospital. I felt trapped. I had tried to kill myself, and I couldn't tell my parents why, at least not yet. Now I was made to spend the next 30 days of my life in a loony bin.

I was completely freaked out about riding in an ambulance. As was my mother, especially since she wasn't allowed to ride in the ambulance with me. The nurse told her it was hospital policy for suicidal patients. It made me feel like a common criminal. We checked in, only to find that they had no rooms available for me. Apparently, the attempted suicide rate was high that month. They were setting up a temporary room for me just for a few days until a room became available. After a short wait, two female nurses dressed in standard uniform led us down the corridors. I felt like I should have been wearing a standard issued orange prison jumpsuit with handcuffs.

My heart rate surged as I peered into the small room they had prepared for me, which was far from normal looking. It reminded me of a sparse prison cell, except the walls were padded with thick brown fabric. My legs suddenly felt like jelly, and I got an instant hot flash and cold sweat both at the same time. Panicking, I turned to my mom who had lost all color in her face and looked as if she was going to pass out.

'No way!' my mom shrieked, on the verge of hysteria. 'You got to be kidding me. You cannot put my daughter in a padded cell. There's got to be another room for Kerri!'

'No, ma'am, we are full this month,' the nurse said. 'We've tried to make the room as comfortable as possible. As soon as another room comes available, we will move her.' Somehow, that wasn't very reassuring.

I took another look. The room was about 8 feet by 12 and covered with row after row of brown faux leather with thick padding behind it. In the middle of the room, toward the left outside wall of the building, was a tiny window made of unbreakable glass. The ceiling was covered in the same faux brown leather material with the only break in the pattern being a ceiling light in the center of the room. There was a bed in the corner that looked like it had been borrowed from Alcatraz and a battered old bureau against the wall. A thin white robe with a zipper lay folded on the bed, and a pair of slippers lay on top.

Over a week ago, I probably wouldn't have cared; I was suicidal after all. Now I felt different as I hadn't had drugs in my system for more than a week, and the thick fog in my mind was starting to clear. Here I was in this awful place against my will. I had to earn the trust of not only my mother, but also the staff, doctors and anyone else who had the authority to sign the papers saying I was 'OK.'

One of the nurses stayed in the room while my mom helped me unpack. Everything had to be inspected before I could put it away in the battered old bureau. The power cord for my portable cassette player was confiscated since it could be used for strangulation. My BIC disposable razors were confiscated as well so I couldn't slit my wrists. The nurse explained they would keep the razors and provide them for use during shower time only. Anything that could potentially be used to harm myself or others was taken from me, even my belt. These items which I used every day and which I had no idea could be so dangerous, were put in a plastic box labelled with my name.

A staff member inventorying my confiscated items with yellow stickers marked 'inspected' said, 'Your items are still yours, Kerri, but you do not have the privilege to use them as freely as you did before. Once you prove you can be trusted and are well enough to leave this hospital, your items will be returned to you.'

The whole process was demoralizing. I felt like I was truly in prison. The only things missing were the metal bars, a disgruntled roommate, and a disgusting rotting toilet. It was time for my mom to leave. I looked at her with tears running down my face, and my hands balled into fists. 'Mom, please don't leave me here,' I pleaded. 'I promise I won't ever do it again!'

She gave me the biggest hug; it reminded me of the times when I was little and upset. All I needed was a hug from her that fixed everything. I could feel her tears running down the side of my cheek as she held onto me as tightly as she could. Then, she backed away. 'Kerri, believe me, I don't want you to be here at all, but you need to understand, I don't trust you anymore. I don't know why you did this to yourself, and I don't know if you'll try again. Dr. Green said that you were a danger to yourself. I have to take the doctor's advice and keep you here until they say otherwise, or until we see a change in you.'

She kissed me and said, 'I love you. I am only a phone call away. I'll be back to visit each week.' More tears streamed down her face as the nurse ushered her out.

I felt completely alone and terrified knowing I had to sleep in this horrible room. The padded door with a small index-sized window closed behind them. I sat down on the creepy old bed and cried.

They call these places loony bins for a good reason. Strangely enough, I felt like I was the only sane one. This place was full of kids who wanted to kill themselves and had been stopped from doing so. Not a day would go by without one of them trying to finish off what they had started, often with gruesome results.

One day, I was playing solitaire with Jerry, a staff member there. Jerry was such a sweet man, who smelled like sour milk. Being friends with him was my only fond memory of the place. He must have been 400-pounds and wore clothes from Big and Tall. His job was to have extra eyes on us kids, a guard, so to speak. It was really hard to inhale his stench as we'd sit every day for several hours playing solitaire, checkers, and other games while discussing everyday stuff like, how did I sleep, what were my favorite foods, was there anything new to tell from the last visit I had with my family? He was the only one who accepted me as I was and didn't pester me with questions about what I did and how I ended up here.

Suddenly, a teenage boy sitting at a long craft table on the other side of the room caught my eye. He had been busy drawing and coloring when he sat abruptly back in his chair. Placing a pencil in each hand, he proceeded to jam a pencil into each of his eyes. He screamed as blood spurted everywhere. Jerry flew out of his chair and hit the emergency alarm. A handful of staff members came running into the hallway and helped Jerry carry the boy away. I was told to cover my eyes and lay my head down on the table until one of the nurses came and collected me. I watched the manager walk and instruct the staff to get everyone to their rooms. The janitor passed me with cleaning equipment and started to disinfect the area. I never saw the boy again. To this day, I wonder if he survived.

The mental health hospital ran on a pretty tight schedule. Everyone woke up at 7 a.m. Without delay, we had to shower immediately before breakfast, no exceptions. This was followed by rotated activities with the only interruption of lunch. After some mandatory outdoor time, dinner was served promptly at 6 p.m. Everyone's light went out at 9 p.m. Each day was exactly the same boring routine.

The shower routine was an interesting one. We had exactly one hour for everyone to take a shower before breakfast. Because the hospital ran on a tight schedule, we were all expected to be dressed in our robe and slippers and ready to enter the bathroom, shower, and brush our teeth in the allotted time given. A towel was given to you while waiting in line for the shower, and then immediately taken away when you exited. We were handed our disposable razors for shaving as we entered the bathroom and assigned to our individual shower stalls. The female staff would keep an eye on everyone. The razor would then be taken away from you as you came out of the shower before drying off and getting dressed. The whole charade was an assembly line, with each person allowed only five minutes in the shower.

When an attempted suicide is an everyday occurrence, you tend to become immune to it. A sort of numbness sets in, and soon you almost don't notice it like a regularly scheduled fire drill. It's routine. There are no surprises because you've come to expect it. A popular place where someone would try to kill themselves was the bathroom. One girl who had asked to take a bath somehow managed to obtain a plastic bag. When no one was looking, she slipped it over her head and submerged herself in the bathwater. They found her in time. You had to be careful with the razors in the shower. Any accidents could be construed as an attempt to hurt yourself, for which there would be severe consequences. Once I was in the shower and in the process of shaving my legs, I accidentally cut the skin on my right ankle. I screamed out in pain and quickly started to bleed. Before I could do anything, I heard heavy footsteps closing in on my stall. Within seconds, my shower curtain was pulled. 'Drop the razor, and put your hands up!' shouted the female staff member.

I immediately dropped the razor and placed one hand on my bleeding ankle and the other up in the air as if I was under arrest.

'I swear I wasn't trying to kill myself again. I accidentally cut skin off my ankle,' I said. I was then forced out of the shower to be examined on the spot, naked and all. At 13, I was not comfortable getting naked in front of anybody. I had never felt so violated. When the examination was done, and the lady confirmed with a nurse it was indeed a shaving accident, I was then allowed to towel off. She gave me a Band-Aid, and I was escorted back to my room not long after. My razor was confiscated once again and stored in a bin behind a door affixed with a red sign that read STAFF ONLY— KEEP OUT!

Among our everyday activities, we would have a daily two-hour group session, meeting with staff members and psychiatrists. The staff would usher us into the 'group room' and would try to encourage each of us to 'explore our feelings.' They wanted updates on how we were adjusting here and what we thought of the other patients. How were we all getting along? Did we have any problems? Was anyone threatening to us in any way? This normally coaxed less than half of the group into talking while the rest listened. Next was the psychiatrists' turn. Their job was to find out why each of us tried to take our lives, and in some cases repeatedly tried. Ultimately, they wanted us to admit the reason for ourselves, so they could then attempt to 'fix us'. During these stupid ass sessions, I always felt while they tried to 'shrink us' we were objects, not individual people with individual problems. I think they expected better results as if all they had to do was wave a magic wand, and we'd all be cured of our 'problems'. I felt if they actually took the time to understand us as the individuals we were, there might have been more success during these meetings. I'll admit, it was fascinating to watch, yet most kids like me wouldn't divulge their reasons why. We would only observe the other kids' conversations with the psychiatrists. Whenever the question was posed to me, the same question Dr. Green tried so painstakingly to rephrase, again and again, I stuck to my original answer, 'Because I wanted to.' And they'd always say that my response was not good enough.

The bright points were speaking to my mom several times during the week when I would always beg her to take me out of this prison hole. Scheduled once a week on Saturdays for an hour was the family session. Every Saturday afternoon my mom, George, Joe, my dad and his wife, would join me for a session with the psychiatrist. We would be ushered into the meeting room that held several plastic folding chairs facing each other in a circle.

My father sat on one side with his arms crossed and George opposite, both openly ignoring each other. The idea was to talk about my relationships with my family and further discuss what might have caused me to take my own life. At our third session, my brother decided to share how he was feeling. He described a particular afternoon at home since I'd been away.

'I was lying on the living-room carpet watching one of my favorite shows, and I started to laugh,' he explained. 'I said to Kerri, 'Wasn't that so funny, I love this show. Isn't this the funniest show you've ever seen, Kerri?' I waited for her to say something, and when she didn't, I looked over at the couch, and she wasn't there. She hadn't been there the whole time. Kerri had been gone for over three weeks, and I'd forgotten. That day watching my favorite TV show for me was like any other Saturday at home with her; we'd done that for years. I completely forgot she was away in the loony bin … Sorry … mental health hospital,' he corrected himself. 'I kept staring at the couch feeling sad and angry. Sad she was gone and angry at Kerri for what she had done. I started to cry.'

I couldn't believe it. I was overwhelmed to hear how much he missed me. I truly believed my suicide would be the best outcome for me, but I hadn't considered the effect it would have on my family, least of all Joe. I was the big sister, always protecting him. My mother referred to me as his 'little mother' because I'd always taken care of him and done everything for him. Unfortunately, as we grew up, we grew apart. We hung out with different friends and didn't seem to feel the same way about each other as we once had. At school, we'd make sure not to acknowledge each other. Once we were home and forced to be in the same room, we fought.

I remember a day we fought over something stupid. At the time, it seemed important. Joe didn't realize he had broken a necklace my mom had given me, and that set me off. I charged at him and in seconds, he managed to get me on the floor. He held my face firmly against the carpet and dragged me by my hair, making sure my face never left the carpet until he was done. The next day, I had to go to school with the biggest rug burn on my face. It was humiliating. The only times you would see us enjoy each other's company would be when we were watching TV together or at a family gathering. I truly believed that he hated me as much as I hated him most of the time, and I thought his and my life would have been better off with me being dead.

I looked around the room and saw that his story had affected almost everyone else too, except my dad and his wife. He looked irate, and his wife, well for all the years I knew her, she never seemed to have any other expression except disgust for both my brother and me. She never made us feel welcomed in their home whenever we visited. We again were the burdens, not only to my father but to her as well. We were the baggage that came with her marrying him. She really didn't care at all; she was just there for show. For the past three weeks, my father had not said a word. He had just sat there looking angry. The psychiatrist decided that today was as good a time as any to question him.

'Mr. Phillips, can you think back to several months ago. At any point, when you visited Kerri, did you notice a change in her demeanor?'

My dad said nothing. He zoned out; it was like all the other times we expected him to show up, but he never did. He might have been there in body, but not in mind. The psychiatrist continued, 'I'd also like to know more about you. How have you been dealing with Kerri's attempted suicide? How has your work and home life been affected since it happened?'

He shifted uncomfortably in his chair. My father never liked personal questions. Over the years, I had always asked him about his childhood and my deceased grandmother. He would always tell me he 'didn't want to talk about it.' His face turned red ... I could see he was going to explode.

The psychiatrist pressed him even further. 'How do you feel about your daughter's mental state? Did you notice any changes in her, leading up to her suicide attempt?'

'NO!' He finally looked up at the psychiatrist. 'I have nothing to say!'

It seemed to me as though my father needed counseling more than anyone in this room, especially me, the one who tried to kill herself. After this outburst, the shrink should surely let me go and admit him instead.

'Please answer the psychiatrist's questions. For Kerri's sake,' my mom begged.

'You do understand we are all here so that we can help Kerri heal?' the psychiatrist added.

'I understand quite well, and I am not going to talk about me, my home life, my work or my past!'

'Come on, we're all here for Kerri,' George said.

I was surprised to hear this from George. He seemed like he really wanted me to receive all the help I could from everyone present.

'NO!' He stood up so quickly, knocking over his chair. He rushed out of the room leaving his wife, like the rest of us, speechless.

We all stared at her.

She took a deep breath and finally spoke: 'Um … I think I'll go see what's going on with him,' she said and left the room. Neither of them came back. That was the last time my father and his wife ever attended a family session. They never called or visited me again at the Mental Health Hospital.

Compared to the other kids here, my main problem had always been the drugs; the phenobarbital. As I had been drug-free since the night I overdosed, my mind was clearing up a bit each day. Surprisingly, I had also not had a single seizure. I started to think that perhaps I had grown out of them. Could I possibly live a life without seizures or the drugs to control them? I began to realize that I was going to be okay, even being stuck in this crazy hellhole.

After 30 days in the loony bin, I had seen more than a girl my age should. I felt I was growing up too quickly living here and being exposed to horrific occurrences I wished I never knew about. For once in my life, I wanted to experience a normal life. I didn't know exactly what 'normal' was, still I knew it would be better than the life I had been living for the past seven years drugged up and depressed. I wanted a fresh start; I wanted to learn how to be happy, to excel at school, join in school activities and feel a part of something. The most important thing I learned being stuck here was that I would never attempt to take my life again. I wanted to live.

I had been in the hospital for a little over a month when I asked my mom to sign my release.

'You've got to get me out of here!' I pleaded.

'Just a little longer, Kerri,' she said. 'George, your brother and I want you to get better.'

'I am better. Mom, please, the kids in here are trying to kill themselves every day, it's horrible.'

'Our home has not been the same since you left, and we want to be a hundred percent sure that you are healed and will never try to hurt yourself again. The doctor said that you haven't been participating in your group sessions. You've not given them any real information explaining how you've been feeling. They believe you are still a threat to yourself, and that you'll try again.'

'I won't. I'm feeling much better. It was the drugs making me feel that way. I haven't had any drugs at all this last month, and I haven't had any seizures either. Please, Mom, I can't stand to stay in this place for another day. I want to come home,' I begged.

She sighed. 'I'll talk to the doctor about it. That's all I can promise you right now.'

We started to talk about what was going on at home; when she was planning on returning to work and what Joe was up to. She asked about my routine, looking for anything different from what I had said last week. We struggled to have a conversation. I wasn't in the mood for chit-chat, certainly not here. I couldn't stomach the idea of witnessing one more attempted suicide, one more patient losing it. Watching them as they were held down and forced to put on a straitjacket before being dragged into the padded room I once stayed in. I wanted to feel normal. A staff member popped their head in to let my mother and I know that our time was up.

As she was leaving, she turned around to look at me one last time. I think she must have seen something in me that she hadn't seen in years because she returned a few days later, and against the doctors' advice, she signed my release papers.

* * *

Pulling up to our home was amazing. I almost had forgotten what it looked like. Our home was small, a ranch design with three bedrooms, one full bath, living room, and kitchen, and was surrounded by a forest of trees. Our next-door neighbor on one side was 20 plus feet away and on the other side were acres of forest. Our street was a main cut through for Mac Trucks. There were no sidewalks and only a few streetlights. If you chose to go for a walk, you had to be extra careful of the speeding cars. The exterior was painted a dark red with white shutters. Entering our home through the front door, you were immediately in the living room. Nothing had changed; the TV was in the far corner next to the fireplace, the three-seater couch was against the light colored paneled wall, the laundry basket full of clothes to be folded was sitting on the two seater couch on the opposite wall like it was the night I attempted to take my life.

I walked slowly through the living room, taking it all in. The narrow hallway connected all the rooms, and the kitchen was behind the living room. I walked into the kitchen to get a drink and noticed my mom's calendar on the fridge, penned with upcoming appointments. George's steel-tip boots were in their usual place in front of the side kitchen door that we never used. Exiting the kitchen and walking down the hallway, it only took seven steps to pass the bathroom on my right. Joe's and my parents' rooms were straight ahead. Joe's messy room was on the left, my parents' room was in the middle, and mine was on the right.

I was relieved to be home, to sleep and wake up in my own bed. There is a saying that you don't appreciate something until it is gone. It's true. I was grateful for everything, even the smallest things like taking a pee when I wanted and not having to ask permission to get a glass of milk while walking from one room to the next without an escort. The thought of never wearing the assigned white robe and slippers made me feel extremely thankful. I woke up to an abundance of light streaming through my open bedroom window, something I hadn't seen in a long time. I loved the way the sun reflected off my walls and felt the breeze from all the trees in our backyard. Looking around, I admired my shelves, which held all of my hair accessories, curling iron, and hairspray. On the opposite wall was my collection of porcelain masks I had amassed since I was ten. I had forgotten all the details of beautiful colors and designs on them. It was great to no longer see plain white walls; it made me smile to view the several different posters of Johnny Depp from his series *21 Jump Street*.

*I'm really home. Yesterday truly did happen when my mom came, signed me out, and we took the few belongings I had!*

What a day this was going to be. I could stay in my PJs and enjoy the comfort of my home, feeling completely safe among my family knowing they were not going to interrogate me anytime soon or on a regular basis. I wasn't on a tedious schedule anymore. I could sit in my bed, pick up one of my books and read the hours away. I could just be me and deal with what was to come one day at a time.

Everyone else seemed pleased to have me home too. For a while, we all got along together, and the intermittent arguing stopped for a bit.

The doctors tried to convince my parents that I would not last long at home and that I would try to harm myself again, probably within the first few days. My release, therefore, came with a set of conditions. If I violated any of them, I'd be sent back to the mental hospital for a much longer stay.

The terms of my release were as follows:

1. I had to ask permission to use anything seen as potentially dangerous, such as a steak knife, which was carefully supervised during dinner. Either that or my food would be cut up for me. My shaving routine resembled the schedule I had in the looney bin, once again closely supervised, and as soon as I was done with it, my razor was locked up in the bathroom.
2. Medicine, even aspirin for a headache, had to be administered by either my mom or George from the now padlocked medicine cabinet.
3. I had to visit a psychiatrist once a week; she would assess my progress. This was mandatory. No exceptions.
4. I was not to be left alone under any circumstances. The doorknob on my bedroom door had to be removed, and my door was to be left ajar and never closed.
5. Lastly, I had to promise my mother that I would always tell her how I felt and be completely honest with her, no matter what.

That last rule has stayed with me to this day and has become a part of who I am.

Almost two months had passed since my attempted suicide. It was the end of June 1987 when I returned home. I had missed the last month of seventh grade and the graduation ceremony into eighth grade. School was out on summer break until after Labor Day weekend. It was a blessing not to face my classmates just yet. The two foot tall 'Get Well Soon' card that had sat in my room at the hospitals and now stood on my bedroom nightstand was a constant reminder from my classmates and teachers that they knew exactly what I had attempted to do. I guess Hallmark doesn't make 'So happy you didn't succeed in killing yourself' cards. Could you imagine the teacher walking into the card store and asking an employee 'where are the attempted suicide cards?' There were so many signatures; I don't think I even knew half of these people. It made it a little easier that school was over. I wasn't sure how I was going to face everyone. I had two more months to figure that out.

Now home, you would have thought I would have jumped at the chance of being FREE to come and go and hang out with my friends like I did before. Instead, I started to become a recluse. TT had come calling several days after I returned. She was so excited to see me. As I came to the door, she leaned in and lifted her arms towards me. She wanted to hug me; I could tell she had missed me. I had missed her too, but I felt very withdrawn from my old life. I took a step back; I wasn't' able to accept this affection from her. I still felt incredibly ashamed of myself, and I wasn't ready for her forgiveness. I was starting to fall into a new form of depression, so scared of having to deal with those people who knew what I had done. TT had witnessed it all. How do you look into your best friend's eyes with her knowing what you had tried to do? It was too much for me. I wasn't ready to let her in.

'It's so good to see you!' TT said to me. Her smile broke my heart as I felt the same way. I didn't know how to express my gratitude for what she and her family had done for me.

'It's really good to see you too. How have you been?' I didn't know what else to say.

'Nothing's changed here. You know how it is around here. Can you come out and get some fresh air with me?'

'I'm so sorry; I can't come out right now. I hope you can understand. Maybe later?'

I could see the hurt on TT's face. I am sure she had a ton to tell me about, and I assumed a million questions to ask me. 'Okay. I'll come back in a couple of days, and we'll do something. It's summer; we have to jump in my pool and see the rest of the kids. They all miss you too.'

'I'd like that.' I lied. I wanted to tell her how I was feeling, and why I couldn't come out, yet I didn't wish to disappoint her with the truth.

'Okay, I'll see you in a couple of days; I'm so happy you are home,' TT said smiling.

I smiled back and gently closed the door. I watched her walk down the driveway and continue down the dangerous street. We didn't have any sidewalks, and it was a cut through for our town. No one ever drove the speed limit. It was always a risk walking to each other's home. I made sure she didn't see me watching her.

TT tried for several weeks to coax me out of the house, but I just couldn't. I was still extremely ashamed of myself. I never intended her to be there that night. Knowing what she witnessed upset me greatly, and I still didn't know how to deal with it. Her excitement quickly turned to anger. I never wanted to hurt TT, and yet I did. Soon, she stopped trying. I pushed her (and anyone else that came calling) away.

I no longer went out riding my bike around the neighborhood. I felt it was easier to hide inside my home, turn on the TV and watch the drama in other people's lives through soap operas like *Guiding Light* and *The Young and The Restless* while comforting myself with fried Pillsbury Dough Biscuits. In my home education class, I learned how to turn biscuits into donuts by scooping out a hole in the middle of the biscuit. Watching the dough submerge and expand one by one into a heated saucepan with vegetable oil was mesmerizing to me. A few minutes later and voila, I had a dozen donuts all for me. I had never been one to eat when I was either stressed or upset. Unfortunately, after coming home from the loony bin I found it difficult to adjust. I had no idea how to rehabilitate myself back into my life. I knew my family was healing as well, so I couldn't really count on them either.

When I was on the phenobarbital, the only thing that made me feel better was watching TV. It transported me into another life; a fantasy where there were no seizures, no hospital visits, no drugs, no parents bickering over me or my brother. Neither anxiety nor depression existed here either. I could give in to the fantasy and leave my unhappy world behind for an hour or two.

*The Love Boat, Fantasy Island, Solid Gold, The Million Dollar Man, The Bionic Woman,* and *Battlestar Galactica*; these shows comforted me. I wouldn't feel lost; for a short time I could be a part of that world.

The best show of all was *The Monkees*! I never missed a single episode. The Monkees were a rock band who had their very own TV show from 1966 to 1968, followed by a comeback in the mid-80s through re-runs. The handsome foursome of Mike, Micky, Peter, and Davy. They had a bit of everything in their show; drama, comedy, romance, and music. For me, the biggest reason I was completely transfixed on the show was Davy Jones. He possessed distinct differences; for starters, he was the shortest band member. He played the piano, tambourine and guitar, which made him unique to me. His accent was mesmerizing, not at all like the other boys. My mom said that he was from England. I had never heard an English accent before and had to listen very carefully to understand what he was saying. My whole view of the world changed. Up until then, I had assumed everyone spoke with the same American accent that I had. Coming from a small town in New England, you don't realize how big the world really is.

I was spellbound by Davy's voice. I fantasized like I'm sure a lot of girls did, about meeting him. I wanted to fall deeply in love with him and live happily ever after. I knew right then and there that an American boy wouldn't do. I wanted to marry an Englishman.

My sessions with the psychiatrist every week didn't help me feel any better about my life. She would show me flash cards with blotted pictures on them and ask how I felt when I looked at them. I swore that my mom was throwing her money down the drain with this lady. It was a waste of time; it was mentally exhausting showing me multicolored blotted pictures one after the other and asking what I saw and how they made me feel. Looking at the weird pictures annoyed me, and made me angry because I thought the sessions were stupid. After several more appointments, I tried to get my mom to stop the sessions. Unfortunately, she declined. The sessions were meant to help me accept what I had done and try to forgive myself, which was easier said than done. At the very least, I could say that after more than two months without any seizures or phenobarbital, I was starting to become the person I think I was always meant to be. A person that could laugh easily and was no longer confused and knew that she could handle schoolwork. I felt quite smart and certain that when I returned to school, I'd be able to complete assignments. I was determined to do well in school, and for once could think about wanting to have a future. I was not entirely sure what that was. Nevertheless, I was full of hope. Something I was not able to feel for as long as I could remember.

It had been almost three months after I had attempted suicide. One very hot and humid night in August, my mom and George called Joe and me out from our rooms into the living room. Looking at each other, Joe and I thought we were in trouble.

'It's been a very long and difficult time these past twelve weeks. We all have been through so much, and I feel as a family we need to reconnect,' my mother said. She then looked over to George.

'Your mom and I have been talking about things we could do. We had planned to do this in the New Year, but with all that has happened, we have decided to move up our plans before you both go back to school,' George said.

Joe and I kept looking back and forth at each of them, not sure where this was going. To our surprise, they felt we all deserved a break, and a vacation, which was long overdue. We were going on a trip that would bring our family back together again and put the past behind us.

'With that being said, what do you both think about going to Disney World?'

Joe and I looked at each other in disbelief. Joe was the first to speak, 'Duh, what do you think we think? YES!'

'What he said!' I chimed in.

'Great, because we leave first thing in the morning!' my mom said, smiling.

# CHAPTER 5 – EPISODE FROM THE TWILIGHT ZONE

A vacation to Walt Disney World was the trip of a lifetime for us. Joe and I couldn't believe it. We had always wanted to go, and now it was happening. Since I returned from the looney bin, my relationship with Joe began to improve. I loved that we were talking and connecting again. Something we hadn't known how to do over the last several years.

One day while I was helping him clean his room when he said, 'You almost died, and you were gone for over a month. It was the worst month of my life. I kept thinking what if TT didn't call. I am so glad you're alive Kerri, but if you had died, I would have hated you; I would never have forgiven you.'

The tears streamed down my face and started to soak my shirt. I hugged Joe and didn't want to let him go. I had forgotten how much I missed this; we hadn't hugged in years.

'I always thought you hated me. I figured your life would be better off without me in it.'

When Joe and I were little, we would sleep in each other's bed the night before Christmas. One year when I was little around four or five years old, I wanted to sleep with Joe one Christmas Eve. We had so much fun that night excitedly talking about Santa and what he might bring us that we started to swap beds each year and it became our special tradition. There were always presents under the tree from my mother and lying in bed we'd try to guess what each other's presents might be based on the size of it. We'd talk and talk until, finally exhausted; we'd fall asleep and dream about Christmas morning. The night before we left for Disney, we told our mother we wanted to sleep in the same bed like we used to all those years ago.

'Go for it,' my mother said.

They didn't care; they were happy to see us getting along again. Try as hard as we could, Joe and I were too excited to fall asleep, and we pretty much talked the entire night. We had heard about the new Michael Jackson 'Captain E-O' attraction at Epcot and were anxious to see it. I wanted photos with all the characters, and Joe was excited to walk through the Magic Kingdom and wanted to go on all the rides. He wasn't picky; he wanted to get out of the house and have a change of scenery. I felt the same way. Just as the sun was about to come up and we both started to doze, the alarm went off.

'Ahhh!' I screamed. I was so startled by the alarm that I fell off the bed.

Joe groaned under his pillow. I climbed back up and shook him.

'It's today, weirdo, get up!' Joe wasn't a morning person, and there was simply no time to waste.

My parents' alarm went off several minutes later, and I heard grumbling. Within seconds, I saw George leave their bedroom, and I knew the first thing he'd want to do was put the kettle on. I left Joe's room and went to see my mom.

'Morning, Kerri, today's the day! We didn't want to tell you weeks in advance because the wait is torture. We figured less than 24 hours was a better bet. It was nice to hear you getting along.'

'I know. It felt like old times. I've missed him,' I said snuggling up to her in her long T-shirt styled nightgown. She looked as happy and excited as Joe and I was.

'Well, remember this moment, and try not to forget how close you two really are, especially when you both start annoying each other later on.'

At that moment, George called my mom from the kitchen to let her know a cup of tea was waiting.

She kissed me. 'Now go get ready,' she said, and then got up to head to the kitchen.

It took us an hour to get out of the door. We loaded up the car with our suitcases and made our way to the Airport. Neither Joe nor I had been on a plane before. We were excited, and extremely nervous.

'Kerri,' Joe leaned over to me in the back seat of our car. 'Can you believe this is really happening? I'm so excited; I can't stop smiling!'

'Me too, my cheeks are starting to hurt.'

Looking at the enormous plane we would be getting on was daunting and surreal at the same time. We were speechless with mouths gaping open like fish underwater. Boarding the plane was surprisingly quick and thankfully uneventful; our seats were the first row of four in economy class. As we lifted off, this trip to Florida felt like a new lease of life, and the best part was nobody knew my darkest secret. I could be Kerri.

Everything about the trip excited us; the drinks and the peanuts on the plane, riding the escalator to baggage claim, even something as mundane as picking up the rental car. I felt it was the perfect day; Joe and I didn't argue, not once.

* * *

We checked into two adjoining rooms at the Marriott Hotel on International Drive, our home for the next seven days. After dropping off our luggage, we set out to explore while our parents unpacked. I don't know if it was the Florida sun, the palm trees, or the lack of drugs and having a completely clear head, but I felt euphoric. It had been so long since I had felt any joy. Suffering from crippling depression at such a young age, I couldn't remember what happiness felt like. I finally realized that the reason I wanted to kill myself was because I had been in pain for so long; mentally and emotionally, and I couldn't stand the dysfunction between my family and new step parents. I wanted to be FREE from it all. Coming to Florida and getting away, helped me understand the true meaning of happiness.

I leisurely strolled my way to the pool, taking my time admiring landscapes and flower beds full of exotic flowers I didn't know the names of, accented by decorative rocks. I had never seen so many beautifully potted flowers, rows and rows of palm trees. It was my first time in Florida, and it was as if all of my senses had been suddenly heightened. My senses had been dulled for so long, practically nonexistent. For the last seven years, I felt completely withdrawn. Here in Florida, the world seemed big again. As I walked to the pool, I enjoyed taking off my flip-flops and running my toes through the freshly cut grass. I'd never felt grass like this before; it felt crunchy under my toes. It had been a long time since I'd been outside; I laid down on the grass and enjoyed the sunrays on my skin. It was so peaceful lying there with my eyes closed. Minutes later, sweat started to form on my forehead, and I got up and looked for the pool.

Approaching the pool bar, I heard Caribbean music and noticed the Marriott had laid out a nice buffet. A waiter with a name tag that read 'Gus' watched me as I approached the table.

'Welcome to the Marriott, would you like to try some delicious fruit and some freshly squeezed juices?'

'Thank you. I've never tried any of those fruits or had freshly squeezed anything.' I pointed to a platter of slices of orange and green colored fruit. 'What are they called?'

Gus was tall, about six feet, and his muscles were clearly defined under his shirt. He grinned at me and said, 'That's cantaloupe and honeydew melon. Here, try some; take a glass or two of the freshly squeezed orange juice. I promise you will enjoy it.'

I couldn't help but blush ... 'Thanks.'

I grabbed the bowl from Gus, picked up a tray, poured two glasses of orange juice and walked to an empty table with an opened umbrella. I started to eat as Gus came by once again to hand me a napkin.

'I truly hope you have a great day on your vacation,' he said.

After having my fill from the buffet, I walked over to the pool and picked out a lounge chair, where it looked like a party was about to start. I arrived at just the right time.

The party was an all-day event sponsored by Tommy Bahama. The entire deck was decorated with Tommy Bahama advertisements, and a sales representative was busy selling suntan lotion, suntan oil, shirts, towels, shorts and bathing suits. I walked over to get a better look at what the salesman was selling as I had never seen this type of brand before.

'Can I smell the lotions, please?'

The representative turned around. He was wearing a Tommy Bahama shirt and matching shorts. On his left shirt pocket, I noticed a name tag reading Bob. He towered over me. Smiling, he said, 'Hello there, Bob!'

I chuckled, confused. Was he saying hello to himself?

He began to laugh.

'Don't worry, beautiful. I say that to all the new guests.'

'Oh, okay,' I said.

'It's a Caribbean joke. Sure you can smell the lotions.'

Bob picked up a bottle of lotion and handed it to me.

'Do you like the smell?'

'Yes, thank you.'

'Are your parents around? Are they looking for some fun Tommy Bahama attire, lotions, and oils? This is not my entire inventory; I have more in a supply closet in the hotel.'

'They are back in the hotel room … Is there going to be a party?' I asked Bob.

'Yes, every Saturday the hotel staff and I put on a big 'to do' for all the guests who arrive on the weekends. It's great fun, and there are games and prizes. I also do a bingo for the adults, and the winner gets to choose some lotions, bathing suits and some funky cool Hawaiian shirts like mine,' Bob said pointing to his shirt.

The lotion smelled so good, like Play–Doh; I had to try it.

Bob watched me spit out the lotion. 'Smells like Play-Doh, huh. That's what all the kids tell me. Well, it was nice talking to you, beautiful, but I gotta get back to work.'

Walking away, I saw other adults mosey over to check out his wares. It was obviously very lucrative for him. He had all these people from all over the world flocking to this vacation spot of a lifetime who were not prepared for the Florida sun.

'Who's in the mood for some FUN? Who likes to play poolside games?' shouted a blonde woman holding a microphone. She worked for the Marriott; the only item that didn't match her uniform; blue blouse and tan colored shorts, was a large straw hat.

Other staff members joined in with their microphones, inviting all the kids to the poolside where they had set-up several games. Soon, she was surrounded by kids.

'My name is Kelly. I'm the manager of FUN here at the Marriott, and I must say I am a bit disappointed. This whole time I have been calling for you all, I didn't hear any of you answer me. So on the count of three, I need to hear who wants to join in on some fun and poolside games? One, two, and three!'

Every kid screamed as loud as they could.

'We are going to divide you all up into groups, and we'll send you all to different stations!' shouted Kelly.

In the biggest tub I have ever seen, comparable to a washing machine, piled high and ready to overflow were water balloons of every color imaginable. Near the limbo stick and stand was an assortment of Hawaiian leis, grass skirts, and coconut bras. Kelly then announced we would have to put on a piece of clothing for every pass we did under the limbo stick. To the right of the limbo stick was an abundance of hula hoops. The only time I had seen that many were in a Toys R Us commercial.

Joe and I were excited to join in on the games. I almost won the limbo contest. Unfortunately, I ended up knocking the stick off the last rung as I crawled under like a crab. The water balloon toss station was my favorite because it reminded me of the time I was on the baseball team. As for the hula hoop station, Joe and I sucked at this; we didn't stand a chance against the other kids. After an hour, the kids who won each game were then placed into a small obstacle course. Though I wasn't a finalist, it was one of the most special times for me to be outside, enjoying being surrounded by other happy kids and feeling alive. It was the best fun Joe and I had in forever. Life was good, and I just needed to focus on the positive.

The pool party kept us occupied all afternoon. The Marriott staff played a variety of Caribbean music as we swam and played in the water. Later while my mom and George sunbathed and lounged with beers and cocktails, Joe and I rented some board games and played at one of the patio tables.

That afternoon, I met Sophie in the swimming pool.

As the pool wasn't packed, I felt comfortable enough to jump in and have some time by myself. For the last month, I had pretty much spent every day alone inside my room, but I had been active outside for hours now and was starting to feel overwhelmed. I needed some time to relax. I casually swam across the length of the pool when a girl with cropped blonde hair appeared out of nowhere.

I choked on water from surprise.

'Hi, I'm Sophie, what's your name?' she said with an English accent. She was so pretty, with her bright blue eyes, button nose, and beautiful rosy cheeks; she reminded me of a pixie I'd seen in the movies.

Gathering my breath again, I told her my name and asked her where she was from.

'I'm from West Yorkshire, England. Where are you from?'

'I'm from New England. How old are you?' I asked.

'I'm thirteen.'

'Me too, we just arrived today. When did you get here?'

'We've been here enjoying Florida and Walt Disney World for the last eight days. I have another week left.'

'Wow, that's awesome. We leave next Saturday.'

Sophie swam under the water, touched the floor of the pool and resurfaced.

'Can you dive and do cartwheels off of the diving board?' I asked as I struggled to stay afloat.

'I can dive, but I've never tried other tricks off of the diving board.'

'It's pretty easy; I'll have to show you sometime.'

'That would be fun.'

'Great, well it was nice talking to you. I am going to get out now.'

I swam to the pool ladder when Sophie called my name.

'Kerri, I haven't made any friends my own age since I got here. Would you like to be friends?'

'Sure,' I said nervously.

Luckily for me, that was it. We had a lot in common being the same age; we became friends immediately. During the rest of the pool party, we enjoyed relaxing on the lounge chairs talking and sunbathing. Later in the afternoon, we had lunch at the pool bar; burgers, fries, and Sophie tried her first Shirley Temple. After lunch, we wandered the hotel grounds together on our own. We eventually came back to the pool where my parents were, so I could introduce Sophie to them. I didn't want them getting worried or thinking I disappeared. I was still on probation, to some extent.

'Who's this?' my mom asked putting her book down. It was nice to see her relaxing in her new bathing suit on the pool deck lounge chair. George was asleep in the lounge chair next to her. I introduced Sophie and told my mom where she was from.

'My brother Joe is around here somewhere.'

'I think the traveling, sun and activities have wiped him out,' my mom said. 'Sophie, do you have any siblings?'

'Yes, I have two older brothers and an older sister.'

'Wow, big family. 'That's very nice. Would you two like to have some pop?'

'What's pop?' Sophie asked.

'It's an individual glass bottle of soda. My parents bought Joe and me a six pack of Coke to celebrate our first day of vacation. Would you like some?'

'Yes, that would be nice.'

Sophie and I grabbed our glass bottles of Coke and wandered the hotel grounds again, looking for what else might be happening.

Being on vacation, I found I had a lot of freedom to do things I was not normally permitted to do at home. If I were with Sophie, I could pretty much go anywhere. She was my new vacation buddy, my new partner in crime. Our crimes usually consisted of drooling over boys wearing Speedos (I'd never seen a boy wear that type of bathing suit before) at the pool. Sophie and I would gossip and giggle as we picked out which ones we wanted all to ourselves.

It was dinner time, and Sophie and I had to get back to our families.

Meeting my family back at the pool, you could tell we were all tuckered out after a full day of traveling and enjoying the pool party activities. We could have easily called it a night, but we didn't because we were all starved and needed to get showered and changed for dinner.

'I've been looking at the map here for dinner, and there are quite a few choices.' My mom fought off a yawn. 'I was thinking IHOP. We could celebrate a very successful first day with breakfast for dinner, what do you all say?'

We devoured four plates of scrambled eggs, bacon, sausage and a small stack of pancakes. It wasn't customary for us to talk during dinner. Typically, we ate dinner watching the TV stations frequently being changed, one after the other. Without the TV, we made small talk. Talking about what we'd like to do when we visited the Magic Kingdom in the morning. After dinner, we walked back from International Drive to our hotel rooms.

* * *

The next morning, Joe and I headed out to the pool after breakfast while our parents got ready for our first day at Walt Disney World. Joe made a beeline straight for the pool, but I didn't because I felt this incredible sensation. It's hard to describe. It felt as if an invisible force greater than my own will was stopping me from entering the pool and urging me, turning me around, propelling me to go to the Jacuzzi. It seemed strange to want to get into a hot Jacuzzi in ninety plus degree weather, especially when I'd never been in one before, and this strong urge demanded me to try it out. I turned around, leaving the cool pool behind. As I neared the Jacuzzi, I noticed there was a boy already in it.

I stepped into the boiling water and felt my skin tingle, not believing I was doing this. I felt an instant hot flash travel from my feet to my head as my body temperature soared, and I quickly glanced at the boy to see if he noticed how uncomfortable I was. I didn't want him to think I couldn't handle the heat, so I plopped in, submerging my entire self under the bubbling water. I came up brushing my hair back from my face and then moved over to the wall of the Jacuzzi and sat on the built-in seat. I sat there, a little uneasy, as I slowly adjusted to the temperature. I got a good look at the boy. Wow, he was so handsome and different looking compared to the boys back home. He didn't look like he was

American. I guessed he was either 15 or 16 years old, with beautiful hazel eyes, tanned skin, dark brown wavy hair with full lips, and the best part he was wearing a black Speedo. I had seen Speedos in magazines and on those boys at the pool, but this was the first time I had the privilege of seeing one up close and personal. I was very pleased and thankful for whatever that sensation was to get me into this Jacuzzi. I couldn't stop admiring him. The boy finally looked up and returned my gaze, and we sat there staring at each other. I waited for him to speak first. Growing impatient, I motioned to speak when suddenly someone jumped in and broke the awkward silence. It was my annoying brother.

'Whoa, that's hot!' he shouted and then dove under just as I had.

I rolled my eyes and glanced back at the boy. He appeared amused. He watched my brother dive under the water a few times, and as he came up a third time, the boy spoke.

'You're going to hurt your eyes doing that mate,' he said, as Joe dived down for the fourth time. 'There's a lot of chlorine in here,' he turned to me and grinned.

I didn't understand a word he'd just said. However, I knew where I had heard that accent before. He sounded just like Davy Jones!

*He was British! Oh, my God, I found my British boy, right in front of me. This was too good to be true!*

My brother came up for air. 'It's too hot in here,' he said. 'I'm going back to the pool.'

Thank goodness for that. I really wanted the British boy all to myself.

I turned back to the boy. 'Hi, my name's Kerri, what's yours?'

'T\*%@&#,' he said.

'Um, I'm so sorry. What did you say your name was again?' This was so embarrassing.

'T\*%@&#,' he said again and smiled.

He had told me his name twice, and I was embarrassed to have to ask again.

'Hey, Kerri, is that you?' I heard from a distance.

I looked up and saw George approaching the Jacuzzi. *Oh, great! I knew he'd want to say something seeing me sharing a Jacuzzi with a boy.*

'There you are. Oh, wow, it's only the second day, and you've already landed yourself a boyfriend!' said George.

I felt my face burning with embarrassment. Then it got worse.

'What's your boyfriend's name?' he asked.

I looked at George and then back at the boy whose name I didn't know. I was trying so hard to be cool in front of this boy. Nothing was working in my favor.

My face was turning bright red, and I felt a hot flash down my back, and my armpits began to bead with sweat.

Since I was not able to answer, George took matters into his own hands.

'Hi, I'm George, what's your name?' he asked.

'Trevor,' he replied.

Just then, I heard the boy clearly. I am not sure why I finally understood him, but I jumped at the chance to redeem myself.

'Yes, this is Trevor, and, Trevor, this is George,' I said quickly.

At that very moment, I knew with all my heart that this was a defining moment in my life and that Trevor was the 'Davy Jones' of my dreams. We were meant to meet. I had this overwhelming feeling that something brought us together. He was mine, and I was going to make it so. I had a new purpose to my vacation. Not only was I going to have the time of my life at Walt Disney World, I was determined to take the initiative and hopefully make Trevor my vacation boyfriend.

'It's nice to meet you, Trevor,' George said, and then turned to me grinning, 'Come on, Kerri, we're ready to go,' he beckoned.

I didn't really want to leave, but it was time to go.

'It was really nice meeting you. Maybe I'll see you later at the pool sometime?' I said, hopeful.

'Yes, I'd like that,' he said looking pleased.

I got out of the Jacuzzi and followed George back to the room, looking behind at Trevor every few steps until we turned a corner, and I couldn't see him any longer.

It was a short drive to the Disney World resort which, back then, comprised only of the Magic Kingdom and Epcot. We were overjoyed as we passed under the welcome sign. Continuing down the road to the Magic Kingdom, I could hardly believe we were actually there. It was surreal. This was really happening.

'Oh, my God, we're actually here! This is awesome!' Joe shouted. His enthusiasm was contagious, and I couldn't help whooping and shouting with him.

George parked, and we made our way to the monorail station. Joe and I sat on our knees pressing our hands against the glass, mesmerized, catching glimpses of Cinderella's Castle, Space Mountain, and other attractions as we got closer. We were like two dogs hanging their heads out of the car window, tongues happily flapping in the wind.

'Mom, George, do you see Cinderella's Castle! Look over there, is that Space Mountain? I am so going on that!' I said.

'Yes, this is amazing. George and I have never been here, either. This is just as exciting for us as it is for you two.'

We passed through the Contemporary Resort before arriving outside the park gates. Disney was still celebrating their fifteenth anniversary, and they were giving out random prizes as you went through the turnstiles. Waiting in the long line to enter the park, I kept hoping I would win a prize. This day was pretty amazing, why wouldn't I win? Passing through the turnstiles without a prize, I was disappointed, but that feeling didn't last long because Joe and I were the lucky kids who were in the most magical place in the world. Walking past the stroller rentals and through a small covered entrance, we eventually arrived in the Magic Kingdom! It was then that the realization of where I was finally hit me. We all stood there for a moment in awe, soaking it all in, the grand train that whooshed over our heads, a short tunnel that led you into the park so the first thing you'd see is Cinderella's Castle, and the words "WELCOME TO MAGIC KINDOM" beautifully created out of the brightly-colored bushes and flowers. I turned to find my parents standing head to head going over a map of the Magic Kingdom.

At that moment, I needed to tell my mom and George how sorry I was, and how much it meant to me being in Walt Disney World.

'Mom, George, I know we've had a rough three months, and I know I am to blame for that. I need you two to know how I appreciate you both taking us. I am sure this trip wasn't cheap, especially after everything that's happened. I just want to say for me anyway, thank you.'

My mom looked at me; she was smiling whilst crying. 'Kerri, you have no idea how happy we are to be here and have you alive. You and Joe are *my everything*. Now, let's focus on the day and not worry about the past.'

I started to cry, and they both hugged me. Joe, not one to show his emotions easily unless he was angry, just stood there, staring at us. My mom went up to him, placing her arms around him. 'Let's go, there is so much to do and see here,' she said.

We followed her under the railway station and ambled down Main Street USA. It truly was magical taking in the ambiance, perusing the shops. Joe and I couldn't wait to take photos with Mickey Mouse and other Disney characters.

Main Street USA was designed to resemble a turn of the twentieth-century town center. Inspired by Walt Disney's hometown of Marceline, Missouri, the street is a recreation of a slow, relaxed and carefree atmosphere of happy times. Coming to the top of Main Street, we all posed for photos in front of Cinderella's Castle before running off to find the first ride.

It was surprising how many rides we were able to take considering the time we had to wait for them.

'Arrrghh! I hate the Florida sun! It's killing me!' my brother complained.

'We are all sweating, not just you. It's at least 90 plus degrees. You have to be more patient, just stand here and drink water. The more you complain, the worse it will be,' I said.

'Shut up! It's hot, and I'll complain if I want to.'

'Well, that didn't last long,' said my mother.

'What didn't last long?' I asked.

'You two getting along; I was hoping it would last more than a day and a half.'

I held my tongue. I wanted to argue that he was being a pain in all of our asses, as usual, and that made the time standing in line feel unbearable, although I had to admit to myself, the amount of fun we had during the rides made up for the shitty complaints my brother constantly dished out.

Out of the six themed lands; Main Street U.S.A, Adventureland, Tomorrowland, Frontierland, Liberty Square and Fantasyland, my favorite was Fantasy Land. 'Fantasyland is dedicated to the young at heart and to those who believe that when you wish upon a star, your dreams come true.' I loved reading that statement as you entered the theme park. I was in a place in my life where I was starting over, and I needed to start dreaming and expecting my dreams to come true. It was a blast to enjoy the many rides in Fantasy Land; It's a Small World, Peter Pan's Flight, The Many Adventures of Winnie the Pooh among others. Joe's favorite was Frontierland; where guests could relive the American Old West, from cowboys to Native Americans. The rides he wanted to go on over and over again were Splash Mountain and Thunder Mountain Railroad. We hadn't been on a roller coaster since we were little, and Splash Mountain and Thunder Mountain Railroad were thrill rides for sure. For me, climbing to the top of the mountain in a seat that was shaped like a log and anticipating the drop down the waterfall in Splash Mountain was fantastic.

After a full day, I couldn't believe it wasn't over. We still had several more days to return and enjoy the parts of the park we didn't have time to visit on our first day.

Sophie and I made plans to meet up at her hotel room that night at 6 p.m. Since I had introduced my mom to Sophie, my mom felt confident I could be trusted and agreed to let me go out shopping and get some dinner with her. It was such freedom to be on my own and know I didn't have security guards, cameras and staff watching my every move as I wandered through the Marriott grounds on my way to Sophie's room.

Approaching her door, I stopped for a second and thought how lucky I was to have met a new friend who knew absolutely nothing about my past. I was free to be myself. I knocked and waited for Sophie to open the door.

The door opened, and a woman, whom I assumed was her mom, stood there wearing only a see-through slip. She was bare-chested, her overly enlarged breasts pointing straight at me. She may as well have been completely naked. For a minute, I thought I had imagined the scene right before me, or maybe I was finally having that psychotic break I'd heard so much about at the mental hospital. This couldn't really be happening, could it?

'Hello, dear, how are you? I'm Sophie's mum. You must be Kerri.' She pulled me toward her for a big and uncomfortable hug; my face squished in between her perky breasts. I stood there dumbfounded, not knowing what to do or say.

Besides my mom, I had never seen another woman's breasts or another naked woman before, so this experience was completely out of my comfort zone. This was obviously a European thing, or maybe it was only their thing?

I was 13 years old and wouldn't call myself exactly worldly yet, but I had never been greeted in this way in my life. I had witnessed and experienced so much in the loony bin; still nothing had prepared me for this. In my panic, I felt the urge to laugh hysterically. Thankfully, I managed to subdue it as she finally let go of me.

'Yes, hi,' was all I could manage to say.

'Come on in, love,' she said, gently pulling me in.

'Sophie, it's Kerri. Hurry up and get ready, dear,' she called over her shoulder.

Don't look at her breasts, I kept telling myself. Keep your eyes up and look at her face, the ceiling fan, a lamp, something else. Don't look down, and for God's sakes, don't look mortified.

'Okay, thank you very much.' I forced a smile.

'Hi there, my dear, it's nice to meet you. I'm Sophie's dad.'

I turned my head, to see Sophie's dad, sitting in the corner and reading the paper, completely in the nude, except for a pair of black socks. I nearly lost it again. His legs were crossed and thankfully the newspaper he was reading was covering his penis. Looking up from the paper, he gave me a winning smile as if this was completely normal and in no way out of the ordinary.

I did all that I could not to freak out and run out of the room screaming hysterically. I needed to act like this was all normal, somehow. This was definitely an episode out of *The Twilight Zone,* and the music sprang into my head as I tried to keep it together. It was as if I had been transported into another surreal universe, perhaps dreaming. Sophie then came out of the bathroom and confirmed that this was, in fact, real life.

'Hiya, Kerri,' Sophie said. She was wearing only panties. She walked past me over to the closet, proceeded to pull out her clothes and got dressed in front of everybody.

I kept wondering, besides being British, was this family part of a nudist colony?

'Hi, Sophie,' I said, giving her full eye contact, making sure once again not to look her thoroughly up and down while trying to keep myself composed. 'How are you? Have you all had a great day today?' I nervously asked.

'It's been a brilliant day, how was yours?' she said, still proceeding to get dressed.

'Mine was the same.'

I decided to smile and mind my own business as best as I could. The flowered print comforter on the double-sized bed was a great place to keep my focus and helped me feel a bit calmer. I was raised to be polite and respectful, and that was the approach I was going to take while in the Twilight Zone. I was not going to engage in any small talk while waiting, although if I were asked any further questions, I'd make sure their eyes were the only contact I had. It felt like an eternity in that room. I wanted to get out of there as fast as I could. Luckily, Sophie was a quick dresser. She picked out a two-piece soft pink shirt and skirt, put it on, gathered her purse, slipped into her tan flip-flops and bid her parents goodbye.

'Mum, Kerri and I are going to International Drive for dinner and to look at some shops. We'll be back later.'

'Sophie, do you have enough money, dear?' asked her dad.

'I'm good, thanks.'

'Sophie, no later than 9:30, we have a big day tomorrow.'

'Okay, Mum.'

'It was nice meeting both of you,' I stammered, clumsily reaching for the doorknob.

'It was lovely to meet you too,' said Sophie's mum. Her dad had already tucked back into his newspaper. I made sure to wait after all the pleasantries before I ran out of there.

Fifteen minutes later, we were on International Drive. We felt very grown up and excited to be able to go out on our own without adult supervision. As we wandered down International Drive toward the shops and restaurants, I told her about my Jacuzzi encounter with Trevor.

'Seriously Sophie, the attraction I have for Trevor is stronger than I have ever felt for anyone. Does this make any sense? My mom says it's just puppy love. I disagree, I truly feel like it's more than that. What do you think?'

'Honestly, I have never felt that kind of pull for someone. I have been attracted to many boys and one in particular, I think, was my biggest crush, but I've never fallen in love with anyone, yet. I've been witness to my brothers' and sister's relationships; I do not want to deal with all of that right now.'

'I guess being the youngest of four has its advantages. Are you always being spoiled and given everything you want?' I teased.

'It certainly has its advantages. I mean I am here with my parents, and they only have me to enjoy it with. So I love all the attention. I pretty much can have what I want. It's brilliant!'

'You know what's brilliant is your accent and all the cool words you use! I could listen to you and Trevor all day. So tell me, any cute guys you've wanted to meet here?' I asked.

'To be honest, I just want to look.'

'Gotcha. But if you were me and had visualized falling in love with a British boy for as long as you can remember and then you actually meet him in person, what would you do?'

'Well, I can tell you are attracted to him. I say you only live once, right? So go for it!'

Boy, if she knew how close to death I'd been. I totally agreed with her. You do only live once, and meeting Trevor was more than an opportunity.

We passed a leather vendor selling handmade bracelets, belts, purses, and bags, so we stopped to browse.

'Excuse me, sir. These bracelets are beautiful. How much for each one?' I asked.

'Five dollars. If you want it engraved, that will be another five dollars,' the vendor replied.

'Which color should I choose, Sophie? I want to get one for me and one for Trevor. I think I have an idea.'

'I prefer the brown leather,' said Sophie.

I ordered one with Trevor's name and the other with mine. I had the vendor decorate them both with hearts at the beginning and end of our names. The minute the vendor had finished Trevor's bracelet, I immediately put it on my wrist.

Sophie and I were having too much fun to stop now. Instead of going to a restaurant, we decided it would be more fun and cheaper to buy some hotdogs.

When we got back to my hotel room, Sophie and I hatched a plan and thought it would be best to tell Trevor how I felt about him through a letter. The letter totaled three pages on the hotel stationery. I had watched so many movies where the girl added her perfume to the love letter she wrote for her special guy. I lucked out and added the perfect touch by dowsing each page with the free perfume sample from the room. After I licked the seal on the envelope, I was immediately overwhelmed with the feelings of excitement of the possibility of falling in love with Trevor and terrified if he didn't feel anything for me. I didn't know how Trevor felt about me and wondered if I was going too far, yet the 'pull' I felt the other day was nothing I ever experienced. All I knew with all my heart was that I was 'meant' to meet him, and I didn't want to lose the opportunity of letting him know just because of fear.

'Are you ready?' Sophie said.

'Well, it's not like I fly to England every day.'

We found him by the pool. He was relaxing on a lounge chair; so incredibly good-looking. I loved how curly his hair became from being wet. His hazel eyes, rosy cheeks and full lips seemed to be accentuated by his darkening tan. I hid behind the bushes as Sophie delivered the letter and bracelet with my name on it. She handed it to him and explained what it was. He looked embarrassed, slightly adjusting his position in his lounge chair. Starting to read my letter, I saw a small grin form as she turned and walked away. Sophie walked back to where I was hiding. I thanked her and asked if he said anything about me.

'He is cute. I think he really does like you,' she said.

'You really think so?'

'I've done this before. There's something between you two.'

'I really hope so,' I gushed.

## CHAPTER 6 – BECAUSE OF A MOUSE

On the third day, we visited EPCOT; The Experimental Prototype Community of Tomorrow. It remains one of my favorite Disney theme parks because I look forward to seeing what Walt Disney's Dream Imagineers will bring to life next.

The best attraction that year, at least in Joe's opinion and mine, was the 3D Captain EO Adventure starring Michael Jackson. We had never seen a movie in 3D before, and we were blown away. We thought Michael Jackson was excellent in portraying the silly space captain with his hysterical alien misfit crew. We must have seen the movie at least a half dozen times throughout the vacation.

As soon as we arrived back at the hotel after 5 p.m., I headed off to the pool on the off chance I'd be able to find Trevor. As I neared the pool, I saw Trevor jumping in and out of the pool and swimming with two smaller boys. The slim boys looked like twins with their tanned skin, matching Speedos, and same blond hairstyles. In fact, they closely resembled Trevor. The only noticeable difference was in their heights, and I could tell they were younger than my brother. Throwing my towel onto a lounge chair, I jumped in and swam over to him.

One of the boys smirked at us. 'Oooh, Trevor's got a girlfriend,' he chanted.

'Shut up!' Trevor said, kicking water at them.

'Who are those boys?' I asked.

'Those are my two little brothers,' he said. 'That's Alec. He's ten and terribly annoying. And that's Ben. He's nine and just as annoying. I guess you could call them twins.' He pointed at each one. 'They're such pains. They keep following me around.'

'I know what you mean. I have a younger brother. He's twelve.'

'Oh, the boy who jumped into the Jacuzzi the other day?'

'Yep.'

We swam away from his brothers who were trying to splash water at us.

'How old are you?' I asked.

'Fifteen. Sixteen in December. And you?'

'Fourteen,' I lied; I wanted to impress him.

We headed to the side of the pool. As he lifted himself on the ledge, I noticed he was wearing the bracelet I had bought him with my name on it. I felt a jolt of happiness. I then showed him the second bracelet I had made with his name on it. He blushed.

'How long have you been here on vacation?' I asked.

'We got here a week ago, Saturday,' he replied. 'We leave next Saturday morning.'

'Wow, you've had two weeks? We're here for only one. We leave on Saturday as well.'

I dived back in, and Trevor dived in after me.

I told him what grade I was going into and how I wasn't looking forward to my classes.

'My favorite subject is transportation.'

'Transportation, huh?' That was a subject we didn't study here.

'Yeah … When I get on the bus and come home.'

I laughed. 'So you don't enjoy subjects like English or art or anything like that? I'm not very good at art, but I do love to read. What about you?'

'I don't like school very much either. I would say my favorite subject is math. And I don't mind art,' said Trevor.

'Math is my worst subject. Are you a part of any sports or clubs?' I asked.

Trevor was about to answer when I saw George coming around the corner. Our time was up. As we said goodbye, Trevor said he'd be staying at the pool all day tomorrow. And so would I.

My family and I went out to dinner at one of the restaurants on International Drive. I wasn't really engaged; I just sat there making small talk. I couldn't stop smiling; I kept thinking about Trevor. I envisioned us swimming, finding out more about each other. If I were lucky, maybe he'd want to have lunch. It wasn't every day you met the boy of your dreams.

* * *

'Aaaant! Aaaant! Aaaant!' the blaring noise from the alarm woke me from a dead sleep.

'Agh! What is that?' Joe screamed from under his pillow. 'Shut it off; oh, my God, shut it off!'

I jumped out of bed, tripping over my own feet and walked over to the alarm clock. I had completely forgotten where I had set it down.

'Sorry, Joe. It's the alarm clock. Just go back to sleep. I'm turning it off.'

'Why did it come on? We're at the pool today, and Mom said we can lie in until we wanted to.'

'I know, but I have plans with Trevor. I didn't want to oversleep.'

'Ooooh, so you really like him?'

I didn't have to look at Joe to know he was smirking at me.

'Does he feel the same way about you?'

I should have kept my mouth shut last night ... 'Go back to bed! I'll be out of here in five minutes. Forget I ever said anything, and don't you dare come to the pool and start harassing me in front of him. I mean it, Joe. You come to the pool and embarrass me, and I'll make you regret it.'

'Geez, you can't take a joke anymore. Whatever. Close the door on your way out.'

'You got it.'

I picked up my stuff that I had prepared the night before and went into the bathroom. I changed into my bathing suit, grabbed some food from the hotel table, scarfed it down my throat as quickly as I could and made my way down to the pool. I reserved two lounge chairs with my towel and a T-shirt and then jumped into the pool. I kept eyeing the clock. Every minute that passed was torture. Thirty minutes later, Trevor arrived with his brothers in tow.

Alec and Ben were dragging their towels along the patio, whispering and making faces as they walked behind Trevor. He did his best to ignore them.

'I set up two chairs over there for us,' I shouted over the busy pool to him.

He nodded and walked over, dressed in his signature black Speedo, T-shirt, and flip-flops. He took off his T-shirt, dropping it on one of the chairs and dove in.

Mom had bought me a brand new bathing suit for our vacation. I saw it hanging in the hotel gift shop and was instantly attracted to the colors that started with electric royal blue, followed by a layer of sea blue which then faded into a lighter baby blue throughout. I never wanted a piece of clothing so much in such a long time.

I got out of the water several times to jump, dive, and do cartwheels into the pool. I was showing off a bit; when you like a guy, you go a little overboard to impress him.

'Did you get a new bathing suit?' he asked.

'Yes, just yesterday. I love it,' I replied.

'It's really pretty. It looks good on you.'

'Thank you very much.' I was so flattered; I couldn't stop smiling.

*Yes! He noticed!*

I felt like I was on my very first date. We spent the morning swimming, splashing, talking, flirting and joking around. The hours seemed to tick slowly by. No matter how much time we spent in the pool or when we took a walk around the hotel grounds, we could keep our conversation. I never felt uncomfortable or pushed trying to think of something to say. It was effortless talking with Trevor. I never experienced this with any other boy; it felt as if I had known him my whole life, and it was all because of a mouse, Walt Disney's mouse. I was so pleased our brothers were not around to interrupt our day together. As the afternoon approached, Trevor asked me if I'd like to have lunch with him by the poolside.

*The boy of my dreams asked me to lunch. Is this really happening? I dreamed about this happening all night, and the whole day has pretty much come true!*

We sat down with some burgers, fries and cokes.

'What do you do for fun back in England?' I asked.

'The usual,' he answered, 'hanging out with my friends after school; I ride my bike, roller-skate, take my dog Roxy for a walk.'

'Hmm, I like those things too, except I don't have a dog. Do you like to read?'

'Yes, I also like photography. We have a dark room at home, so I print my own black and white pictures,' he replied. 'I'm also a member of the Drama and Operatic Society in the next town.'

'You do opera?' I tried to imagine Trevor on stage in full costume singing Madame Butterfly.

'No, it's just called an operatic society. We do plays, musicals, and stuff. The last one we did was called Irene,' he explained.

'That's cool,' I said. 'Do you play any sports?'

'Not really, just swimming. Do you want another coke?'

'Sure.'

We got up to go and refill our drinks.

'Since I'm going to be sixteen soon, I've also started looking around for a part-time job.'

'Oh, where at?' I asked.

'Not sure yet, there aren't a lot of places with positions open, so my options are pretty limited. I've been going to the local supermarket every Saturday and talking to the manager there. He says he will keep me in mind. Unfortunately, I have to keep going in to remind him.'

'I've had babysitting jobs off and on. This year, I want to focus on school and work towards good grades. I had a bad year last year, so I want this year to be a lot better.'

'Oh, why did you have a bad year? What happened?' he asked.

*I am such an idiot; I shouldn't have been so honest. If he knew the truth, he might not want to know me anymore.*

'Uh, well it's a long story, and I don't want to talk about it right now. Maybe another time.'

Trevor paused for a moment. We shared an awkward moment of silence.

'Kerri, I wanted to ask. I was hoping maybe we could go out for dinner before we leave.' He started looking at the ground, and his ears turned a deep red ... 'What do you think about that?'

'I would love to go out to dinner with you.' I smiled.

'So what do you fancy eating when we go out to dinner this Friday night?' he asked.

'Fancy, I really like that word and how you say it. I've never heard anyone say that word before. It's nice. Um, well, I've never been on a date before to be honest, so I'm not sure. When we go to International Drive, can we decide then? I like being spontaneous,' I said.

'Sure, that sounds good.'

It was wonderful how we got on so well. I had never felt at ease with someone so quickly before. I loved everything about this 'New Start' vacation where nobody knew of my past. I was a different person here, the person I felt I was meant to be if it wasn't for the pony accident. Being in Florida, enjoying Disney World, it's hard to believe six weeks before I had been in a mental health hospital for attempted suicide.

Five o'clock was fast approaching, and I knew I'd be sought out for dinner by my mom or George. They had spent the day with Joe at Wet N Wild down the street. I thanked Trevor for a lovely day, grabbed my towel and T-shirt and walked back to the room.

* * *

The next morning, my family and I left the hotel early to go to the Character Breakfast at the *Empress Lilly* in Disney Village, now known as Downtown Disney. Designed to be a full-size replica of a paddle steamer riverboat, the *Empress Lilly* took us back to the days of Mark Twain's Mississippi River, with Tom Sawyer and Huckleberry Finn. The Character Breakfast was the first of its kind at Disney World, and being a very popular venue, required reservations.

We got there early and were assigned to a table with a German family of five, who were probably the heaviest family I had ever seen.

Breakfast was delivered, and we had photos taken with Mickey and Minnie Mouse, Donald and Daisy Duck, Goofy and Pluto. At the time, it seemed a little strange to me that the German family didn't once get up to greet and take pictures of their own. When we finally sat down to eat, I realized why.

They had eaten everything. The platters piled high with bacon, sausages, and eggs that had been placed in the middle of the table had been completely cleared. They had obviously taken advantage of our photo shoot distractions to gobble down as much food as possible.

My mom caught the attention of a waiter and called him over.

'Excuse me, sir, can we have some more eggs and bacon? The other family has had more than their fair share,' my mother asked.

'We are all very hungry, and there are only fruit and biscuits left,' George added.

'I am very sorry to hear that, ma'am. Unfortunately, we have pre-portioned breakfast items per each table, and we will not have any more eggs and bacon prepared until the next sitting,' replied the waiter.

'You've got to be kidding me. For what we paid for this breakfast to eat and have photos taken with the Disney Characters, this has been a complete rip-off!' My mother was outraged.

'I'm very sorry, ma'am,' the waiter replied.

'That's it; we're leaving. We'll have to go somewhere else to eat!' George said.

Joe and I knew better than to argue with them. My parents glared at the German family and ushered us out of the restaurant, noisily muttering how unfair the situation was, and that we were never coming back. We drove around for about thirty minutes before we found a reasonably priced breakfast at IHOP.

We spent the entire day in EPCOT's World Showcase, wandering through each pavilion window shopping and sampling some of the foods. We stayed quite late and I, unfortunately, only had an hour at the pool with Trevor. I told him about visiting England in EPCOT.

'You guys make the best fish and chips I've ever tasted. Do you know why you named fries 'chips' when we call them thinly sliced potato 'chips'?' I asked.

'Not sure why. All I know is we call potato chips 'crisps' because they're crispy. We ate at the English Pub when we went through EPCOT the other day as well. I enjoyed the culture. Coming here for Disney is a big treat for us. Each year we go on holiday in France.'

'Wow, you get to see France every summer? That's pretty amazing. I'd love to see France one day. What do you do there when you go?'

'We typically go camping and stay in a caravan. Being the oldest, my job is to walk to the campsite store each morning to buy freshly made bread and croissants.'

'Your camping trips sound awesome. I love freshly cooked bread or bread in general. Every time we go out to eat, I make sure to hide the hot bread rolls, so I can have them all to myself.'

I was having such a good time talking to Trevor that I hadn't paid attention to the time. Joe came running and shouting my name, embarrassing me in front of Trevor once again.

'Let me guess, it's time to go?' I said to Joe as he caught up to us out of breath.

'Yup,' was all he managed to say.

'Trevor, what are your plans tomorrow? Do you think we can see each other again before our dinner date on Friday?'

'I know my parents are jam packing a lot of activities before we leave, so I'm not completely sure. I'll come back to the pool after we're done, and hopefully, we can see each other then.'

I was disappointed I didn't have a definite time to make plans, but anything with him was better than nothing.

'OK, once we are done with Busch Gardens, I'll come find you.'

I wished I could kiss him. I wanted to the moment I laid eyes on him in the Jacuzzi. I didn't know him well then, and I never felt such a strong attraction to any other boy before. I knew Trevor was shy, and I didn't wish to scare him off with being too forward. So I pushed the feeling aside.

'See you tomorrow,' I said.

Turning around, I saw that Joe had not waited for me as I thought he had. He was running again, almost out of sight. I ran after him, knowing George didn't like to be kept waiting.

* * *

My family and I had never been to Busch Gardens and had heard a lot of good things about it. We were told the rides were amazing, and the safari was incredible. After several hours, we realized that most of the rides were old and closed for repair, or looked scary to go on. We loved going on rides; still we were not thrill seekers. We did manage to go on a couple of mild roller coasters that made both my mother and me nauseous. The only fun thing we did as far as I was concerned was to take the safari tour. We booked a two-hour tour and boarded a big jeep that had an observation roof. You were encouraged to stand and observe the animals at each stop. The guide drove us behind a convoy of other Jeeps filled with excited families. To see up close the many protected animals, the guide drove us into their habitat. It was awesome to witness the cheetahs, meerkats, gorillas, elephants and giraffes living peacefully among each other. We agreed the amusement park itself was a waste of time and money except for the safari, which we all thoroughly enjoyed.

That evening, after dinner, Trevor and I met up at the pool again and discussed what we wanted to do on our last night together.

'Would you like to dress up? I brought a nice shirt and trousers with me for when my family and I went out to dinner. I can wear that if you like? Or we can dress casual and eat outside with a food vendor,' he suggested.

'I like the idea of dressing up, and I could wear one of the sundresses I brought. That would feel like a 'real' date to me.'

'I'd love to see a dress on you. I've only seen you in your bathing suit, not that I'm complaining.'

My cheeks were beginning to turn red; I loved his compliments.

'OK, so we know what we are wearing, what should we eat?'

'I really like most types of foods, except Italian. Their food is too creamy for my taste. Other than that, I think I'm good,' Trevor said.

We agreed to dress up for dinner and meet at 6 p.m. for an early night since he was headed back to England first thing the following morning. He told me about the five-hour time difference and how horrible the jet lag was. I had no idea since I had never flown out of the United States.

After we made our plans, I had to meet up with my family back at the hotel room. I said goodbye to Trevor, wishing I could kiss him for real and not wait for our date night. I was still nervous about who should be kissing whom and didn't wish to come across as pushy. He waved me off, and as I was just about to go around the corner toward my hotel room, I made sure to take one last look. He was so gorgeous watching me walk away; he stood there wearing a white V-neck T-shirt and black Speedo. His dark brown hair was wet with curls having just come out of the pool. His skin, a golden brown, framed his hazel eyes, which seemed to sparkle when he looked at me. Not to mention I always felt butterflies when I thought about his soft, kissable lips. I was in heaven. Not only did I find my Davy Jones, which for me at the time was just the dream of meeting and falling for a British boy, I truly lucked out; he was more than I could have hoped for. Compared to Davy Jones who was much older and much shorter than me, Trevor was taller, a teen like me and because of that, we had a lot in common. I knew nothing about Davy Jones except for his talent as a singer/actor and pretty face. Trevor was more than just a pretty face; he was incredibly smart and funny. He always made me feel important when he listened to me talk. He truly was the nicest boy I had ever met. It's morbid to think, but I kept wondering if I hadn't tried to take my life would I have had the opportunity to have met Trevor? I walked back to our hotel room with the feeling that I was in love. I had never felt this way for anyone else before. For the first time in my life, I understood what being in love meant. For once, I didn't feel like someone's problem, I was wanted and accepted for being me. I couldn't stop smiling.

* * *

My family and I spent our last day in the Magic Kingdom. Each ride's wait seemed longer than the next; luckily we still managed to ride most of our favorites twice. Although I was whisked around on the rides with my family, my mind was far away with Trevor and our pending first date. I felt a little guilty that my thoughts were somewhere else on our last day. I had a good idea of how expensive this trip must have been, and I was grateful, yet I couldn't stop thinking how much I wanted to spend my very last day alone with Trevor. Not just the evening, I wanted the entire day. Throughout the day, I would constantly check my watch, counting the hours until 6 p.m. By three o'clock, I was beginning to feel very excited and anxious. Our date was three hours away, and my parents were not showing any signs of stopping our activities.

When it was 5 o'clock, I finally asked my mom what time we were leaving.

'Well, it's our last day here, so we decided to stay until it closes,' she answered to my dismay. 'We're going to have dinner in the Magic Kingdom, and then stick around for the Main Street's Electrical Parade and fireworks.'

'What?' I cried. 'I agreed to meet with Trevor tonight; we've been talking for several days now at the pool about going out to dinner for our last night together.'

'NO. YOU'RE, NOT.' She looked at me in shock, leaning down so only I could hear what was coming next. 'EXCUSE ME, what makes you think you're going out with some boy on your own? Have you forgotten you are only thirteen, Kerri? And after all we've been through over the last few months ... NO ... Not going to happen!'

She scared me. The way she leaned into my face, she reminded me of my father.

'But, Mom, you let me go out to dinner with Sophie.'

'Going out with Sophie is completely different. Plus, George and I have never met him or his family. What in the world makes you think this would have been okay?'

'We are only going to dinner. Why is that any different?' I asked.

She didn't answer me. She just turned and walked away. By not answering me, she might as well have kicked me in the stomach; I felt as if I was going to be sick. I had no way to contact him and let him know I wasn't going to be there. I didn't know which hotel room number he was staying in, and I'm pretty sure he didn't know my room number either. I didn't even know his last name. This was supposed to be our evening together, a night where we could spend our final magical moments, and I was quite sure we both had wanted that first kiss. I felt terrible. It was never my plan not to show up. What would he think of me? I followed after my mom.

'Mom, PLEASE! It's not like he's from around here. He lives all the way in England. I'll never see him again.' I started to cry.

She ignored me.

I cried the entire night. When we went to dinner, I ate very little and mostly pushed my food around my plate. I HATED my parents at that moment. I hated them with a passion and wandered behind them furious. I watched the rest of my family enjoying themselves while I was feeling heartbroken as we walked through the crowds in the Magic Kingdom. My parents were insistent on finding the 'perfect spot' to watch the electrical parade show. Despite everyone else thinking how fantastic it was, I couldn't enjoy it. All I could think about was whether Trevor was still at the pool. He probably thought I stood him up and was mad at me. I couldn't blame him. If it were me, I would feel the same way. I was consumed with guilt, feeling nauseous, wondering if he had waited for me and for how long? Worst of all was that I would never see him ever again. I had planned on taking photos of us tonight, and now the only thing I had from our vacation was the bracelet I made with his name on it and the memory of our time together. I would never have the opportunity to explain why I didn't show up and be able to say a proper goodbye.

The evening dragged on. I was hoping at any moment my mom would give in and take me back to the hotel so I could, at least, see him one last time, but no, she was adamant and we stayed until the very end. We didn't head out until the fireworks had finished and the park was closing. On the ride home, I wondered whether there was a small possibility that if I went to the pool when we got back, he'd be there. No, who was I kidding? Trevor, his brothers, and parents were most likely sleeping, their suitcases packed and ready for their early flight back to England the next morning. It was well past midnight when we finally parked the car in the hotel parking lot, and I was too late. It was all too late.

We walked to the hotel rooms, and I opened the door with tears running down my cheeks. I switched on the lights and noticed something on the floor right below me. It was an envelope with my name on it.

*You've got to be kidding me. Was this a joke? Were my eyes playing tricks on me?* I didn't trust what I was seeing, but the proof was right there lying on the floor. I knew exactly who the letter was from. I just didn't understand how. How did he find out which room I had been staying in? I took a deep breath, dried my eyes and carefully opened the letter.

*Dear Kerri,*

*Hi, how are you? I missed seeing you today. I thought you were spending today at the pool and then later going out with me for dinner, but I'm guessing perhaps you went to see the Electrical Parade. I only ask because you had mentioned it to me this week while we were hanging out. I hope you are having a great time this last night on your holiday. It was so very nice to have met you and spend time with you at the pool. Thank you again for your bracelet and letter that went with it. I plan on wearing it daily to remind me of you and our time together on holiday. I wish I was able to see you one last time and say a proper goodbye. If I don't see you before you leave, this letter will have to be my goodbye. PTO. Anyway, please write to me, so I know you got my letter ok.*

*Love, Trevor*

*Love, had I read the word love?* I was relieved to read he loved me too.

I re-read his letter again. He wrote his address on the back of the letter. I didn't lose him after all, and now I had a way to contact him. I didn't know how he found my hotel room, but it didn't matter, I thanked my lucky stars that he did. I lay on my bed, closed my eyes and silently said a special thank you to whoever or whatever made all of this happen. I read the letter several more times until I couldn't keep my eyes open any longer. Gently putting the letter back into its envelope and laying it under my pillow for safe keeping, I shut off the lamp on the side table. I closed my eyes and easily drifted off to sleep relieved that Trevor was still in my life.

# CHAPTER 7 – PAR AVION

Coming home, I felt as though I had been away for months and had almost forgotten why we had left in the first place. This was my 'new reality', I had started to feel anxious because I was back in my small town where gossip travels quickly. I assumed the rumors had started while I was away and, of course, those rumors of me trying to commit suicide were true. School was starting after Labor Day weekend, and I knew I couldn't avoid it any longer. I knew I would be bullied with weird stares, whispering, and gossiping. I was not looking forward to it one bit. As far as I knew, I was the only kid at school who had attempted suicide. I wish my parents could have sent me to another school. Unfortunately, we only had one middle school in town, and unless my parents packed up and moved out of town, I had to go back. Except for TT, I wasn't sure who else knew. I couldn't have expected anyone to keep their mouths shut in this situation. Those who didn't know were sure to find out sooner than later in this small town. I started to feel overwhelmed with worry, not knowing how the beginning of my school year was going to turn out.

I knew I couldn't predict the outcome, but there was one way I could escape my reality, which was through letter writing to Trevor. Alone in my room, I pulled out my stationery set. I wanted to tell him what had happened on that last night and make sure he knew how I felt about him.

*Dear Trevor,*

*I just got home from vacation, and the first thing I wanted to do was to lie on my bed and write you a letter! I was given my new stationery set two Christmas's ago, and it's been sitting in my hope chest collecting dust ever since. I've always wanted to use it and send letters. Unfortunately, I have never had anyone to do that with. Now that we have met, I can finally make good use of it.*

*You have been on my mind the entire plane ride home! Actually, you have been on my mind since the first time I met you on vacation, and especially last night when I was not able to meet you. First of all, I'd like to say I am so sorry, Trevor, that I was not there. Yes, I was at the electrical parade show and hated every minute of it. All I could think about was you and our dinner plans. My mom wouldn't let me go out to dinner with you, especially since I never asked for her permission. My parents had already made plans to go out to dinner and then go back to Magic Kingdom for our last night there. Unfortunately, I was not allowed to change them or go out with a boy they didn't know. I have felt so terrible not being able to see you one last time and say a proper goodbye to you. Kissing you goodbye was definitely something I wanted to do. In fact, I have wanted to kiss you since the very first time I saw you in the Jacuzzi. I just didn't have the guts to do it.*

*How long did you wait for me at the pool? Thank you so much for finding my hotel room and putting the letter under my door. How did you know what room I was staying in? We never mentioned our hotel room numbers or last names. It was so awesome to have met you. You definitely made my vacation more amazing. It was exciting to hear your accent and finally understand you! Ha, Ha! Unfortunately, I'll be starting eighth grade very soon. You have no idea how much I am dreading it. With meeting you and receiving your letters, I think eighth grade might be a more enjoyable and tolerable year. How long do you think it will take to receive letters from one another? My mom said we live over 3000 miles away from each other 'across the pond' as the saying goes. Well, I definitely talked your ear off more than you did mine while on vacation. Please fill me in on what this year is going to be like for you and your daily activities. Would love to hear what it's truly like to live in England. Could you also send me some photos of you, your family and where you live? It would be great to see your home, neighborhood, hangouts, etc. I've never written letters to anyone before besides what was required in school, so this is going to be so much more fun! By the way, what does P.T.O mean?*

*I love you, Trevor.*

*Love, Kerri*

It cost me 50 cents to send the letter, and the post office clerk said it could take 1-3 weeks to arrive in England. I had been told more than once that my handwriting was worse than chicken scratch, so I hoped that somehow my letter would make sense.

I had never written letters overseas before, and the whole process was very exciting. This was a new experience, and I couldn't wait to hear back from Trevor. Every day I would stand by our mailbox for our mail lady, Beth.

After I first sent my letter to Trevor, I made sure to tell our post lady Beth all about him, how we met and our letter writing. I was hoping by telling her that she would keep a look out for his letters.

On the third week, Beth stopped by with a smile. 'Let me guess, waiting for Trevor's letter? You are so committed. I've never seen anyone wait by their mailbox every day anxious to receive someone's letter they just met.'

'Of course, I am. I know you might think I am being very silly, but you wouldn't understand. He's more than just the boy I met on vacation,' I said smiling.

'Well, I figured that much, and I think I'll be making your day because it's finally here!'

'Oh my God, are you serious? Give it to me, please!' I screamed at Beth while holding myself back from tearing the letter out of her hands.

She winked at me as she handed me the letter. I was so overjoyed I, hugged her.

I had known Beth for the past year when she started her career with the post office. Her wavy brown hair was always pulled back into a ponytail, which showed off her beautiful green eyes and rosy cheeks. Every day without fail, she greeted me with a welcoming smile. When I first met Beth, she immediately reminded me of the beautiful Irish girl character I was reading in one of my Danielle Steel romantic novels. We became good friends. After meeting Trevor and starting our letter writing, I was eager to confide my new relationship with someone who wasn't from school, and Beth was first to come to mind. She had always been supportive. Every time we talked, she seemed genuinely happy for me and would make time in her busy day to ask how I was doing. Beth was the big sister I never had. I could tell her anything.

I thanked Beth and ran into the house. I flew into my bedroom and dived onto my bed, calming down just enough to open his letter carefully and begin to read.

*Dear Kerri,*

*Hi, how are you? I hope this letter finds you and your family very well. I am back at home now and, of course, back at school. I am now studying and working hard for my first set of official exams in April. I only have time now to do what I really want at the weekends, so I have to spend my time very wisely. I'm sitting on my bed at the moment thinking of you, writing you this letter and listening to my Michael Jackson's L.P. Bad, which always seems to remind me of you and our holiday together.*

*I got your letter this morning. What a wonderful surprise, I'm really pleased. You should be back at school as well by now. So you will be entering the eighth grade and dreading it. So sorry to hear this, does anyone really like school? Not me, that is for sure. I hope your year there will not be as bad as you think. I didn't expect to meet anyone on my holiday, and I feel I must be honest with you. You have a brilliant personality and are quite outgoing unlike myself; I was a bit nervous to be around you at first. I haven't dated much at all, and I haven't liked a girl as much as you. So it was really nice to get along so well, and it worked out great that our holiday schedules allowed us some down time together. It was nice to spend the entire day with you at the pool and have lunch too; I really enjoyed it.*

*Thank you for letting me know what happened. I was worried you were running late when you didn't show up at the pool on time because you always came when we made plans to meet up. After half an hour, I got worried about you. It's not what we planned, but I am glad you were safe and okay. Please do not be so upset, I understand why your parents wouldn't let you come to dinner with me. I really did want to kiss you goodbye as well. In fact, I had wanted to kiss you for the entire holiday, like you I didn't have the guts to do it. That is why I really wanted to have one last night with you and make sure I got that kiss before we had to say goodbye.*

*To answer your question, I had waited for you for two hours. I would have waited longer. Unfortunately, my parents came to find me and told me since you were nowhere to be found, we would be off for dinner and some fun on our last night in Florida. I wanted to say I am sorry I wasn't very easy to talk to when I first met you, (believe it or not) I really like you a lot and would love to see you again. Do you think that would ever be possible? Maybe we could make plans for the future, maybe this coming summer? If that cannot happen, then could I at least have a photo of you and of where you live? My first time to the States was Florida. I would be interested in seeing the differences between states. Show me your town and anything else you think would be interesting to me. The pictures you wanted are included here; me, my dog Roxy, and my home. By the way, 'P.T.O' stands for 'please turn over.'*

*How was your plane flight home?*

*You're not going to believe this, Alec and Ben showed me where your room was. They had followed you back to your hotel room one time without you knowing. I had no idea that they did this. I was so upset when you didn't show. My dad figured you probably had to go out with your family for the last time to Disney World and maybe see the electrical parade show. He suggested I write you a letter and give you our address. I told him I didn't know where your room was, I also didn't know your last name in order to find out your room number from the reception desk, and that's when Alec and Ben confessed. As much as they irritate me, and I wished they would leave me alone when I wanted to spend time with you, if it weren't for them, I'd never have known where your room was.*

*Look, I've written two letters now so far, which is a great effort for me! Ha! Seriously ask my parents! I dislike school very much and homework; it takes me forever to complete my assignments. I cannot wait to hear the post come through the door and see your next letter to me! We always know when the post has been because our dog, Roxy lies directly under the post slot in the door and he gets hit by the mail every time. You can hear his constant barking for five minutes or so as if he's telling off the postman. It's hysterical. You would think he'd sleep elsewhere. Can't wait for another letter from you, so when you write back, please put the date it was written, also, the date you sent it so as to see how long it takes to get through. I miss you, Kerri, so don't forget to write, and don't forget the photos. Goodbye.*

*I love you, Kerri.*

*Love, Trevor*

*P.S. Sorry it's late*

*P.S.S. When are you turning 15? (So I can send you a birthday card on your special day)*


Mystery solved. Looking up at my ceiling, I lifted my arms and shouted as loud as I could without alarming the neighbors, 'Thank you, Alec and Ben!' The word love was written several times. HE LOVES ME!

My first love. Was I his first love as well? I hoped so.

So what if we had an ocean between us? It wasn't going to deter me from making Trevor mine. I'd write a million letters to him if I had to.

I pulled out my special stationery from my wicker hope chest and sat down again on my bed. I was excited to write several pages answering his questions. I had some questions of my own, and I wanted to fill him in on what was going on since I last wrote.

'What are you doing?' asked George sounding slightly annoyed.

He startled me; I didn't hear him come in.

He stood in the doorway covered in dust and dirt from his work. He looked annoyed with me, and I didn't know why.

'I'm in the middle of writing to Trevor. I received a letter from him, and it's important I write back ASAP because the mail takes so long.'

'Did you start your homework?'

'I have some, but it can wait,' I replied, not looking up from my stationery.

'We have rules, Kerri, and you need to follow them. You should put that away and focus on what's more important.'

'George, this will only take a few minutes, and this is what makes me happy. Doing homework doesn't make me happy. I do it because I have to, not because I want to. I'll start it right after this.'

I wanted to shut the door, but, I had to keep my door ajar at all times. Plus, I didn't have a handle to shut my door with.

'I understand meeting Trevor and writing to him makes you happy, but you must follow our rules. I don't want you failing out of school after all we've been through.'

This was a weird statement coming from George of all people. I really didn't think he understood or cared about how much Trevor meant to me. He never went through what I did, so how would he know? He'd never shown much interest in Joe and me. Never attended any 'meet the teacher nights.' Acting like a father that cared now about my schoolwork was out of the ordinary.

Him hovering around was starting to piss me off. What was his problem? Did he have a bad day at work? Was I the one he needed to take it out on? I wish I could tell him off and ask him to leave me alone, any talk-back would have got me in more trouble, and so I had to bite my tongue. I just wanted to write the letter; it's not like I was being unreasonable.

'I hear what you are saying, but let me finish this letter, and I'll put it away and get on with my homework. Like I said, it's not a lot, and I can get it done quickly. No problem really.'

'I don't appreciate you talking back to me, Kerri.' He leaned against my doorframe and folded his arms across his chest. 'When your mother gets home, we'll need to talk about your attitude.'

Now I was furious. 'George, I do not have an attitude. I have been told what to do all day at school. I literally got home and received Trevor's letter. I was really excited to receive it. I would just like some privacy and to feel like I have a little freedom. Can't you understand that with all I've been through?

'I'll be talking to your mother, and this might have to be brought up at the psychiatrist's visit.'

'I'll make it easy for everyone; why don't I stay in my room and hide away? I hate going to school and those shrink visits anyway. They're a waste of money. All I do is look at blotched pictures of ink dots! It makes no sense. I don't think she knows what she's doing because every time I leave, I feel more confused than when I first walked in. All she does is ask the same questions every week. I don't want to go anymore. Why don't you tell Mom that I am done! What else do I have to do to prove I am not a threat to myself anymore?'

George didn't seem to know what to say to that, so he closed my door. I didn't care about his threats. I was relieved.

I was ostracized at school; I didn't feel comfortable hanging out and playing with my old friends. I still had moments of loathing myself and had to fight the thoughts of *so what if I did die?*

I was overwhelmed with my daily routine of trying to meet everyone's expectations. The only thing that made me happy and helped me continue with my 'new miserable reality' was Trevor! I had this amazing new love in my life. He made me so happy. Why would George want to interfere with that? It was just a letter!

Truthfully, Trevor and his letters were hope for a future I couldn't imagine before. I enjoyed daydreaming and envisioning a fantastic life as an adult. These letters were something I looked forward to. Having a connection to someone outside of my attempted suicide was wonderful. Reading Trevor's letters gave me hope for thinking about my future and finally being happy. My family and I were doing our best to move on after what I did. For me, it still felt like the same old routine. I didn't want to cause any more problems or come off as having an attitude. I was happy and grateful for being home, that didn't mean I was happy at school, or my life was suddenly perfect and my attempted suicide never happened. My current reality was hard; it was better than when I was constantly depressed. Unfortunately, now I had to deal with all I had done, and how I was being treated at school and home. I was finding out who I was and trying to build stronger relationships with my brother and mother. As for George and I, we might have clicked when I was five, but not anymore. No matter how much I tried to see George differently, we didn't get on. Overall, the dynamics of my household hadn't changed. I enjoyed reading Trevor's letter and would re-read it until I received another one. I hoped my life would get better at some point; wishing people at school would forget and hopefully start to talk to me again and not look at me in that way anymore. And maybe one day, I could be reunited with Trevor, and we could have that kiss and something more.

*Dear Trevor,*

*First, thank you so much for sending me yet again another letter! I have waited anxiously every day for our regular post office lady, Beth. I would ask her every day if I received your letter. She would typically say 'No.' Today, I didn't need to ask. She was excited, and I knew she had your letter. She thinks our writing letters to each other is very romantic! I second that! Before she left, she winked and said, 'Happy Reading.' She is so nice; I do really like her.*

*With all the music that is out there, why does Michael Jackson's LP* Bad *remind you of me and our holiday together? I like that track. It is very good. My brother and I are huge fans of Michael Jackson. I really enjoy the history of Michael and his brothers getting into the music industry when they were all little in their group The Jackson 5. My brother loves Michael Jackson* so much he actually asked my mom to buy him the red leather jacket (she bought a fake leather jacket look-alike, of course) and the white glove (the white glove was a replica that was mostly bedazzled than anything remotely close to the real thing). Why you ask? He was Michael Jackson for Halloween! It was very cool of him to be Michael Jackson, also kinda weird to see a little 'white' Michael Jackson with bright blue eyes and blond hair. I've enclosed several photos from our Disney World vacation that my mom had developed per your request as well as pictures of our home and some of our town. I hope you like them. Right now, it's the fall season and my favorite time of year. I love watching the leaves change colors! No matter how many times I watch this happen, I am still mesmerized. You don't normally see such breathtaking colors in so many different shades. It's better than a rainbow. Being born in the fall doesn't hurt either. I feel very connected to this season. I don't mind raking the leaves up because I always get the chance to then jump into them. When you take a drive during the weekends through our town, you can smell several yards burning leaves, and that is the best smell! I make a point to roll my window down all the way so I can enjoy the scent. I wish I could bottle it up and bring that scent into the house.

I have a confession to make, and I do hope you will not be angry with me or not like me anymore. After we first met, I was so excited to talk with you and have you like me. Because of this, I was afraid if I told you my real age you wouldn't be interested in me. I was 13 when we met, almost 14. In fact, I turned 14 this past September. So you are a bit older than me, and I am more than fine with that, but not sure if you are okay with me being younger than you are. So sorry for lying, I do not like to lie and pride myself on not lying, but I thought this time around I had a very good reason to. When is your birthday? I'd love to send you some American type gifts or something you are wanting or interested in? School is in, and it's horrible as I predicted. I am in eighth grade now. You might as well call this grade 'HELL' and be done with it. I wear your bracelet every day and look at it often to remind me of the unforgettable vacation we had together. Our vacation feels like a million years ago now. I wish we were still in

*Florida enjoying our time at the pool and planning more hangouts and finally having that date. Your bracelet brings all our memories back and always cheers me up, especially at school when the boys are giving me weird looks over it, and the girls stare at me all the time. It's uncomfortable, and I don't like it one bit.*

*I love your photos, thank you. Why are they all black and white? Is that special film you are using or did something go wrong with the color?*

*Please do me a big favor and hug your family for me. I am so grateful that your brothers followed me back to my hotel room. It is a bit creepy, I agree, but, in this case, I am glad they did it. I am also very grateful to your dad for coming up with the idea to write me a letter in the first place. Believe me, I was a mess the night we were supposed to meet. I cried a lot and didn't talk to my family for the entire evening after I was told I couldn't go back to the hotel. I truly believed I would never see you ever again. Now we don't ever have to worry about that, which makes me happy!*

*Halloween is finally here this week, and it's one of my favorite holidays ... Do you all celebrate Halloween? Do you hand out candy in England and dress up and have parties? Or is it more an American tradition?*

*Roxy sounds hysterical. He should definitely find a new sleep place. He looks so tiny and sweet in your photos. We do not have any pets, not even a goldfish. My mom has told us most of our lives that she is very allergic and for that reason we cannot have any pets. I wonder why the breeders you bought Roxy from gave him that name. It's weird, I agree. If I had a dog, I'd want to call him Charlie. I've always loved that name for a dog.*

*Well, believe it or not, even though I talked your ear off on holiday, as you call it, I can actually run out of things to say. I know I've written a million pages here, but I think I'm done, cannot think of anything else to tell you. I better be going; I have homework to do. Not that I want to do it, and I haven't started any of it yet. Please write me as soon as you can. I love receiving your letters, Trevor! They really brighten up my day or month for that matter!*

*I miss you so very much, Trevor, and love you so very much too.*

*Love, Kerri*

And so our correspondence to one another began. We both received a letter once a month. Not being a part of school sports or any other activities made me feel like a recluse. Trevor's timely letters gave me something to look forward to and brought back memories of how we first met. I still laughed at myself for not understanding him at first in the Jacuzzi. The first letter I wrote him and sprinkled it with hotel perfume and watched how his ears turned red. My favorite memory was our full day at the pool and having lunch together.

Sophie and I had exchanged addresses before we said our goodbyes at the Marriott. Sophie's letters meant a great deal to me, and our friendship grew deeper and stronger. It was as if a wall had collapsed through our letters, allowing us to open up.

Every couple of weeks, we'd receive a letter from each other. It was exciting to receive two letters a month from each of my new best friends, which both came from England. And it gave me the needed escape from school life.

My entire year of eighth grade was a dreadful experience. Each day seemed more difficult to get through than the day before. Most days, it was a push to get out of bed. I felt I had to put on a mask for my family to show them I was feeling much better, and all would be okay. Every day when I got out of bed and knew I had to go to school, I was quickly reminded that I was "that girl" who tried to take her life. Groups of kids would shy away from me as I walked down the halls. Others would stare at me as I walked past them, and I'd try to imagine what they were thinking. I didn't know how to talk to anyone, and I understood why they didn't know how to talk to me. Every now and again, a person would be brave enough to start a conversation with me only to stutter uncomfortably when they ran out of things to say. We'd look at one another, share an awkward silence and walk away to our next class. I coped by shutting myself off, to the point where even today I can't remember much about seventh or eighth grade at all. All I could remember were the letters I got from Trevor and Sophie, letters that gave me a reason to look forward to the next month.

Trevor and I knew how crazy the post office would be during the holidays, so we sent Christmas presents to each other early before the madness ensued. In mid-October, my mom took me shopping. On the way there, we sang songs in the car together, enjoying each other's company. My mom was super busy commuting and working all week, and I knew her free time was precious, so I was grateful for her time and for giving me money to buy his gifts. She knew he was an important person and a positive influence in my life, and she encouraged our letter writing by regularly driving me to the post office and paying for the stamps several times a month.

I picked out a gold link chain for his sweet sixteen, and some clothes and candy for Christmas. In return, he sent me a silver necklace with several entwined hearts and some Cadbury's chocolates. I wore the necklace every day. During study periods, I would often take the necklace off to admire it, and I would daydream about us being together. It wasn't ideal to be in love with someone who lived so very far away. Nevertheless, I was still determined to make this work. His letters were more than just words on paper. They were a form of hope, something I needed; I craved them because I was able to escape my daily life once pen hit paper and finally become the girl I always wanted to be. Trevor didn't know my past; he knew me as the fun amazing girl he met on vacation. Not only did we fall in love, but Trevor was also my best friend, a true confidant, and as time went on, our letter writing enabled me to start dreaming of a future I would never have thought possible.

*Dear Kerri,*

*Thank you for the chain, clothes, sweets, and photos, they mean a great deal to me, and I will treasure them always. The reason the photos are in black and white is because black and white photography is one of my favorite hobbies. We've converted a spare bedroom into a darkroom where I have all the necessary equipment to develop all of my photos that I've taken. Anyway, some colour photos I am taking now should reach you in the near future. So please look out for them, and I do hope you like them. The reason Michael Jackson's L.P. Bad reminds me of you and our vacation (we call it holiday) together is we both loved the Captain EO ride in Epcot and Bad was released the week we got back from our holiday. Most importantly, my favourite track on that record is "I Can't Stop Loving You" and, of course, that's how I feel about you and I listen to it most days when I get home from school.*

*You being thirteen and not fourteen doesn't make any difference to me. It wouldn't make you look much different or act much differently; maybe you'll be a better mathematician now that you've turned fourteen. Ha, ha! I love you just the same at your current age as I did when we met. Well, I will be turning sixteen this December, five days after Christmas. I am trying to get to see you, maybe in the summer, like an exchange in which I come over to stay with you, and you come and stay with me, for a week each. Let's say it would be fun and educational. What do you think? It would definitely be a lot cheaper than a holiday as we would only have to pay for the airfare. My dad said it would be a good idea if I could earn the money. What about your parents? Do you think they will think it's a good idea as well? I really hope so. So there's something for you to think about. I've been thinking about it a lot lately, and I really hope we can manage it.*

*We do not celebrate Halloween here, at least not in this house, or my neighbourhood. We do celebrate each year on November fifth; it's called Guy Fawkes Day. I can hear you saying "What's Guy Fawkes Day?" Well, I'll try and sum it all up. My history teacher would be proud. In 1605, on November fifth, a man named Guy Fawkes attempted to blow up the Houses of Parliament and failed. The failure is celebrated by lighting bonfires and setting off fireworks. It's a lot of fun. I'd love to be able to take you to see and experience it.*

*Roxy is a King Charles Cocker spaniel, and his breed of dog is normally what you find walking around with their owners here in our village. I like Charlie that is a great name for a dog. It's getting on, and I have a ton of homework to do, but before I go, here's something I've been working on at school and thought you would really like it.*

*I've been learning and practicing French lately so……………….*

*Au revoir*

*J'aime tu*

*I love you*

*Trevor*

*P.S. Au revoir means goodbye*

*P.S.S. I think you can work out what J'aime tu means*

*P.S.S.S. Another letter should reach you in about 2 weeks. Please write back. I LOVE YOU.*

I continued to write to Trevor, but all of a sudden his letters stopped. Months went by with no word from him. I went over everything I had written to him, wondering if I had said anything that would make him stop writing to me. I couldn't think of anything. His letters to me had been so regular. Why didn't he reply? *What if something had happened to him?*

# CHAPTER 8 – ALEC

Without Trevor's letters, I felt a bit lost. My life at home was unraveling as well. When we went to Disney World, it was as if my attempted suicide never happened. There was no stress, no fighting, nothing but fun, wonderful outings to the parks and relaxation days at the pool. It seemed as if the division between the three of us and George was no longer there; we were a family. I was hopeful once we returned home everything would change for the better. Unfortunately, resuming our routines, us at school and our parents at work, everyday life stresses seemed to seep back in, and it felt like we never had that vacation.

My relationship with my mom and Joe was improving. Unfortunately, my relationship with George, no matter how much I tried, was poor at best. I felt I had to walk on eggshells in our house and shouldn't really say how I was feeling or admit there might be a problem between us. I wished we could have moved house. I think a truly fresh start would have been better therapy than the continued shrink visits. Sometimes, I would have nightmares and wake up in a cold sweat remembering my time in the loony bin. I never told my parents because I felt it would only make it worse. Although, I was no longer on my medication, the sensation of being a burden never left me. I didn't want to hurt my family any more, and so I kept my feelings locked up.

My relationship with my father had always been chaotic, and he was a person in my life I couldn't count on. I have a few vague memories of him from when he was married to my mother, sadly most of those memories are of him being angry; when his temper would inevitably get the better of him, and he'd blow up and start screaming and you were so scared because you didn't know what he would do next. For example, when I watched him throw our living room lamp against a wall or the time when he put his fist through the apartment wall, in response to an argument he was having with our mother.

There is one happy memory: I remember wanting to run away - I must have been three or four years old - I can't remember why I wanted to do this, I just did. I packed all my fake food into my Fisher Price shopping cart; I added some clothes and my favorite baby doll. Toddling out to the back of our apartment building, I saw my dad was cooking hot dogs. He asked me what I was doing, and I told him I was running away.

He said, 'OK, but before you go, do you want to eat a hotdog? Wherever you're going could be a long journey.'

I said, 'Yes, please.'

And that was it, I sat down to eat some hotdogs with him, and I forgot all about leaving.

I was four years old when my father left us for a year before our parents' divorce was finalized. I remember feeling it was my fault and having repetitive nightmares. When my father returned a year later, he joined the Police Academy and started dating a lot of different women.

There are other memories with him after they divorced; playing the card game fish with pennies and going to local nature parks for fishing. Because of his new life being single, he chose not to show up for our planned weekends together. One day in the winter when Joe and I were little, we sat on the icy front steps of our apartment building waiting for hours in the cold, but he never showed up. This became a pattern over time.

I always felt bad for Joe; at least I had my mom, and we were close, but Joe deserved a full time dad. Unfortunately, our father was not interested in having us in his life, and this impacted Joe's life more than it did mine.

By seventh grade, my brother's natural blond locks were fading into a dark brown. He wanted to change it. One day, he came to ask for my help.

'Kerri?'

I was in my room reading.

'I'm in my room, Joe.'

'Yeah, stupid of me not to come here first; you're always in your room.'

I stared at him.

'Can I help you or did you come in her to irritate me! Cause I really don't need it today.'

'Sorry, still no letter from Trevor?'

'No, it's really bothering me. I keep wondering what the hell I've done wrong. I keep re-reading his letters looking for something I might have missed, but there's nothing.'

'I'm sure he's been busy after the holidays. He'll write soon enough.'

'Thanks.'

Joe told me his predicament, and I thought about it. Bleach would be dangerous. It would be way too expensive at our local salon to have a hairdresser change his color. Then it came to me.

'How about Sun-In? It's a chemical that lightens your hair. It's not too expensive. We can probably get some at CVS and get it done this weekend. If you don't like it, it will rinse out over time.'

A couple of days later, he purchased Sun-In. My brother put his faith in me, and I did the best I could. I sprayed a good layer over his head, covered his hair with a towel and had him sit on the side of the tub.

The time was up, and I came back. I took the towel from Joe's hair to admire my handiwork. The Sun-In had definitely lived up to its name. At that moment, I found myself suddenly unable to form any words...

Pulling away, Joe jumped up to look in the mirror. 'What have you done to me?' he gasped.

After getting over my speech impediment, I eventually managed, 'It's kinda cool. It's not the exact color we wanted, but it's much lighter than before.'

'Kerri, it's ORANGE!'

'Okay, it's orange; no need to yell at me.' I shampooed his hair to calm him down, but it didn't make any difference. He left the house wearing a hat, slamming the front door on his way out.

After that day, he didn't talk much more than a grunt here and there.

*Great, not only was I worried about Trevor, now I had to worry about my brother hating me and how he was going to be treated at school for this new hair color change.*

The following Saturday, my brother went to spend the weekend at our dad's house. I didn't go because I couldn't forgive him for the way he acted in the hospitals. Not surprisingly, he didn't make an effort to make amends with me.

When Joe came home, he had tears in his eyes.

'What's wrong? Did you not have a good time with Dad?'

'Thanks to you, Dad thought it would be hysterical to call me 'Sally' all weekend long. He said I'm either gay or a girl with my hair like this. I tried to explain, but he wouldn't stop teasing me. I don't know why he thinks it cool to tease me. I'm his son, doesn't he care?'

'He doesn't, Joe. You know what he's like. Why we expect anything different from him is ridiculous.'

'Yeah.'

I walked over and gave him a hug. Surprisingly, he accepted it; we hugged for a good moment.

I released Joe so I could look at his face. He was still crying.

'Joe, it's really going to be OK; your hair will grow out, or you can buzz cut it. As for Dad, I wish I could say he's going to change, but we both know by now he's not. I am probably the last person you want to talk to, but I am always here for you if you need me.'

'I know.'

Joe hugged me again and then walked away.

What made matters worse was when Joe returned to school that Monday, he was ordered to remove his hat for the entire day. Some of Joe's friends asked what had happened, and he confided in them. Unfortunately, one of those friends told another, and by the end of the day, I learned some bullies were calling him Sally and other inappropriate terms. Until he got that buzz cut a week later, he was continuously picked on.

Our mom still fought for support payments from our dad. Joe wanted to have a relationship with him, even though when they did spend time together, ten to one Joe would come home upset from comments or suggestions made by our father to him. Our dad would always find a way to pick on my brother with each visit. It was a time in Joe's life when he was changing and becoming a teenager and dealing with puberty. Like me, he definitely needed a father figure in his life and being a boy I believed even more so. There was no connection with George. I had always felt George was jealous of any time my mom spent with me, but I felt it more when she was paying attention to her one and only son. He needed a father figure; he didn't need jealousy from George or our dad's anger issues focused on him.

Seven months went by, and I stopped checking the mailbox every day. I happened to be outside when Beth our mail lady came one day in late August, and I ran over to collect the mail from her. She beamed at me as she handed over a letter with a familiar Air Mail stamp on top. I was shocked. I stood looking at it for a few moments, debating whether I should open it. I noticed his address had changed. When did that happen? Did this mean that he hadn't received all the letters I sent over the past seven months? Confused, I ran to my room and gingerly opened the letter.

*Dear Kerri,*

*Before you read this letter, please take a seat cos this is the worst letter I have ever had to write in my life. It's taken me 7 months to write, and I've written this letter over a million times in my head.*

*To start with I will say how very sorry I am for not writing to you since Christmas, and it's not because I'm mad at you, or because you've done something wrong or I've found someone better because I couldn't possibly find anyone better than you.*

*Can you remember my two little brothers? How can you forget the little pests, Alec and Ben? Anyway, the older one of the two, Alec, was killed in a road accident on his bike in February. He had turned 11 this past October. It was a Sunday afternoon, and he was on his way to a swimming competition in the next town when he pulled out in front of a speeding car. He was hit full on and killed instantly. The rest of the swim team drove by in the bus a few minutes after it had happened. The bus driver stopped to help and saw it was Alec. Alec's coach got off the bus and held Alec until the police and EMTs arrived. Needless to say, they cancelled the competition.*

*It was too painful to continue to live in our small town, where everyone knew us and knew what happened. My dad got a new job shortly afterwards, and we moved once I finished the school year. Please take note of our new home address above, it should be used from now on.*

*We are all still coming to terms with Alec being gone. It hasn't been easy. It's so quiet in the house. We had to box up all of his stuff from the old house. I think Ben is taking it the hardest that I can tell. Alec and Ben were inseparable. My parents are trying to get on and be brave for us. We miss him so very much. You really don't think this sort of thing will ever happen to you.*

*Right now, I'm sitting in our new home, which is nice just not the same as our old house. I've met some new friends since we moved here from school and around the neighbourhood. I've finished my exams, and now I've got myself a full-time job at McDonald's until I go back to school in September then I'll need to go part-time. The job isn't too bad; it's nice having some money I can call my own. Do you have a job? Are you allowed at fourteen? Well, you are closer to fifteen now, aren't you? Your birthday is coming up in September, right?*

*I'm on holiday the same week you and your family are going camping in Walt Disney World's Fort Wilderness, but we are staying a week longer. We are going to the South of France for our holiday. We usually rent a caravan for a couple of weeks. It's definitely not going to be the same without Alec. I was hoping to get to see you this summer, but I'm sure you can understand with all that has happened since Alec's death, it wouldn't work out. I've already started saving up to try and get us together. How could I not try and see a beautiful girl like you?*

*Anyway, I hope you feel happier now that I've written to you. Please know I am truly sorry to have upset or worried you. Please write and tell me how you are and what's happening your way and send me a postcard from Florida.*

*I love you.*

*Love, Trevor*

*P.S. I miss you.*

*P.S.S. Love Always*

Alec is dead!

I was completely stunned. How was it possible? I felt guilty for even being mad at Trevor. I cried, imagining what they all must be going through. I immediately remembered the day I met Alec. He was walking with Trevor and Ben; the boys were dragging their towels on the pool patio giggling the entire time. When we were in the pool together, he'd splash water at us, crack jokes and constantly tease Trevor and me. What a troublemaker he was. In a lot of ways, he reminded me of Joe.

My mom came home and found me crying on my bed. I showed her Trevor's letter. She was as shocked as I was, and she held me as I cried.

'I don't know what to do,' I sobbed.

'Just carry on with your writing as you normally do. Don't stop writing. Don't ever stop. Make it as normal as it can be under the circumstances.'

I was desperate to call Trevor and comfort him. I needed to hear his voice.

Sitting there alone on my bed, holding Trevor's letter, I understood what my mom was suggesting for me to do, but I still felt useless. I felt that I needed to show that I wanted to be there for him and his family, sadly I kept coming up short on how.

I decided not only to write a letter to Trevor, but also to include a message to his brother and parents. I wanted them to know how lucky I was to have met Alec. If it wasn't for him, Trevor and I wouldn't be talking now. Most of all, I wanted to express how very sorry I was. How much I wished I was there to help them through their difficult time. I still didn't think it was enough, but it was all I could think to do.

* * *

A week later, my family and I went to Disney World again. This time, we drove down with three other families. The other two families drove RVs, which blew our pop-up tent camper away by comparison. We also invited my aunt and our cousins. My aunt was often asked if she was my mom. They didn't exactly look alike, but they were similar in height around 5'7', both had short brown hair, oval faces, and hazel eyes. As for my cousins, regardless of their six years age difference, they took after their father's fairer side; both having light blond hair with striking blue eyes.

George had put a canopy on the back of his two-seater Ford truck. He constructed a makeshift seat that was made out of a foot and half of thick spongy foam and cut it into the shape of a small two-seater couch. The seat was covered with a red cotton fabric cover and placed up against the back of the cab. That is how we traveled the 1100 miles down to Orlando. In the 100 plus degree heat of summer, Joe and I baked in the back of the truck with our aunt and cousins. We didn't talk much because we all dozed off and on from the unbearable heat. When we did talk, it was only to complain about our cramped space, non-stop sweating, or lack of water. At times, we asked our aunt to bang on the window for a bathroom break while George and my mom sat up front in the air-conditioned cabin. We had asked if the window could be kept open to give us a little taste of the cool air, but George refused saying he didn't like the noise the open window made from the wind blowing in. We also asked if we could open the back hatch to the canopy. Unfortunately, that wasn't allowed either because it was illegal to be traveling like this in the back of his Ford truck. I felt like we were being smuggled across the country.

Thankfully, we had vented windows on each side of the canopy that allowed some air to flow through. Every few hours, my aunt would bang on the front cabin to get them to either open the back window for a few minutes or stop so we could stretch our legs. Every time we'd do this it would annoy George because he wanted to stick to a schedule and to pull over every couple of hours wasn't part of his plan. After a while, he told us to quit complaining and deal with the heat, and we'd soon be there. Due to us all being squished together, every time we stopped for breaks, I felt like we were coming out of a sardine can. The amount of sweat and smell on the five of us could have probably filled a couple of gallon jugs. My aunt eventually squeezed herself into the front seat of the truck until it became too uncomfortable for all of them. George would pull over, and my aunt would be sent to the back again. She'd do this several times throughout the drive. The other families would overtake us on the highway in their luxury RVs, waving and laughing at us as they drove by; it would piss me off, and I wanted to flip them the bird.

We finally arrived at the Disney Wilderness Campgrounds and put up our camper tent. The camper tent comfortably slept five, so this was going to be a stretch accommodating the seven of us.

After setting up camp, we took a tour of Fort Wilderness. Not having camped here before, my parents wanted to check out the amenities and find out what our options were getting to Disney parks besides a car. We learned that you could take a boat over to the Magic Kingdom and get the monorail over to Epcot. That was definitely something I was excited to do. The itinerary was pre-planned, and the first two days were to be spent relaxing at River

Country Waterpark after the long 24-hour drive. The remaining days we'd be in Disney World.

After our tour of Fort Wilderness, we packed some lunch for later, grabbed our beach gear and walked to the water park. Walt Disney and his team created the most adventurous looking waterpark I'd ever seen. River Country Waterpark was built using the water from Bay Cove Lake and featured a rustic wilderness theme. It didn't look man-made to me; it looked as if it was magically built from the existing rocks and boulders. It took a team of men and women known as Disney's Imagineers to design and construct the entire waterpark. I read it took three years to complete and was described as an 'old-fashioned swimming hole with a twist of Mark Twain's Huckleberry Finn.' Our cousins who were younger than me and Joe were extremely excited; our parents said we could stay all day as long as we made sure to check in with them for breaks and lunch.

I'd never seen so many water slides designed around a mountain and at such great heights. We all took off looking for the biggest water slide to try first. Slippery Slide Falls; two water slides that were super-fast and flushed you out of the tunnels emptying into Upstream Plunge were my favorites.

I wouldn't say I was afraid of heights. However, Whoop 'n' Holler Hollow, which were two water slides, one 260 feet, and the other 160 feet long and drained into Bay Cove, a sand-bottom lake, made me think twice.

Joe, my cousins and I wanted to challenge ourselves with the Barrel Bridge, a bumpy bridge with barrels beneath it. It was hysterical trying to hold onto the ropes for fear of falling as the bridge swayed back and forth.

We ended up spending most of our time in the open lagoon area of Bay Cove, which featured a tire swing, boom swing, rope climb and a T-bar drop. The T-bar drop would be considered a zip line today.

Overall, in my opinion, Disney's first water park should be rated with five stars compared to Wet N Wild. If I had my way, we would have stayed for the remainder of the week at River Country Waterpark, but everyone wanted to spend the rest of our vacation in the Disney World parks.

Joe and I made sure when we were in Epcot to take our cousins to our favorite attraction, Captain E-O. My aunt and cousins had never been to Disney World before, so it was awesome to go on the rides, spend a full week enjoying each theme park as well as the food in Epcot's different countries. The best time I felt was spent camping and hanging out at night by the fire. My family and I ended up riding almost all of the same rides in the Magic Kingdom like we did last year. The only differences were the lines seemed longer, and the Florida heat was much hotter since it was the end of August.

This was my second trip to Disney, and I knew what to expect besides having fun; a lot of walking and long lines, but my aunt, and cousins didn't. They were more exhausted than the rest of us by the end of each day. We all enjoyed the weeks' vacation, but it seemed to pass much more quickly than it did the year before. The previous year's vacation had seemed like an eternity, and had made me forget the events that had happened leading up to it, but this one seemed to flash by in the blink of an eye. Before I knew it, it was all over, and we were packing up and leaving, starting our two-day convoy home.

I'm not sure what happened on the last day, but somehow George got involved in an argument with one of the couples we traveled and camped with and decided to drive straight home, for 24 hours non-stop. Those hours we were stuck in the back of that truck seemed longer than our weeks' vacation.

I got home to find a postcard from Trevor. He was in France. I immediately wrote back to him to tell him about my vacation in Florida.

* * *

The following month, I started freshman year in high school. For once, I was both excited to go to school and nervous, because I didn't know what to expect. Unfortunately, during those school years, I was still trying to find myself and fit in. It was hard to accept I would always be a suicide survivor, and my classmates knew it. Having gone through years of depression and loathing myself, I would still feel anxious and out of control when faced with the occasional stressful situations with other students. When I felt out of control or didn't know how to work through a problem, I would at times have to fight thoughts of wanting to kill myself, always thinking that would be the easier answer than to deal with my life.

My father wasn't a part of my life; we never reconciled from my attempted suicide and the things he said in the hospital. The relationships at home fell back into the same routines, and nothing really changed between the four of us.

With all that was going on at home and school, I found myself looking for love in all the wrong places. I found it hard to love myself, always feeling ashamed and disgusted and the sensation of feeling like a burden to my family never left me. I had what I like to call my 'destructive years' during sophomore and junior year in high school. During that time, I experienced my first real relationship, and after six months, I lost my virginity at age 16. To this day, I have regretted that decision because I wasn't' ready, and I forced myself to have sex with my boyfriend for fear of losing him and the 'so-called love' I thought I was receiving. The start of my junior year I was out of control. I slept with three more boys, all of which were in my junior year class, and coming from a small town, everyone knew my business. The only reason I finally woke up to the realization of what I was doing to myself was because, during the last time I had sex, after my boyfriend and I broke up, I found out later the condom had broken. I spent the next month terrified, thinking I had truly sabotaged my future. Thankfully I got my period.

Finding out I wasn't pregnant was a turning point for me. I made a decision right then and there that I needed to start loving myself and stop hating myself. I knew my demons of wanting and sometimes thinking of killing myself would arise out of stress or fear. I chose to stop feeling fearful, started to love myself, faults and all because I wanted to live, I wanted a future, and I wanted my own family one day, just not at 17. I was thrilled I wasn't pregnant. I vowed to myself I would wait as long as I needed to find Mr. Right, and I would not sleep with him until I was 100 percent sure I was going to marry him.

It had been four years since I met Trevor, and I still kept in touch, and even though I had other boyfriends, I realized I never fell in love with them for the right reasons. I was just trying to fill a need. With the other boys I had dated, I was always trying to please them and be what they wanted, so I could feel wanted and have the attention I desperately needed. With Trevor, he met me when I was 13, and I was finding out who I was after the attempted suicide. I had been off my meds for months, and I was learning who it was to be the real me. I never pretended with Trevor; I was always truthful, and in our brief week together fell in love for the first time. We had loved each other and became the best of friends over the years, and I realized I still loved Trevor. No matter what stage I was in my life, I loved receiving his letters. I still needed his connection and to think, 'What if?'

I decided to concentrate on my studies. Because of my vow, I did not date seriously or have sex again for the next four years.

Meanwhile, Trevor started Sixth Form. Sixth Form College is similar to American High school Honor Classes. It's considered a college in that it is an educational institution in England, Wales, Northern Ireland, among others. Students aged 16 to 19 typically study for advanced school-level qualifications. Trevor began studying for his A-levels. We still wrote to each other; however, I noticed a shift in our relationship as we started to date other people. One thing we never mentioned was our other relationships. When I wrote him, I'd tell him about my first driving lesson, joining the softball and field hockey teams, and sent him photos of my school proms. He wrote to me about leaving McDonald's to go and work for Pizza Hut for double the pay, changing schools and taking his A-levels, and his love for music that resulted in a huge collection of tapes and LPs. Deep down, I think we still longed for one another and didn't wish to hurt each other's feelings. Throughout those high school years, Trevor was a constant reminder of the wonderful vacation, and the boy whom I fell in love with after a horrific time in my life. Trevor was the boy who gave me new reasons to be happy; a boy who would always be my Davy Jones.

I was your typical high school student; overwhelmed from always studying, trying to keep good grades as I worked a part-time job and had my own car. I made sure to join in some sports because I needed the social interaction. I loved softball and joined the team in sophomore year. I played second base, had a strong right arm, catching most of the balls that came my way. I would practice daily with my team, and during our season managed to hit two home runs. I thought in the fall, I'd join field hockey as a friend convinced me that it was an awesome sport and that I should try it out. It might have been awesome for her, sadly it wasn't one of my favorite sports because every time I got on the field, I was literally chased after by another girl with a thick stick, and she meant to use it on my person if she needed to steal the ball and ensure winning a goal for her team. One day out of the field, I had forgotten to take out my earrings (my ears are double pierced) and got hit on my right ear. That hit stung like a bitch, but what hurt the most was pulling my ear away from my neck; my earrings got stuck in my skin. I never forgot to take my earrings out before practice or a game again.

School and I didn't really get along; the only thing that made it worth attending was History and English class and seeing my best friend Melani. I had other friends, but I was closest to Melani. She was the complete opposite of me in height; I'm 5'9 compared to her 5'. She was beautiful with a strong jawline and independent spirit to match. I was jealous of her long brunette hair that she could style perfectly. My hair, on the other hand, had a mind of its own, and ten to one I'd be throwing it up in a bun or a ponytail not to have to deal with it. Like me, Melani was an avid book reader. At times when we hung out, we would sit in silence together; we didn't always have to talk. Sometimes, I'd catch her intelligent brown eyes daydreaming of future plans, and her positive attitude inspired me as much as my determination inspired her. We could always cause each other to burst into hysterics with all our crazy stories, and her laugh was contagious. She amazed me with her ability to play any sport, and I admired her for that. We had a lot in common: our parents had divorced when we were young, we had younger siblings in the same grade, and we both despised high school. We were inseparable in our senior year after she moved back from Florida. Although we had a couple of classes together, we spent most of our time together after school and on the weekends. I enjoyed hanging out at Mel's home.

I really enjoyed English class because I love books and still enjoyed escaping my reality and would allow my mind to plunge deep into a books story line. I would become the heroine of the book going on adventures, seeing the world and never having a fear or care in the world. I also understood poetry, enjoyed reading Shakespeare and didn't mind the essays required. Outside my daily routine in high school, I didn't have concrete ideas on what I wanted to do for the rest of my life. Melanie felt the same. We both knew we wanted to get out of our small town. The day of high school graduation was like a bird escaping a cage for me. I felt completely free. We were both extremely excited to be done with high school, even though we were not a hundred percent sure of what we wanted to do afterwards. While Mel and I applied and got cleaning jobs at a local hotel for the summer, Trevor was two years older than me and on his way to a university.

I didn't have a 4.0 or the finances needed to attend an out of state school. I didn't like school enough to accumulate a huge college bill for my mother for a degree I was unsure of. After trying out a home-based travel and tourism course during the summer after high school graduation, I realized only then that I might be short-changing myself and should apply to local colleges for a travel and tourism degree.

I quickly enrolled at Bay State College in Back Bay, Boston, in hopes of obtaining an associate's degree in travel and tourism. After finishing college, I had dreams of an exciting travel career, one where I would travel each week or month to new and exotic places. I interviewed and got the job with a company called National Leisure Group that owned Filene's Basement Vacation Outlet. My duties were to answer the phone and book domestic and international flights for customers. Not exactly what I had in mind, but it was a start.

After the first 30 days, I quickly learned my job was far from the exciting career I thought it would be. In my interview, they said it was a traveling job. Unfortunately, the only traveling I did was from my four by six cubicle to the fridge in the kitchen during my lunch break. Each time I took a booking, I became jealous of my customer's travels, wishing I could go with them, rather than being stuck in a box day after day.

Around the same time, Trevor finished university. Over the years, we had always said in each of our letters how we'd love to visit one another. I quickly realized after almost three lonely months employed and four years celibate that I was still completely in love with him. I wanted to explore the possibility of having a special relationship with Trevor now that we were in our twenties and employed. I sent him a letter asking if it would be okay if I could visit him in England and nervously waited for his reply.

# CHAPTER 9 – OUR FIRST KISS

It had been seven years since Trevor and I first met in that Jacuzzi. Now, almost twenty-one, I was thinking more and more of him. What he was up to, and with whom? Did he still think of me as a best friend or could there be more?

Throughout the years of exchanging letters, we had always talked about visiting each other, sadly we were too young and never had the money to do it. Making less than $5.00 an hour working as a part-time employee doesn't get you very far.

With my job at Filene's Basement Vacation Outlet came a regular salary and benefits that included discounts on all flights, hotel stays, and car rentals. My plan was to save money and then use my accumulated discounts and vacation time to visit Trevor.

I gave Trevor my work number and asked him to call me and see if we could make it happen. Trevor was now twenty-two and had graduated from university. He was working part-time and living at home with his parents. He would, of course, need their permission.

It was a Wednesday, and like most days, it was slow. Trying to look busy, I rested my hand on the manual pretending to read, but in reality, I was dozing. The phone rang, and I pounced on it, grateful for something to keep me busy.

'Thank you for calling Filene's Basement Vacation Outlet, this is Kerri, how can I help you?' I sang on autopilot.

'Hi, Kerri, it's Trevor,' he said in his thick British voice.

I dropped the phone. 'OH MY GOD! It's Trevor. It's him, oh my God, oh my God,' I screamed to my co-workers.

They started laughing at me. They knew I was crazy about him. How could they not? I had pictures of him plastered all over my cubicle. I suddenly realized that this call was long-distance and calmed down a little. I composed myself and picked up the phone. All I could hear was laughing. He was laughing at me, along with another male and female. I had no idea his parents were on the line too.

'I'm sorry,' I said self-consciously, feeling my cheeks burning, 'it is so good to hear your voice.'

'I'd hoped you would be surprised.' He laughed. 'It's good to finally speak to you again.'

We had never had the opportunity to call each other before, due to the expensive phone bill. This was the first time we'd heard each other's voices in seven years.

We managed to talk about dates. I say, 'managed' because I was having a tough time understanding him again; his accent was so distinct. After 15 minutes and cutting through the communication barrier, we decided on August 25 through September 4. I had only started my new job and was afraid that I might lose it if I flew off to see him immediately. Besides, I needed some time to save for the flight. I also liked the fact that August would be exactly seven years since we first met.

The only problem was now I had to wait 64 days to see him. I figured by the time the day arrived to fly out to England, I would have enough money saved to pay for the flight, but I still needed spending money. Looking at the exchange rate, I needed, at least, a thousand dollars. The American dollar was valued less and would be halved when exchanged for British pounds. I asked my nana for some help, and she was so happy for me; she said 'Yes' on the understanding that I would pay her back. Of course, I agreed.

From the moment I hung up with Trevor, time ticked by slower. Those 64 days seemed to painstakingly drag as if time somehow knew and was making me suffer. I was learning very quickly that sitting in a four by six cubicle for eight hours a day, five days a week was as boring as hell. Each day was exactly the same; after my morning commute, I'd take the elevator to the 4th floor and put my lunch in the fridge. Then I'd plant my butt in my seat surrounded by three and a half gray fabric walls; just tall enough for some privacy, but short enough that anyone could lean over and look in. For the first four hours of the day, I'd wait for a call to book a flight – domestic or international. During the summer, you would think my phone would ring off the hook, but it didn't. All of the calls were customers wanting to book all-inclusive Sandals, Beaches or cruise vacation packages. Most days, I had a novel with me and would read the hours away or take a nap waiting for my phone to ring. I would break the monotony with half an hour for lunch, and then I'd repeat the morning routine for the rest of the day until 5 p.m. Working in the Travel and Tourism industry was not going to be the exciting and exotic career I had imagined. I had a calendar in my cubicle, and every day I checked off the day's square with a large red X, counting down the days until I could see Trevor again.

The weekend before my journey, I was packed and ready to go. Unfortunately, I still had to work four torturous days.

Two days before my trip, I went to the mall to purchase a box of Bazooka for the airplane cabin pressure and a new set of panties. I then threw all my 'old panties' away.

A day to go, and alas, it was then I noticed that the new set of panties were not the sexy panties I thought they were. The label read 'Extra-Large.' I groaned inwardly, envisioning Trevor's face at the sight of the granny panties, but it was too late to exchange them now.

The day finally arrived. On Thursday, August 24, my mom drove me to the Airport to catch the Virgin Atlantic red eye flight to London. I was so excited; I had been packed and ready to go for days. I made my way to the gate only to find that my flight had been delayed due to a mechanical issue. Virgin needed to change planes. I was pissed.

Are you kidding me?

I threw my bags down and forcefully stuffed my ticket into my fanny pack.

Walking up the terminal, I headed towards the bar to calm my nerves. Two hours and three cocktails later, chatting with my fellow passengers, I boarded the plane very drunk. I cheerfully greeted each seated passenger I passed while looking for my seat.

As the plane lifted into the air, I was feeling very light-headed and happy … I couldn't wait to see my 'Davey Jones'. The last photos I had of Trevor were two years old. He was dressed up in a girl's white silk pajamas for a University Co-ed Pajama Party. He wore a short-sleeved button down top with shorts for the bottoms. He had a big pink bow in his hair with bright red lipstick and blush. His long sexy legs were nicely covered in black lace stockings. He pulled off drag pretty well. It would be hysterical if he showed up in that get up. But I had no idea what he looked like now …

I could hear my mother's voice nagging, 'Now, Kerri, do not expect too much. Don't put all your eggs in one basket.' I sighed, pulled out my eye mask from my carry-on, covered myself with the airplane blanket and attempted to get some sleep.

The minute the plane landed, I got off as fast as I could and joined the longest queue to clear immigration.

This took longer than I thought. Finally arriving at the immigration gate, I handed my passport to the officer who was portly and bald with an unnecessary comb-over. He looked at me strangely, mumbling something with such a thick accent I almost didn't understand what he said.

'Miss, how long are you staying in the UK?' he repeated.

'Oh, about ten days,' I replied.

'Do you have your return ticket?' he asked.

'Yes, I do, somewhere,' I fumbled in my carry-on bag and handed my return ticket to him.

'Where will you be staying?' he continued.

'Um, at my friend's house,' I told him. 'I have his name and address here.' I handed him a piece of paper with Trevor's address on it.

'Do you have a romantic involvement with this boy?' he pressed me.

'Um, no,' I answered him. Well, at least, not yet, I thought.

'Are you planning on getting married during your stay here?' he stared at me, his comb-over flopping down the side of his neck.

'Err, no.' A girl could dream, though, right?

'Do you plan on living in the UK if you were to get married?'

'Um, I guess; I don't see how this is relevant?'

Furiously stamping my passport, he waved me away with a gruff, 'Have a good day … Next!'

Well, that was weird, I thought.

Next stop, I headed for the bathroom. I needed to make sure I looked decent. The last time Trevor saw me, I was a 5'4" gangly teenager, with short brown hair with bangs. Looking into the mirror, I saw a young woman who had grown an additional five inches, my hair was all one length and laid three inches past my shoulders; my lips were fuller, and something I was quite proud of now: my breasts and hips.

I added more eyeliner and mascara, brushed my teeth and hair and finished with lip-gloss.

I was going for, you-haven't-seen-me-since-I-was-thirteen-and-boy-have-I-changed-sexy-look, not the just-slept-several-hours-on-an-airplane-and-look-like-a-complete-mess-look. Unfortunately, my hair was not cooperating with me that morning. After several attempts, I realized it was useless, threw my hair up into a ponytail and headed off to claim my suitcase.

I got there as my bag came out on the conveyor—good timing. I collected my bag and waited outside for Trevor to pick me up. I stood there for almost an hour and slowly started to panic. What if he got the dates wrong? What if he didn't really want me to come or his parents changed their minds? Did he go to the wrong airport? What if he stood me up?

Eventually, I lost all patience. I thought of all the effort I had made to get here: borrowing money, taking time off from a new job, ordering a new passport. A lot of planning went into this trip. As I was getting ready to gather my suitcase and head inside to look for a telephone to call Trevor and give him an earful, I felt a tap on my shoulder. I turned around, and there he was.

Standing before me was a tall, dark and handsome man. It was Trevor. He was no longer the 15-year-old boy I met in a Jacuzzi. His hair had darkened from a light brown to black, and his voice was much deeper. He hadn't shaved and had a five o'clock shadow. He shaves? I thought. For some reason, this never dawned on me. He wore slightly tight jeans that nicely showed off his bum and wore a brown leather belt that reminded me of the bracelets I had bought for us. I noticed his gray cotton V-neck shirt had a button undone, showing off a tuft of black chest hair. I had an urge to run my fingers through it.

'Kerri, I am so sorry,' he gasped, out of breath and his face a little flushed. 'My granddad and I saw last night on the Teletext that your flight was delayed, so I was planning on getting here later.' He paused, 'This morning, we checked the Teletext again and saw that your plane had made up the time and landed early. I rushed here as fast as I could.'

'It's … it's okay.' I was so shocked to see him that I stuttered.

Was I upset? Not in the least! Those hazel eyes, those full lips, his smile, and to top it off the accent! I had forgotten I was mad at him. He looked as if he had stepped right out of *GQ*. I kept thinking, doesn't he know how attractive he is? If he does, he doesn't act like it.

'Kerri, welcome to England,' he said smiling, bending his head toward mine and kissing me full on the lips.

Life bustled around us, but for those few seconds, time stood still for me.

*Our first kiss.*

For me, this was an important moment in my life. It was gone, but I was still replaying the moment. Standing there in the busy airport, his lips finally pressed against mine. I felt a bit faint, and my legs had gone to jelly. I knew right there, at that moment, that this was the man I was going to marry. I had no doubts, whatsoever. The only question I had was, did he feel what I felt, and if not, how I was going to convince him?

Smiling, we picked up my suitcase and made our way to the parking lot. I decided that, over the next ten days I'd make things official between us. I could hear my nana's and my mom's voices in the back of my mind, nagging me still, 'Now, Kerri, do not expect too much; don't put all your eggs in one basket.' Screw that! My basket was full, and I was going to chuck it out of the window! I had one shot to finish where I left off; I was going all in.

Having been up for well over 24 hours at this point, I was a little hyper. Loudly chewing Bazooka gum, I talked his ear off in the car. Trevor had asked me about my flight, and I explained how much I had to drink and was still wired from that. I was this crazy American girl, hyped up on several drinks, running on a few hours of sleep and now with a sugar rush, obnoxiously popping bubbles in his ear while we cruised at 80 mph down the motorway. I kept wondering if he thought 'what did I get myself into.' Thankfully, Trevor seemed as excited as I was to see him, and our conversation flowed so easily. Just like when we first met.

As we drove, I kept admiring Trevor and his driving skills. I'd never ridden in a car that had a stick shift. Trevor made driving 80 miles per hour in morning rush-hour traffic look easy. Watching his strong hands steer, maneuver between cars and shift into gears, the muscles in his left arm would contract, and it was quite sexy, really. I started to feel warmth spread over my body as I envisioned those same hands all over me. I had to stop myself on many occasions from reaching out and touching him as we were driving. I loved the control he had over the car. Rushing down the highway, I never felt so safe.

A couple of hours into the drive, I began to settle down. I started to feel a lot calmer as we pulled into a restaurant called Little Chef to get some lunch. After ordering our meals, we sat down with some burgers, fries and drinks. Sitting across from him, I noticed his chest hair again.

'Wow, I cannot get over your chest hair!' I exclaimed loudly. Several patrons turned around and stared at us.

'Shhh! Please,' Trevor whispered, embarrassed.

I lowered my voice. 'Oh, I am so sorry. I just reacted … It's a shock to see how much you've changed. You were not great with sending me updated photos. For starters, you didn't have any chest hair, and you certainly didn't shave then either.'

Embarrassed, his face and ears were turning bright red again from my honesty. I knew how reserved the British were compared to us Americans. You would think he should have expected this from me. I was always straightforward and honest in our letter writing. Maybe my personality was a bit disarming in person.

I tucked into my lunch, which gave Trevor an opportunity to tell me about himself. '… My mum, married young and had me at nineteen. My birth father was verbally and physically abusive, so my mum left him when I was nine months old and moved us back into her parents' house.'

'I'm so sorry to hear this; my dad was too.'

'Oh, I didn't know that about you.'

'I didn't want to tell you something like that in a letter.'

'I understand. The good news is I don't remember living with my birth father. I only remember living with my grandparents.'

'I'm sure your grandmother enjoyed having you with her.'

'She did. My grandmother was like my second mother to me. She looked after me until I was four while my mom worked at the local electric company, that's where she met my dad. They then married quickly, and my dad legally adopted me as his son at the age of five. Alec was born when I was four years old, and Ben came eighteen months later.'

The similarities of his story with mine really hit home for me. Over the years of our letter writing, we had never gotten this personal.

We headed back to the car for another hour or so drive to his parents' house. As we entered Trevor's hometown south of Birmingham, I immediately fell in love with it. I felt like Alice from Wonderland; transported into an exciting and completely different world.

I loved the architecture of the homes; they didn't look like the homes I grew up in. More like small cottages. They reminded me of the small towns I had visited in historic Boston and Martha's Vineyard. Their main streets were not paved; they were covered in cobblestones. Each home or small business had skirt-styled roofs and was closely squeezed against its neighbor. Trevor's town was quaint compared to the homes and retail plazas in my town. Everyone drove on the left side of the road in their mini vehicles that were really matchbox-sized cars compared to the cars in the States.

We arrived at a two-storied brick home. The Gardners had a one-car garage, and the door was the tiniest I'd ever seen compared to the garage doors in the States. Inside, Trevor said they had four bedrooms, and one was used for his dad's study. Trevor collected my suitcase, and then gentlemanly opened the door for me. I could get used to this. We walked into the house and took the first door on the right into the living room where we found his mum, sitting on the couch cross-stitching. She got up and gave me a warm, welcoming hug. Moments later, Ben, now seventeen, came down the stairs to welcome me as well. Ben hadn't changed much, but there were obvious differences; older, shaving, and as tall as his big brother. Trevor's dad was still at work and would be home later. Trevor showed me the rest of the downstairs. Through their small kitchen or dining room sliding glass patio doors, you could access the backyard; the British call it a back garden. My house's backyard was much larger and surrounded by pine trees; theirs was landscaped with brightly-colored flowers and a vegetable garden. Trevor took me back through the kitchen and up the stairs to his bedroom where I'd be sleeping. It was arranged that he would be sleeping on a camp bed in the study during my stay.

Trevor's room on the second floor was warm and inviting, but definitely a boy's room. I was quite impressed how organized his room was compared to my brother's rat's nest at home. A twin-sized bed sat in the corner. The comforter, curtains, wardrobe and night side table, were gray with matching white and red stripes. Three shelves on the wall held his growing collection of LPs, tapes, and a few CDs that had not long been on the market. Trevor told me that music as well as new movies are released first in Europe before coming to the States. The double-paned window was above the bed. I tried it out and noticed there was no screen. I figured they didn't get many bugs. Trevor put my suitcase on the bed, and I unzipped it and started to unpack, putting my clothes away in his bureau and wardrobe where he had cleared out some space for me. I really appreciated the time he took to make room for my clothes. This gesture made me feel like we were becoming more and more official.

'I'm sure you would like to stretch your legs. Fancy a walk around town?' Trevor asked.

'That would be great.'

We meandered through the town center, and as we walked down the cobbled high street we held hands and kissed for the second time; a real kiss, this time, not a peck. It was a French kiss and full of passion. We made our way across the main road and around the corner into the park, stopping every so often to kiss ... He had the softest lips like I was kissing butter. We played on the swings for a little while, and flying with the wind in my hair next to him was glorious; it felt like time had stopped and transported us back to when we met as teenagers, enjoying being together, without our parents governing our every second. We laughed, each trying to out swing the other. I wanted to win, so I jumped off at the highest point in midair. I was surprised when Trevor followed suit. We landed hard on the ground, winded and laughing. He rolled over to me, and I leaned in for another precious kiss.

We were surrounded by other families enjoying themselves, and the park was vibrant, full of color from all the decorative park benches, swing sets and climbing frames. Amongst all the kids and families hanging out and playing, I decided this would be the very best place to take our first photo together. Feeling so incredibly happy, I wanted to capture that moment with him. I asked a lady passing by if she wouldn't mind. We plopped down on a patch of grass and made ourselves comfortable for the photo. I stretched out on my left side and put my left arm under my head, and Trevor lay behind me, wrapping his right arm around my waist while leaning on his elbow.

'Can you believe that was our first ever photo together?' I said to Trevor.

'Really?' 'I thought for sure we had taken at least one when we met,' said Trevor.

'Everyone is so nice here in your town; it was nice of that lady to take our photo,' I said.

'It's a nice town, very small and at times not much to do, but my friends and I tend to visit the pubs regularly and hang out. Do you like pool or darts? We could go later and play if you feel up to it after your long flight.'

'I haven't played either, but I am up for anything while I am here.'

I took more pictures of him as we wandered around the park. He sat on top of a metal fence and made silly faces; fish kisses and then appearing very serious while I snapped away. We played on the swings for a little longer and then walked home. We hadn't said it to one another, but I felt we were acting like we were officially a couple, who hadn't seen each other for a very long time. It felt completely natural for our arms to be wrapped around each other, stopping to make out every few hundred yards.

All that time had been worth it. When we got home, we went straight up to his room, laid down on his bed and made out for a while. Trevor's hand wandered up my shirt and under my bra when there was a knock on the door. Trevor's dad walked through with an all-knowing grin.

'Hi, Kerri, I'm Nigel. It's nice to meet you finally. After all these years of writing letters to Trevor, I feel we practically know you.'

I re-adjusted my bra and pulled my shirt down as I walked over to hug him. 'It's so nice to meet you as well,' I said, blushing.

It was obvious the mood was broken, so Trevor and I headed downstairs to see if we could help his mum with dinner.

While we were waiting for the roasted potatoes to finish cooking, I handed out the Patriots sweatshirts that I had brought as gifts from Boston. Everyone seemed pleased.

We all got on so well that I didn't feel like a guest at all; I felt like a member of the family.

After dinner, Trevor and I headed out to his local pub, The Spring Meadow.

We sat down at a corner table on the bar side of the pub, Trevor with a pint of bitter and me with a pint of sweet cider. I found myself becoming more and more confident, with each new drink.

'Trevor, I think you should know I came here to be more than friends. I am not looking for a fling.'

Trevor's eyes widened over the rim of his pint. It was then that he hit me with the news. 'I have to be honest with you, Kerri. I have a girlfriend, Nicola,' he said. 'We were at university together and have been going out for about two years now.'

I stared at him, completely heartbroken. Every fiber of me, devastated.

'What? We've been kissing all day. You gave me the impression that you felt the exact same way I do,' I smiled weakly, trying to keep a brave face.

'I know,' he said, 'I've been looking forward to you coming, and I had hoped that we would pick up where we left off. I didn't want to say anything about her because I thought you might not come if I told you.'

'You're right.'

I tried as hard as I could to hold back the tears. It was no use.

'You need to understand I haven't been in love with her for the last year. Our relationship is more a friendship. For the last six months, I have wanted to officially break up, but I don't wish to hurt Nicola because we were friends first, and I care about her. We live together at university with other roommates, and it's been very difficult to try and break it off with her.'

Since that day when I promised my mom I would not hold things back, I've had difficulty keeping my feelings and opinions to myself. Today was no exception. I let it all out. 'I think there was a reason why we met in Florida all those years ago. If Alec and Ben had not known where my room was, if you hadn't left me a letter with your address, then we wouldn't be here right now.' I paused to take a sip of my cider, which aided my courage. 'Ever since you first called me at work, I have not stopped thinking about you. I couldn't wait to get here, to see you and to tell you that I want us to be more than friends. If you don't feel the same way, I understand.'

I hadn't meant to pour my feelings out to him today in this pub of all places ... Maybe this was best. At least, he would know where I stood.

He stared back at me, speechless for a moment. I didn't expect his face to turn beet red, and then thankfully, he smiled. 'Who said I didn't feel the same way? I've been thinking about you lately too. I've often looked at your pictures on my wall that you have sent me over the years and wondered if there was ever a possibility we could be together.'

I didn't expect him to be in a relationship, but I was relieved he didn't love Nicola anymore. The fact he'd been contemplating over the years like I had if there was a possibility of being together was still music to my ears. I felt a huge smile spreading. 'You have been thinking about me?' I asked.

'Yes, of course, Kerri; you were my first love. Did you ever wonder if we'd be in a serious relationship if we lived in the same country?'

'Yes. I just never realized you had as well.'

'Let's talk more about this tomorrow, you look tired,' Trevor said. 'We should go home. Do you realize you've been up for thirty-three hours?'

We drank up and walked home, our arms around each other.

I took a well overdue shower and laid down on Trevor's bed. A huge wave of exhaustion came over me, and I yawned.

'Come here,' Trevor whispered as he picked up my comb.

Unwrapping the towel from my head, I laid my head on his lap as he softly combed my wet hair. I was feeling closer to him every minute, closer than I've ever felt to anyone before. We cuddled and kissed for a while afterward.

'I wish you could lay here with me all night,' I said, beginning to doze off.

'It could probably be arranged. I'll talk to my dad in the morning.'

'I wish you didn't have to leave me,' I whispered, trying to keep my eyes open, fighting the sleep my body desperately needed.

'I let you go seven years ago,' he said softly. 'I'm not letting you go again.'

We kissed for a while longer. I was fighting sleep as he tucked me into bed. Trevor gave me one last kiss on my forehead, and then I watched him leave for his camp bed in the study.

## CHAPTER 10 – HOOK, LINE, AND SINKER

I woke the next morning with a hangover. I had lost count of how much alcohol I inhaled during my thirty-something hour jet-lagged day. I could hear Trevor and his family moving about in the kitchen.

'Oh, good morning.' Nigel smiled at me as I wandered into the kitchen, 'Did you sleep well?'

'Yes, thanks,' I replied.

I looked across the room at Trevor, and he turned and grinned at me.

'Would you like a cup of tea?' he asked.

'Hmm, yes please.'

We sat down at the kitchen table with our tea next to Claire and Ben. Trevor made me shredded wheat with hot milk for breakfast, and slowly I started to feel better.

We took his mum's car about half an hour south to Cheltenham. He showed me the house where he lived when he was four after his mum met Nigel. We then parked at the Park and Ride and took the bus to the town center. Trevor paid, the gentleman that he is. We wandered through the shopping center, holding hands, cuddling and kissing while we window-shopped. I purchased a headband, barrette, shower gel and kiwi lip gloss at the Bath and Body Shop and some postcards at a vendor's booth to send home.

We stopped for lunch at Peppers Café—an oriental chicken stir-fry for me and a cheese, lettuce and tomato club sandwich for Trevor. As we sat waiting for our food to arrive, I took the necklace off Trevor's neck and slid my high school senior class ring over it.

'What's this for?' Trevor asked.

'I want you to have this as a memento. I don't ever want you to forget me,' I replied.

'That's not a possibility,' Trevor said.

He examined the ring and said, 'Thank you ... As he let my ring drop onto his chest, you could hear a loud thump. It's heavier than it looks, do you mind if I put it on my finger?'

'No, that's fine,' I said. 'I chose a boy's ring when I selected it from the catalog. The girl's ring choices were too dainty for my taste. It will probably look like it belongs on your hand more than it ever did on mine.'

Trevor took my ring off his necklace and slipped it on his right middle finger. It was an amazing fit and looked great on him. Trevor wearing my ring made me feel like we were committing to one another, definitely an upgrade from the bracelet I gave him when we met.

'What do you think?' Trevor asked.

'I think it's a perfect fit,' I replied.

Our lunches arrived, and we wolfed them down. My hunger surprised me, probably still soaking up all that alcohol from the day before. We ate quietly, enjoying each other's company.

We went home after lunch and headed up to Trevor's room where I wanted to rest from still feeling the jet lag. I sat on his bed, and he joined me.

'I wanted you to meet my friends, so I arranged for all of us to meet later tonight at our local pub.'

'OK, that sounds like fun. Who's coming?'

'Libby, Dave, Mark, Theresa and possibly Allison.'

'You went to school with them?'

'Yes, we met when I moved here and started Sixth Form.'

'Do you like to dance? They all wanted to go clubbing after hitting some pubs,' Trevor asked.

'Yes, I love dancing. The last time I danced at a club was three years ago during my senior year in high school.'

'Great. You look tired; you're probably still feeling the jet lag.'

'I am. It probably didn't help I drank so much on the plane and at the pub last night.'

'Do you want to take a nap?' Trevor asked.

'That would be nice, will you join me?'

'Of course.'

Normally, it's not always easy for me to fall asleep, but because it was so warm and comfortable in Trevor's arms, I soon fell into a deep sleep.

* * *

We got up around six o'clock feeling refreshed and quickly took showers and got ready to go out clubbing, leaving at seven o'clock. Trevor agreed to pick his friend Mark up, before meeting up with the rest of their group at the Horn and Trumpet Pub. I was thrilled to meet his friends and to see first-hand what he was like with them and what they did for fun on a Saturday night. Everyone was nice and welcoming and made me feel part of the group.

After a couple of drinks there, we left for Images Night Club. I hadn't been to a nightclub in ages. I'd had two pints of sweet cider and already had a buzz on. We all had a few more drinks at the bar before hitting the dance floor. Once there, it seemed we stayed on the dance floor for most of the evening. Dressed in black leggings, a white sports bra and a see-through sweater that seemed to become even more see-through with the strobe lights, I looked and felt pretty provocative. We danced closely, and every now and then, Trevor would lift me up in the air and twirl me around, bringing me back down for a madly passionate kiss. The first time he did this, I was shocked at first being lifted in the air, and it was exhilarating. I was also impressed he could lift my 140-pound frame. Each time, thereafter, our kissing was longer and heavier to the point that we couldn't keep our hands off each other.

'I want to take you to bed and make love to you,' Trevor whispered.

This had been something I had wanted to do with Trevor since I arrived. I believed in my heart he was the man I was going to spend my life with, and I knew he was being truthful with wanting to finish his relationship with Nicola. From what I understood, the relationship had been over for a long time, and I didn't doubt Trevor would make it official soon.

He took my hand and led me out of the club. Looking back at his friends on the dance floor, I felt bad not saying goodbye, but I'm sure they knew why. We were both too drunk to drive, so we took a taxi home, kissing and fondling all the way to the door. We crept quietly, well, as quietly as we could, up to the bedroom. He laid his duvet cover on the carpet.

I stood there watching him, filled with love and feeling a little nervous. I was definitely out of practice and knew making love to him for the first time wouldn't be a one night stand. I was starting to sweat a little, unsure of what I should do next. Also, I really wanted to stay there in the moment and watch him make the first move in making love to me.

Trevor turned around and said, 'Are you sure you want to do this?'

I was touched he really wanted to make sure I was okay; he didn't want to rush me. I felt all my life I was meant to meet him and be here at this moment and for the first time, I was going to make love for all the right reasons.

'Yes, I am sure.'

'Come here,' Trevor said, moving closer. We were now inches apart, and his beautiful hazel eyes were fierce with love. I knew I could trust him. I started to smile, and my anxiety lifted a bit. He put his arms around me and pulled me close. Trevor leaned in, and our lips met. I felt his tongue touch mine. Soft at first then hard and searching. His hand cupped the back of my head, and I felt enveloped in him.

His lips left mine. He began tracing a line of soft butterfly kisses down my neck. Down... My heart was pounding so fast, I thought it might explode. Then a sudden rush of heat coursed through my body. 'Trevor,' I sighed. This was our moment. Forgetting everything else, I quickly pulled off his shirt and unbuttoned his pants. At the same time, he undressed me. Our warm, naked bodies embraced and entwined as we slowly made love on the floor.

Exhausted and satisfied, we laid in each other's arms.

Trevor lifted my chin to look at me. 'I love you,' he whispered.

'I love you too,' I said, leaning my head in for a kiss.

We moved back to the bed, pulled the duvet over us and cuddled.

\* \* \*

We slept in late the next morning, in no rush to go anywhere. As we walked into the kitchen, we were greeted by huge grins from his parents.

'Good morning, you two. Did you have a nice time?' Nigel asked.

'It was great.'

'I heard you get in late last night. I noticed the car wasn't in the drive?' said his mum.

'We were too drunk to drive home. Trevor suggested we get a taxi,' I said, sheepishly.

Did they hear us last night or did the looks on our faces give us away? Anyway, they didn't seem to mind.

After Nigel and Trevor had driven to pick up the car, we settled down to their Sunday lunch tradition. This was a big to-do in the Gardner household. On every other day of the week, everyone did their own thing, but on Sunday's without fail, the family would get together for a roasted dinner. I had never experienced this in my own home. We never ate as a family at the same table. Every so often, George would cook a corned beef and cabbage meal on a Sunday, which we all loved, but after finishing up in the kitchen, he would always take his plate to the couch in front of the TV and we would all follow suit.

Watching the Gardners preparing for their ritual fascinated me. Ben making the stuffing, Trevor peeling the potatoes, his mum preparing vegetables, and his dad seasoning the meat—everyone worked as a team on a mission. I helped set the table with the decorative table cloth that was usually reserved for special occasions. A recorded Peter Gabriel concert was put on the TV in the living room, playing through the stereo system so we could hear it in the kitchen. White wine and beer were served at noon as we talked about Peter Gabriel and how he was the lead singer for the band Genesis. It was nice hearing how Nigel's love of music was introduced to Trevor at a young age. Now, they could spend Sunday's listening to all their favorite artists or bands together. It reminded me of my and my mom's love of movies and our movieathon Sunday's. Music in this house was a passion, not just something played for background noise. The laughing and joking continued until, at some point, somebody realized that it was well after three o'clock, and we really should make the gravy and come to the table to eat. We all sat down, slightly drunk, to a lunch of roast lamb with mint sauce, Yorkshire puddings, roast potatoes, stuffing, peas, carrots, cauliflower cheese and gravy. It was the first time I had ever tasted any of these things.

We retired to the living room afterwards, and as Trevor and Nigel sat and played records and dished out whiskies and brandies, I sat with Claire sipping on cherry brandy as we browsed through the family photo albums. We went through several albums. I loved seeing the boys' birthday parties. It reminded me of mine with paper chains for decorations and noisemakers. It was cool to see 'pin the tail on the donkey' was a universal game. There was a picture of Trevor holding a present, but he was surrounded by other kids sitting in chairs forming a circle. I was told it's a birthday party game called 'pass the parcel'. The birthday boy or girl starts the game off with a large present, and that present is wrapped with layers of paper. The object of the game is to be the last person to take off the last wrapping paper to find a prize inside. There were several pictures of Trevor and his brothers riding bikes in the neighborhood. Another album held pictures of weddings they attended for family over the years. All of the boys had been in several plays at their schools, and there was an album filled with pictures of their Disney World trip. It was wonderful being caught up with everyone's lives and feeling truly welcomed into their family.

At one point in the afternoon, Ben made a joke directed toward me. 'You're all mad driving on the right side of the road. I think you're all a bunch of nutters,' he said and then burst out laughing.

It was funny watching a very drunk Ben in hysterics over which side of the road Americans drive on. But I didn't want him to think he got the best of me.

'You'd better watch out,' I responded, 'or I'll give you a wet willy!'

Ben's face lost all color, and he looked horrified ... Both Nigel and Trevor's jaws dropped. Claire first looked troubled, and then she started to giggle. I knew 'wet willy' was when you licked your finger and then shoved it in the person's ear. I could tell it meant something different in England, but I wasn't quite sure.

Trevor started to laugh too and looked at me and said, 'Kerri, you're not going to like this but, a wet willy means you plan on giving Ben a blow job.'

My cheeks felt very hot from embarrassment, and I said, 'Oh my God ... there'll be none of that going on.'

We all helped clean up the dinner table and loaded the dishwasher before Nigel and Claire settled down to watch the Sunday evening TV, and Trevor and I took a walk up to the pub to meet his friends Libby, Allison, and Dave.

'Trevor?' his dad called as we were about to head out the door. 'You may want to fill Kerri in on the English meanings of any other expressions that she has.' He laughed.

I could feel my face heat up again. I didn't think I'd ever live that one down.

* * *

The next morning, we took a drive out to the Tardebigge Locks; the longest flight of canal locks in the UK. There wasn't a cloud in sight as we walked along the canal, hand-in-hand, watching the boats coming through. There were beautiful pink roses along the banks, and I picked one for Trevor. He smelled it and then proceeded to arrange it in my hair, standing back afterwards to admire his work.

'England agrees with you. You just fit.'

'I love it here, especially with you.'

We sat down on one of the locks and talked for an hour or so about what we wanted out of life, playfully discussing what our lives would be like together. We covered everything; getting married, our dream home, how many children we wanted to have. We both believed in marriage.

'Trevor, I want three kids. With Joe and I, I always felt when we fought, which was quite often, it would have been lovely to have another sibling to hang out with or one that would understand me. Take my side when needed. A sister would have been nice, or so I think anyway.'

'I want to have two boys and one girl.'

'Well, I want four; I think an even number would work better. And I don't care if they are two boys, two girls, or all the same sex. I just want them to be healthy and happy. That's more important to me.'

'What type of house would you like to live in?' he asked.

'I am not sure, but I do know it needs to have at least four bedrooms. After living in a ranch styled home for 11 years, I know I want to have a two-story home like yours. I am partial to a farmer's porch. Do you know what I mean?'

'Does that mean a country-style porch or a wraparound? I've seen them in magazines, but they are not popular here in England.'

'I'd love a porch and buy rocking chairs and sit and watch the kids play in the yard or enjoy the view of the neighborhood. I'd really enjoy watching the early morning sunrise or evening sunset. I would like to have a lot of windows. After growing up with dark paneling in our living room, I don't ever want to see it again. It would be great to see the light of the sun reflected off white painted walls. So, I've mentioned my must haves. Is there anything, in particular, you'd want to add to the house, Trevor?'

'I love playing pool, darts and listening to concerts and music in general. I'd love to have plenty of space for a pub room that would hold a decent size pool table and bar.'

'That sounds awesome; I would never have thought to add a pub room to a home, but it makes total sense. I really can vision our home to be. I love it!'

It was great to have such an open conversation with him and discover that our ideas clicked.

As we lay in bed that night, Trevor talked about his brother Alec, and what happened on the day he died. We looked over old family photos of his brother's and then Trevor read the poem that was recited at Alec's funeral.

*Death is nothing at all. I have only slipped away into the next room. I am me, and you are you: Whatever we were to each other, we are still. Call me by my old familiar name; speak to me in the easy way which you always used. Put no difference in your tone, wear no forced air of solemnity or sorrow. Laugh as we always laughed at the little jokes we enjoyed together. Play, smile, think of me and pray for me. Let my name be ever the household word that it always was. Let it be spoken without effort, without the ghost of a shadow on it. Life means all that it ever meant. It is the same as it ever was ... I am waiting for you, for an interval, somewhere very near, just around the corner. All is well. By Henry Scott-Holland.*

'We used to fight all the time,' Trevor recalled. 'One time we were fighting, he was being annoying, and I locked him out in the front porch and wouldn't let him in. He banged on the door and the windows until he got so angry that he kicked the front door window in with his bare feet. The glass shattered all over the floor. It's a wonder he didn't cut himself. He knew he'd be in trouble and would be sent to bed when Mum and Dad got home, so he figured he may as well save them the trouble, and went and put himself to bed.'

I listened to him reminisce about his brother. It meant a great deal to me that they felt comfortable enough to talk about Alec and share stories in my presence.

* * *

We woke early the next morning and laid there cuddling quietly for a while. It was so peaceful to be there in his arms, listening to his heart beating.

'I don't want you to go,' Trevor broke the silence.

I kissed his chest. 'I don't either,' I said. 'I want this to continue, even though I have to go home soon.'

'We'll try and make it work somehow.'

Nigel had taken the day off so we could enjoy an afternoon in Oxford. The city is beautiful. We decided to split up to explore Oxford, the city of the dreaming spires, as the poet Matthew

Arnold once described it. Trevor and I reminisced about our first meeting in Florida as we wandered the streets, marveling at the architecture and watching the people around us. We shopped a little. I purchased new film and batteries for my camera and a blue baseball hat with dark red letters and white trim that read 'Oxford.'

'I'd like to buy you a gift,' I told Trevor. 'Is there something you would like?'

'Not really,' he answered. 'I thought that we could visit the jewelry district in Birmingham later this week.'

'Sounds like an adventure,' I replied.

We continued walking for a few more hours and met back up with his brother and parents for the drive home.

When we got home, we put on some music and had some drinks while dinner was cooking. After dinner, we retired to the living room to play records. We played, sang and danced to Beatles' songs while we slowly got drunk. It was the first time I had ever had sherry, and I was sucking it back like pop. Trevor and I danced to one of the slow songs, and then I danced with Nigel to one of the faster ones.

'Trevor is very much in love with you,' he said. 'Do you know the saying, 'Hook, line and sinker'?' he asked.

'Yes,' I said.

'Well, that's what has happened to Trevor,' he explained. 'We've never seen him this besotted with anyone. I want you to know if you two become serious, Trevor's mum and I would be very happy about that. You are the only girl we've seen Trevor show us how much he is in love, and it's been wonderful to see. Promise me, no matter what happens after you return to the States, do not quit on each other.'

I was so overwhelmed with Nigel's sincerity. Suddenly, I felt completely accepted here.

'I promise.'

# CHAPTER 11 – 3000 MILES

The next morning, we were up at eight o'clock. We quickly got ready and packed the car and were on the road to Yorkshire by nine thirty. We were on our way to visit Sophie, my close friend and pen pal.

En route, we stopped in York for lunch at Pizzaland. We devoured a chicken and mushroom pizza and a side of garlic bread before wandering around the shops and the town ending up at the York Dungeon. We joined the 70-minute interactive tour through the dungeon's dark history. This was where all the thieves, murderers and sometimes the innocent were slowly tortured to death in horrible and creative ways. Each phase of the tour, the actors would re-enact the gruesome tortures on their unfortunate victims. It truly felt like you were back in time witnessing unspeakable deeds due to the special effects and convincing acting. Walking around, we noticed these modern torture devices for visitors. There was a wall with holes inviting you to 'experience' some of the less fatal forms of torture. All you had to do was be brave enough to stick your hand into one of the many holes. Attached to the wall was a talking console. It repetitively advised 'IF' you chose to stick your hand in one of the holes, it could be cut off or worse. It described the worse as your hand sitting in a container that may hold rats and other disgusting unknowns lurking inside. I told Trevor he should do it. He was very apprehensive.

After joking about what might happen, I said, 'Come on and try it. What's the worst that can happen?'

'What you said is exactly what I was thinking, and I don't want to do it,' he said.

'I'm as nervous as you are, but when am I going to be back here again?' I said.

I very slowly put my right hand into the hole. Trevor whispered a creepy noise in my ear that reminded me of a scene in a horror flick right before the serial killer would jump out and savagely stab the victim to death. He then pushed my hand in further. I freaked out and jerked backward, withdrawing my hand as fast as I could, and clung to him. We laughed.

'Stop it.' I laughed. 'I seriously want to try this.'

I placed my right hand slowly back into the dark hole, and it felt like tiny bugs and other unknown things crawling all over it. Unsure of what I was touching, my mind came up with all sorts of disgusting and nasty ideas of what it could be. Was it maggots or cockroaches? I also felt moist substance like slime that you could get out of a can, sharp pointy objects and rough textures that reminded me of thumb tacks and sandpaper. I screamed and pulled my hand out of the hole as fast as I could.

Trevor laughed at my reaction and pulled me in for a kiss.

We moseyed over to the York Museum and walked through the exhibits of York's long history from the early Vikings to the modern day. I found it fascinating that they had Viking swords on display that were almost a thousand years old. We didn't have that kind of history in the United States, certainly nothing that old. We enjoyed walking through each of the exhibits but decided halfway through the astrology section that we should get going.

Trevor drove me to his old village, and we drove past the junction where Alec was killed, past his old house and visited the plaque in the local park dedicated to his brother. Trevor hadn't been there since they left six years ago, and I could tell that it took a lot of courage. We visited the church where Alec's funeral service was held and the crematorium.

Trevor's shoulders looked weighed down after leaving the crematorium. He was silent and looked pre-occupied with his thoughts. I had a feeling he was re-living Alec's funeral.

I walked over and gave him a hug, and he sank his head into my shoulder. I held him tightly for a few minutes until he raised himself again. I could tell he was ready to go.

'How are you feeling?' I asked Trevor as we got back into the car.

'It's like I'm back at the moment when we found out about Alec. I'm glad you're here, but I want to get out of here now.'

'Thank you for showing me. Alec's plaque is beautiful. I can see he was well loved by this village.'

'He was.'

We pressed on with light background music playing in the car. Trevor and I had arranged to meet Sophie at the White Horse Inn. The three of us had a couple of drinks there before following Sophie to her house to change for dinner. We ate at a small local Italian restaurant then walked over to the Fleece Pub for some more drinks. Trevor seemed to hit it off with Sophie much more than I did. I was thoroughly disappointed, feeling a little bit like the third wheel as they talked, laughed and got caught up. I was frustrated. I didn't understand why they had so much more to talk about when it was me who had kept in touch with Sophie over the last seven years, not him. I had always felt Sophie and I were more like sisters than vacation friends. We told each other everything in our letters. Now, it felt like I hardly knew her.

I sat next to Trevor and across from Sophie and was silent the entire dinner, and I felt the same way at the pub. I became jealous. I actually started to think Sophie was trying to flirt and maybe was attracted to Trevor as well. I wrapped my arm around his waist pulling him closer as we sat at the bar.

The atmosphere at the Fleece was dead, so we had one drink and left. At Sophie's house, we made tea and browsed through her photo albums. I felt a little more involved as we talked. Her parents got home a little later and were pleased to see me and to meet Trevor. Her dad kissed me on the cheek and gave me a big bear hug, lifting me off the ground. We all made fresh cups of tea and then sat down in their cozy den. Listening to their conversation with Trevor, I remembered the first time I had met Sophie's parents and how thankful I was that this time they were dressed! It was well after midnight when we realized the time and decided it was time for bed. Trevor slept in Sophie's room, and I shared the guest room with her. I was excited to have some alone time with Sophie hoping to re-kindle our friendship, I was also disappointed at not being able to sleep with Trevor since I only had three days left with him. We both got into our PJs and into the guest bed. Sophie rolled over and turned her back towards me; this surprised me as I was expecting some long overdue pillow talk. Compared to our letters and phone conversations together where we'd talk for hours about boys, sex, and clothes, this was a far cry from what I remembered. I didn't understand what was wrong; on paper we were thick as thieves, yet lying right next to her, there was definitely a distance between us. I should have asked her and got it out in the open. Unfortunately, it was too late as I was leaving in the morning. I wanted the rest of our time together to be as enjoyable as possible. It was upsetting how distant we felt from one another with only a pillow between us, but if I had to speak to her back then so be it. After a few minutes, I coaxed her into a conversation, and we managed to talk for about half an hour about Trevor and me and her current relationship.

'Unlike you two, I am not serious with anyone at the moment. I've been on dates, but I haven't been impressed and do not plan on pursuing any of them. I cannot believe you and Trevor are a real couple. I remember when we met and went shopping on International Drive. You bought those two bracelets, and I gave him his with your note. I would never have thought that you would ever consider a long-distance relationship,' Sophie said.

'I know. I'm amazed myself. Turns out, he's always loved me since we met. Being here, I fell in love with his family and him all over again. I don't think I ever stopped. This makes me really believe we have a future together. Sophie, I want to marry Trevor. He's definitely the one,' I gushed.

'I hope everything works out,' she said. 'G'night.'

And with that she turned back over, shut off the light and went to sleep.

'Oh, um, good night,' I said and turned off the table lamp.

I was annoyed. I expected to have more of a conversation with her. I thought after we talked about Trevor, she would fill me in on what was new in her love life. If I had known that we weren't going to reconnect, then I wouldn't have suggested driving the four hours to visit her. At that moment, I wished we had stayed at Trevor's. At least there we would've been in the same bed.

* * *

Sophie and I got up around eight o'clock and made breakfast with her mom. Trevor slept in a little, resting up before the long drive home. At ten o'clock, we said our goodbyes.

Starting my relationship with Trevor seemed to end my relationship with Sophie. We didn't appear to care to continue to write to each other after that. Because I was hurt, I never asked, and she never gave me a reason. I think our friendship ran its course and faded away without as much as a proper goodbye. The letters just stopped. That never sat well with me. I will always love Sophie and am very grateful to have met her when I did. What a wonderful friendship we had for eight years; growing up and sharing our lives through letter writing.

As we began our drive home, it hit me like a swift slap across the face. I only had four days and three nights left with Trevor.

That wasn't enough time. Soon, there'd be an ocean between us again, and we'd have to resort to more letters and phone calls. I couldn't imagine not waking up to him every morning. This past seven days together, the moments we spent felt so natural; as if we had been sharing this routine for years. The idea of not talking and sharing stories in the car, being in the same room, walking around his town holding hands and kissing whenever and as much as we'd like was unbearable. I was immediately saddened and wanted to cry, but I had to put those thoughts aside and enjoy every minute I had left with him.

Halfway home, we stopped at a mall. Trevor was in need of new sneakers or trainers as the British call them. I found him a pair of white sneakers, size 11 wide and showed them to him.

'Will these do?' I asked.

'Yes, let me try them on to make sure they are a good fit.'

I was happy I could be of help, and Trevor purchased his trainers. Walking around the mall, I found that I was having a great time doing mundane things with him like checking out appliance and kitchen stores. It was fun picking out items we'd like to have if we lived together. We both wanted a food processor, a blender, and I liked his parents' cookware. They had a bright orange set by Denby; it's crafted from cast molten iron inside and out and comes in several colors like red, orange, cream and black. I thought if we ever lived together, the Denby set would be a must have. Surprisingly, we seemed to like the same things; when we didn't agree, we would put the item down until we found something we both liked. As we turned a corner, we came across the Disney store and browsed through.

We played with the huge pile of stuffed animals at the back of the store. Trevor pulled up a large stuffed animal of Mufasa from *The Lion King*. There were holes built in for your hands to control the front legs and another hole at the back of the mouth.

'Hello,' he said as he mimicked the words with the lion's mouth.

'Oh, hello.' I laughed.

'I love you,' the lion mouthed.

'I love you too, Mufasa,' I said. 'You're my favorite character from *The Lion King*.'

He opened Mufasa's arms and wrapped them around my neck for a hug.

'Very sweet,' I said. 'Now your turn.'

I captured Mufasa and made him give Trevor an aggressive kiss on his cheek; he laughed, pulled the puppet out of my hands and threw him back in the bin where he came from.

We continued to browse the store on our own. As I was making my way out of the store, I looked around for Trevor. I found him near the exit hiding something behind his back. He turned and handed me a huge Disney bag with a grin.

'For you,' he said.

Inside the bag was Mufasa.

'You are so wonderful,' I said as I kissed him.

On the way out of the mall, I noticed a hair salon, and we stopped to get my hair cut. My experience was completely different from my local hair salon back home. Normally, I would have to make an appointment. It was a refreshing change to walk in without one. At home, I would have had my hair washed, cut and dried. Typically, a 30 to 45-minute experience, nothing special really. This time, while my hair was being washed, I was offered a warm blanket. I was then escorted to my chair, and another hairdresser came to ask if I'd like a hot cup of tea and a hot towel around my neck while my hair was being cut. Of course, I accepted. After the cut, I had a scalp and neck message at no extra charge. It was the best 60 minutes I had ever spent in a hair salon.

'I had fun shopping with you,' Trevor said as we got in the car. 'I don't normally like going shopping, but with you I actually enjoyed myself.'

'Me too.'

'I feel we've got on so well and so easily this week; it's never been this easy with anyone else,' he said.

*Of course it's easy; we've spent the last seven years getting to know each other.*

In response to him, I pulled Trevor toward me and planted a long kiss on his lips.

We got home around six o'clock, just as Nigel was getting home from work.

He met us at the door. 'How was your trip?'

'It was different than I what expected, but overall we had a good time,' I said.

'That's good, what do you have there?'

I pulled out Mufasa...

Nigel politely smiled. 'You're still buying such things at your age?'

'Trevor bought him for me.'

'Oh,' was all Nigel said.

You could tell Nigel thought it was quite childish of us to buy a stuffed animal, but we didn't care. We were in love.

Peter Gabriel's recorded live concert played in the living room while dinner was cooking, and I sipped my new favorite drink, cherry brandy. We settled in the living room after dinner, and Claire got out the photo albums again. She showed me pictures of Alec and the newspaper articles that he had been in with the Boy Scouts describing the milestones they all had achieved as a troop. Lastly, she showed me a newspaper article about his death and the condolence cards from everyone.

'I'll never forget that day.' Her voice quivered and there were tears forming in her eyes. 'The doorbell rang, I opened the door, and there stood the police officer. He was a friend of ours. He stood there and started to well up. I was confused; I didn't understand. He finally got the words out. 'I am so sorry to inform you, Alec is dead.' I felt sick to my stomach, and the next thing I knew I was punching him; I was hitting him over and over again. Thank God, Nigel was there. He had to pull me off.'

By the time she finished, the both of us were in tears. I looked over at Ben, who was next to the sofa on the floor patting Roxy and watched his face crumple. Ben was so upset he started to sob hysterically, and he had a hard time calming down. Trevor had told me after Alec had died how hard it was for Ben. He loved Alec as much as the rest of them, but they were inseparable being so close in age. Claire went to console Ben, and they left the room. We all watched them leave, and for several minutes no one said anything. To lighten the mood, Trevor played another live concert; Pink Floyd and put the photo albums away. About a half an hour later, Claire and Ben rejoined us. More drinks were poured, we talked, sang and danced until we finally called it a night about one o'clock in the morning.

Trevor led the way back upstairs to his room. We laid on his bed together with the soft moonlight pouring in through the wide open curtains.

'Why do you love me?' Trevor asked.

I pulled away from him slightly offended.

'I'm sorry Kerri; I need to know.'

'OK.' I moved closer to him and placed my head on his chest. 'I've known you since you were fifteen. You were my first love, *and will be my last,* and then that love grew into the most incredible friendship ... Don't you agree Trevor, that we have the most amazing friendship?' I tilted my head to look into his eyes waiting for his answer.

'Yes, I've always been able to tell you anything; I've never felt that comfortable with other girls.'

'See, that's how I've always felt too.' I rested my head back down on his chest. 'To me, you have wonderful qualities that I haven't found in other guys. For starters, you are very genuine. You have such a beautiful heart and soul, and you show it to your family and me. Since I've been here, all you seem to do is want to make everyone happy, which is very selfless of you.

'Now you're embarrassing me.'

'You said you wanted to know why I love you. So shut up and let me tell you.'

'OK, sorry.'

'You should be.' I looked up at him and gave him a playful glare. 'No more interruptions?' I said, threatening to tickle him.

'No more.'

'Well, the list is endless, but I'll go over some more points. You are a great dancer, a wonderful cook, very attentive, you make me laugh, you listen, for some reason you know when I am not in the best of moods and can decipher why. I appreciate that.'

I leaned on my elbows and looked him in the eyes. 'Remember our day at the locks?'

'Yes.'

'When we sat at the locks and talked about our future together and what we really wanted, I could envision you as a wonderful husband and father. I know you would be an amazing provider to our children and me. You would be there for them and let them know how very much they mean to you no matter what. I have never had that with my father or my stepfather, and seeing that side of you makes me fall in love with you even more. I guess I could sum it up by saying from what I've just described, you are everything I've ever dreamed of having in a man to love me, create a family with me and be with me for the rest of my life.'

At this point, I could see Trevor turning a deep shade of red. He was so easily embarrassed. But it was the truth.

After a few moments, he finally spoke. 'Wow, thank you!'

'You're welcome.'

Trevor pulled me to him, fixed our covers, and we fell asleep once again in each other's arms.

* * *

After waking and making dinner plans later that day, we decided to hang out at the house and watch some movies. Trevor picked *The Rocky Horror Picture Show.* I had never seen a musical comedy/horror film before.

I popped in the VHS tape and asked Trevor for a blanket. We wrapped the fleece blanket around us and got comfortable lounging out on the three seater couch.

'My favorite character is Meatloaf,' Trevor said.

'Who's Meatloaf?'

'You have never heard of the singer/actor Meatloaf?'

'No, what's so great about him?' I asked.

'Well, he plays the rocking biker in this film, but I am a huge fan of his *Bat Out of Hell* CD trilogy. I'll have to play it for you before you go.'

'OK.'

I enjoyed the movie, although I thought it was goofy too because there was more singing and sex than horror as I had expected. I did think Tim Curry had sexy legs and played a fantastic transvestite.

Watching *Meatloaf* sing, I definitely wanted to hear more of *Meatloaf's* music and find out *why* Trevor enjoyed it when I didn't think that he was that great.

Soon it was time to get ready for our date. We showered, got dressed up in our Sunday best and went out. Trevor had made reservations earlier in the week at a Chinese restaurant in Chinatown in Birmingham. We were escorted to a cozy table in the corner of the restaurant and started with some drinks and prawn crackers.

The ambience was romantic, lights dimmed and oriental music playing in the background. Each table was beautifully laid with silk table clothes, china plates, and matching cups, and in the center of the table was a lit candle.

'What do you call a box full of ducks?' I asked.

Trevor looked puzzled and thought for a moment and then asked, 'I don't know?'

'Quackers,' I told him.

It wasn't a particularly funny joke; still we couldn't stop ourselves from laughing. The waiter delivered the next course, Peking duck.

Each main course was then brought out at separate intervals. For four hours we sat, ate and enjoyed watching the waiters carrying out course after course of sweet & sour chicken, chicken & mushroom in gravy sauce, BBQ spare ribs, and each dish was served with fried rice. We finished the meal with deep fried banana for dessert. I had never had such a laid back dining experience before. We used to have Chinese takeout every Thursday night at home, but other than the word "Chinese" there was no comparison. It was the best Chinese food I had ever eaten.

I really appreciated the staff making us feel welcome; they were very happy to take some photos of us on our first dinner date. This was the date we had wanted to have on our last night in Florida seven years ago. I never got to wear it, but the night before our date, I had picked out the prettiest sundress that I had brought on vacation. I remember having a dream that night, where I envisioned what our date would be like; getting ready, and then leaving to meet Trevor at the pool. He would have been dressed up in his ironed shirt and trousers. It would have been weird to see him wearing shoes. We had agreed to walk around International Boulevard and eat dinner from the local vendors. What if we chose a restaurant? This was probably how our first date would have felt like. I was thrilled we finally got to experience it. Toward the end of the meal, a man came around the restaurant selling roses.

'I'll take one mate.'

Trevor took one of the red roses out of the basket and handed it to me.

'Thank you so much, Trevor, it's beautiful!'

I had never received a rose from a boy before. The rose was in a long plastic holder. I was excited about that because I wanted the rose to survive the trip home so I could preserve it.

Trevor and I enjoyed the one-hour drive back listening to *Night Ride Home by Joni Mitchell.* It was well after midnight when we got home, and no one was up. I started to cry. I was down to one day with Trevor. I knew I was meant to stay. How was I to do that when all my family was back in America along with my job and my responsibilities? Somehow, we had to make this work.

'Kerri, please don't cry; we'll figure it out.'

'How? It's killing me knowing I have to leave you after tomorrow.'

'I know I feel the same way. Let's not worry about that now.'

Trevor wiped my tears away and made love to me once again. I fell asleep, feeling safe, warm and comfortable with his arms wrapped tightly around me.

\* \* \*

Every day since I had arrived, the weather was blue skies and gorgeous. Today, we awoke to an overcast, rainy Saturday. I was disappointed the weather had changed so abruptly. It didn't matter, we only had this last day together, and we were not going to let the weather ruin it. First on the agenda, Trevor wanted to take me to Birmingham. The town was well known for its jewelry district. I had never seen 350 jewelry shops all in one place.

'Your twenty-first birthday is in a few weeks, and I'd really like to buy you a gift. What do you think you would like?' Trevor asked.

'Everything is beautiful. Let's walk around until something catches my eye.'

We window-shopped for a few hours until I found a small gold ring decorated with emeralds and diamonds. I loved it. We went to have it sized, and, unfortunately, all the stones fell out. The jeweler said there was nothing he could do and advised us to find another ring. My second choice was an amethyst surrounded by diamonds. I had wanted to buy Trevor a ring as well, but because he was already wearing my high school ring, he thought one ring was enough. We both liked and settled on a gold bracelet for his belated birthday gift. I wanted to wear my ring right there, but I didn't because Trevor asked me not to.

'I know you're anxious to wear your new ring, but I really think we should hold off until tonight when we go out for your birthday dinner.'

'Why?'

'You'll see tonight; I promise it will be worth the wait.'

Back at his house, we spent an enjoyable afternoon popping popcorn and watching live music concerts while playing with Roxy. Roxy got tired and made himself comfortable on my lap while Trevor and I cuddled on the couch. I was introduced to bands and music I had never listened to before; Yes, The Who, Sting, and Eric Clapton. Each artist was great; I found I liked them all.

It was a perfect afternoon that thankfully didn't rush by. At 6:00 p.m., Trevor reminded me we needed to get ready for our dinner reservations at 8 p.m.

The whole family got dressed up to take me out for my birthday. We had a reserved table at TGI Fridays in Birmingham. I bought the first few rounds of drinks to say thank you to Nigel and Claire for having me. I sucked back, I don't know how many June Bug cocktails and by the time my gifts were handed to me, I was a bit drunk and awkwardly opened them. Ben bought me a pair of gold earrings, and his parents bought me a gold necklace. I could see now why Trevor wanted me to wait. They all wanted to buy me jewelry and put it on all at the same time. Trevor had brought my ring with him. He slid it on my wedding finger and helped me with the rest of their gifts. I felt like a princess being doted on with beautiful jewelry. The rest of the evening was a blast. More drinks were ordered with our appetizers; loaded baked potatoes and cheesy fries. Our main course was sizzling steak and chicken fajitas. I loved all the attention and the thoughtfulness behind each gift. His parents and brother made me feel really special as if I was already a member of their family, and I didn't want the night to end.

Trevor and I crawled into bed after midnight for our last night together.

We talked for several hours, coming up with scenarios on how our relationship was going to work long distance. We knew we'd have to find out about all the legalities of how we could be together. Trevor had just graduated from university and was looking for a local full-time job. Without any work experience, he didn't think he would be able to work in the States. Before Filene's Basement, I had worked part-time as a travel agent during my second year in college in Boston. Still, I wasn't sure if that would be enough experience if we decided it made more sense for me to move to England.

'I don't want you to go tomorrow, Kerri,' he whispered.

I lifted my head to look at him. 'I don't either. These last ten days have been more than I could have dreamed of. My day to day at work and home feels monotonous and empty not sharing it with someone; it's really going to be difficult to resume that life now that I know what I can have with you,' I said.

We began kissing each other and slowly made love for the last time. After reaching a crescendo, we fell apart, breathless, and lay side by side not talking. I wanted him to know everything about me. I worried that if I told Trevor my past, he would stop loving me and would not want a future with me. There had been many opportunities to tell him. Unfortunately, every time I tried, I chickened out.

Knowing this was our last night together, I decided tonight had to be the night. I started from the beginning; my accident when I was two, my seizures and the medication I had taken. I told him about my suicide attempt and the real reason for my vacation in Florida, to give us all a fresh start.

'It doesn't change the way I feel about you,' he said.

It felt like a huge weight had been lifted. I was confident we could carry on building our relationship knowing I had nothing to hide from him anymore. He loved me for who I was; flaws and all.

The alarm was set at 8 a.m. I quickly showered, dressed and packed my suitcase. It was awful watching Trevor carry my suitcase to his mum's car. I thought I was going to be sick. I didn't want to go; I wanted to stay and continue these amazing days I had with Trevor and his family. I knew I belonged here; I could see myself having a fulfilling life with Trevor. Nigel, Claire, and Ben stood waiting outside by the car. We had got on so well; I knew I would miss them all very much. I hugged each of them with tears in my eyes. They surprised me because they all looked ready to cry too. Trevor packed my case and carry-on into his mum's car. Compared to the constant conversations when I arrived, it was a quiet ride to Gatwick International Airport. I don't think either of us knew what to say. We did manage some small talk during our three-hour ride, talking about what my week would be like returning to work and him needing to get back to university to pack up his stuff and finally end it with Nicola. That made me feel better; but I still felt like I was dying. As if I was being deprived of oxygen. For the rest of our trip, all I could do was cry off and on.

Trevor parked the car farthest away from the entrance, and we made sure to walk slowly, stopping every few minutes to kiss. Once inside, I dragged my luggage, looking for the Virgin Atlantic counter. I checked in for my three o'clock flight only to find that the flight had been delayed until nine. I beamed at Trevor, so happy he hadn't dropped me off on the curbside. The lady at the desk apologized for my inconvenience and gifted me with a pre-paid credit card. It was a wonderful surprise to receive fifty pounds. We decided to check my luggage in, rent a locker for my carry-on and take the train into London.

We caught the Gatwick Express into Victoria Train Station and took the Underground to Covent Garden. Holding hands, we wandered around for a while in the sun, enjoying the hustle and bustle of London. After lunch, we took the underground to Baker Street and spent the pre-paid card touring Madame Tussauds Wax Museum. We wandered around the museum, being silly by mimicking the figures or pretending to be a part of the scene when other guests walked by. My favorite moment was when we'd stop in front of wax figures, making obnoxious faces at each other while snapping shots. We finished with the museum staff taking a photo of us with a wax Arnold Schwarzenegger. We liked it so much that we purchased it and then relaxed with some tea in the café. There was little over an hour left before we had to catch a train back to the airport. We walked around to Trafalgar Square, where Trevor and I sat down on the fountain. It was great to watch all the visitors and tourists enjoying the day as much as we had.

'Let's get a picture of us sitting on top of a bronze lion,' I suggested to Trevor.

'OK, let me ask someone to take our picture.'

Trevor asked a lady walking by if she wouldn't mind taking a picture of us. We climbed on top of the statue; I sat up front while Trevor held me from behind. The lady took the picture, and we thanked her. It was getting late, and we had to leave.

We made it back to the airport by half past seven and sat in the bar waiting for my boarding announcement. To calm our nerves, Trevor and I had a last minute drink and then made our way to the concourse. I broke down and cried again when they announced my flight was boarding.

'I wish you didn't have to leave me.'

'I don't want to go,' I sobbed.

'You'll call me to let me know you got home, okay?' he said.

'Maybe I could stuff you into my suitcase,' I said half-jokingly.

Our attempts at laughing turned into more tears. We stood there holding onto one another, and I kept thinking it'd taken seven years to feel this happy, to be this content in knowing without a doubt that he was the man I was meant to be with, and now I had to leave him. Love could be so cruel. We didn't part until the final boarding announcement was made, and Trevor kissed me one last time. It broke my heart to watch Trevor cry. I'd never seen a man cry over me before. Finally, my name was called for the final boarding attempt, and Trevor had to push me through the gate.

I was the last person on the plane. I quickly stowed my carry-on and slumped down into my seat. I had no idea how this long-distance thing was going to work, but I knew we had to do everything we could to be together, no matter what.

# CHAPTER 12 – TWENTY-ONE

I landed back in Boston after 11 p.m. I went through Customs and Immigration pretty quickly. The daytime hustle and bustle was over, and all the lights had been dimmed. Apart from a few staff, it was spooky walking through an almost empty airport. Making my way over to the luggage carousel, I joined the remainder of the passengers from my flight and waited for it to turn on. The buzzer went off, and we all got ready, looking for our suitcases. One by one, the suitcases trundled past us, looking identical to each other. I made a mental note to buy a bright pink suitcase that would stick out like a sore thumb for my next visit. I had expected to see my grandpa parked outside in his old blue Ford pickup truck since he had agreed to pick me up, but I saw no sign of him. I was about to go back inside to find a pay phone to call him when I noticed a state police cruiser pulling up to the side of the curb. I suddenly had the strangest feeling about that police cruiser, like I had seen it before, but I couldn't place where. The moment it parked at the curb, I knew it was here for me. The officer got out of the car. It was my dad. Just what I didn't need right now!

We had only just started talking to each other again. He had called me before my year-end college exams four months ago saying that he wanted to 'try again.' It had been three years since we had last spoken to one another before this. I had invited him to my college graduation, not expecting him, since he didn't show up at my high school graduation. I was very surprised when he did show up.

'Hi, Kerri,' he said cheerfully as he walked over.

We stood awkwardly looking at one another for a moment before he pulled me in for a hug.

'Um, hi Dad,' I said. 'Is Grandpa okay? He was supposed to pick me up.'

'Yeah, he's fine. I called your mother's house this week to check in with you, and she told me that you had gone to England. I asked when you were returning and figured since I was going to be on duty by the tunnel, I would call your grandparents and let them know I decided to pick you up and save them a trip,' he said.

'Oh, okay, thanks,' I said.

I let him take my suitcase and watched him load it in the trunk before getting into the cruiser. The thirty-minute drive to my grandparents' house was awkward. Sitting there in his cruiser, I appreciated him picking me up, I just wasn't in the mood to talk. I kept thinking of all the times I wished he had showed up for my games at high school or had called to check in weekly and see how Joe and I were doing with our studies. Any action from him that would show us he really did care. That never happened. We only saw our dad when it was convenient for him. Getting married and having a second family only made our relationship more strained and problematic. As much as I'd wanted a decent relationship with my father, with all the problems that we'd had over the last seven years, it was hard for me to trust him and expect that he had changed. I thanked him for the ride, kissed him goodbye, and told him I would call him.

My grandparents were not up when I walked into their house. They had left the small living room lamp on for me. I pulled out the sofa bed and went to bed in my clothes; I was too tired to change.

* * *

In the morning, I heard my grandparents up at 6 a.m. like clockwork. Busy in the kitchen; I heard my nana put the water in the coffee maker for Grandpa and then fill the stove kettle for her tea. Moments later, I could smell the butter sizzling in the wrought iron pan; next was chopping of the onions and grating of the potatoes. It smelled delicious, and I knew he was busy making his famous daily breakfast; potato pancakes. He made the best potato pancakes ever.

It was time to get up; plus my stomach was growling. It would only be a matter of time before my grandpa would come into the living room to wake me anyway and ask if I wanted breakfast.

I quickly showered and dressed; I wanted to fill my grandparents in on my time away.

'Did you have a good time?' asked Nana.

'Yes, it was amazing, Nana. Trevor and his family had planned several activities while I was there. His dad took a day off during the week, and we visited Oxford. While there we had a delicious lunch called 'toad in the hole'. Basically, sausages covered in gravy that is baked in dough.'

'Sounds interesting, 'said Nana.

'For my birthday, they took me out to TGIF's and all bought me beautiful gold jewelry. Trevor got me an amethyst ring, his parents a necklace and Ben bought me earrings. It was a special night. They all welcomed me and made me feel like family. I didn't want to leave.'

'I don't blame you; I am glad you are home, though,' replied my nana.

'How have you been, Grandpa?'

'Good,' was all he said. Grandpa was never one for conversation.

I looked at the clock on the wall and realized I needed to leave and catch the train to Boston. I packed my car and said my goodbyes.

I found my tiny cubicle exactly the way I had left it and settled down for the monotonous day ahead. With all of my vacation time used up on those ten days in England, I felt I had nothing to look forward to but my boring job, stuck in a drab four-by-six cubicle. The only exciting interruptions were when my co-workers stopped by my cubicle and asked me how my vacation went. I showed off my diamond and amethyst ring Trevor had bought me, accompanied by a lot of 'oohs' and 'aahs.' I recounted some fun moments about my ten days.

'The weather was great; Trevor had planned small trips throughout the week.'

'What did you do, what was your favorite?' asked Jill.

'He's from a small town, so we had to drive a lot to get to anything. One day we drove an hour to a nearby town, and we took a mineshaft tour. That was pretty cool, actually. You read about that type of stuff in history class, but to actually walk, well it's not walking, it's practically crawling in those small tunnels where they mined for coal; it was unbelievable... We shopped, went to Oxford and enjoyed his local pubs with his friends. We also toured at Cadbury's Chocolate Factory. We got to enjoy all the chocolate samples we wanted.'

'As for my favorite, it's hard to say; each day was pretty special.'

'Sounds like you both had a great time. What are you both going to do now?' asked Kathy.

'We did. Now we have to figure out how to have a relationship with 3000 miles separating us.'

They all agreed that our long-distance relationship was going to be a hard road to endure, and wished me luck regardless. I appreciated how genuinely happy they were for me, but I needed to find out what my workmate and best friend Robin had to say.

She and I had met at work only months before, but we quickly became the best of friends. While I had left out the more intimate details when I was talking to Jill and Kathy, I didn't hold anything back from Robin.

'I knew you were going to be more than friends when you left. I know you. You're determined. I say do whatever it takes to guarantee that you and Trevor have a future together.'

'You're right, Robin, that's exactly what I was thinking. A long-distance relationship is never ideal for anyone, but it's what we have to do until we can come up with a better plan. I feel happier talking to you. Thanks!'

'What are best buds for?'

After a day that seemed to drag on forever, the clock struck five, and I didn't stay a minute longer. I headed out for the train station. I wanted to get home to see my mom and sleep in my own bed. I sprinted to the train station and made the five-thirty train. Sitting on the train, it was hard to believe that just the previous day I had been in London. I put my feet up on the opposite seat and stared out of the window daydreaming, the scenery flashing by in a blur.

I always enjoyed riding on trains; watching other people interact and imagining where they were going or what they did for a living. I liked making up stories about certain houses that caught my attention and what that family who lived in them might be like. I don't know if other people thought this way, but for me, I'd get a feeling about what kind of person lived in each house from the appearance of their backyard. One backyard in particular held seven old demolished cars piled high on top of one another. The story I came up with was the owner must be a man and owned a junk yard. He liked to bring some of his work home and sold spare car parts. The funny thing was the other half of his yard was neat as a pin with a decent brick patio decorated with lounge chairs. I thought maybe that was his wife's side.

I also enjoyed watching the seasons change from the speeding train; the trees changing color, piles of leaves getting swept up and blown around; dancing snow flurries that would stick and slide fast against the window. As the months passed, I would look forward to seeing the snow melt, and then again weeks later look out at the blanket of trees blooming with new buds. This was something I did when I commuted to Back Bay, Boston during my two years at college. During the ride I would read a book, more often than not, I found my attention always drawn to the window watching life pass by outside in a haze. The train stopped, jolting me back to reality, and I realized I was at my stop. I quickly gathered my things and hurried across the parking lot to my car.

I drove the forty minutes home on autopilot; the jet lag was finally catching up with me. I was surprised I made it through the day at work and was craving some Earl Grey tea and Cadbury chocolate biscuits. In between our outings, Trevor and I would make a hot pot of tea and grab a container of chocolate biscuits to dip. After a few days, it became a routine of ours. I would have to find out if our supermarkets carried the tea and chocolate biscuits here. If not, I was certain Trevor would be happy to send me some.

My mom was already home from work and waiting for me. Seeing her standing there at the window with that knowing look was too much. I closed the front door, dropped my suitcase in the entrance and felt all the emotions I had been holding in all day come flooding forward. I walked up to my mom and threw my arms around her.

'What's wrong? Are you okay, honey?' she asked, softly.

'I love him.'

'You slept with him, didn't you?' she said with a tone I expected and didn't want to hear.

'Mom, I am almost 21, and you know how I feel about him. I am sure you thought that it might happen.'

She let out a huge sigh and continued to hold me as I started to cry.

We separated, and she led me to the couch so we could sit down.

'How is this going to work, living in different countries?' I asked.

'Typically, long-distance relationships don't work out. However, I also know you are determined when you want something. If he is what you want, you know I'll support you. Did you have a good time at least?' she said, changing the subject.

I cheered up and showed her my promise ring Trevor had bought me.

'That's beautiful, Kerri. Did you get him anything? You had mentioned before you left you wanted to buy him a belated birthday gift.'

'Yes, while we were at the jewelry district Trevor mentioned he'd always wanted a gold link bracelet. We found him one, and it looks great.'

'That's good …' She looked at me quizzically, then said, 'You must be tired … Do you want to watch a movie and chill out?'

'Yes, I am. Want to order a pizza?'

My mom ordered us a cheese pizza, and we put on the TV to watch a romantic comedy.

Life at home had not changed in those ten days I was away, but I had. I was no longer content with living at home. I wanted to move out and start a life with Trevor.

Snuggling up with Mufasa was hardly a suitable replacement for Trevor, but somehow it made me feel a little closer to him. The cuddly lion had become a permanent fixture in my bed since I returned home. Trevor's words echoed in my mind …whenever I looked at the lion, I remembered laughing as Trevor had brought Mufasa to life, but now he just sat lifeless on my bed.

Trevor told me he would call at the weekend. It sucked waiting five days to hear his voice again. I had almost forgotten how thick his accent was not hearing it every day. We picked up right where we left off as if no time had passed at all.

He told me about his week: 'I drove back to college dreading the conversation I needed to have with Nicola. As I expected, she was missing me and wanting us to resume our relationship. She expected me to sleep with her in the same bed again and other things.'

'She wanted to sleep with you?' For some reason, I didn't think of that. 'I hope you told her right then and there you were with me,' I said slightly annoyed.

'I did, in the end, but it helped I needed to study and take those final exams. And there was never any chance of that because I'm crazy in love with an American girl I met when I was 15.'

'Good. So were your exams difficult? Are you officially broken up?'

'Long story short, I passed my exams, and I broke up with Nicola.'

'Congratulations on your exams. I knew this week was going to be very hard for not only you but Nicola. I feel bad, yet I am also selfishly very happy because now we can carry on with our relationship without any distractions besides distance, of course. How did she react when you told her you wanted to break up?'

'Thankfully, it was amicable. She had known we had written for the past seven years and, of course, saw all your photos on my dorm room wall throughout the years, so she had a feeling. I am just glad we are able to remain friends.'

'That's great you two can still be friends. I have never known how to do that with my break ups. What are you up to now?'

'Now, I am back home and looking for a job. I need to find a full-time job, so I can save money and come visit you. It's only been a week, and I am missing you terribly. I cannot imagine not seeing you for months on end.'

'I'll call you again on your birthday,' he said.

'I would really love it if you could. Do you think it would be easier for you to call me at work or at home? With the five-hour difference, I know it makes it tough on both of us,' I replied.

'I know it will be late my time, but I really want to be a part of your actual birthday, even if it is through a phone call,' he said.

'That would be great. I wish you could be here now, but no worries, I'll wait for your call. It's better than nothing, right?'

'Right. Love you Kerri.'

'I love you, Trevor. Talk to you Friday, Bye.'

\* \* \*

I was excited to go out yet again for my birthday. The first time was in England at TGIF's three weeks early from my actual birthday. My birthday was on the following Friday. My mom, me, George, Joe, my mom's sister and their parents and my best friend Melani, and her boyfriend, Jamie all met up at the Olive Garden to help me celebrate.

The Olive Garden was packed. I knew it would be busy on a Friday night, but I had no idea it would be so busy that we had to wait almost 45 minutes to get a table. Once we were seated, we excitedly looked through our menus. I overheard my grandparents bickering on what to order. It made me smile because no matter how many years together they still bickered over what to eat at home and when they were out. Most of my family planned to order the spaghetti and meatballs or Olive Garden's signature dish eggplant parmesan. I've had eggplant parmesan and don't care for it. Tonight I was in the mood for something simple. I was going to order their minestrone and bottomless salad with unlimited breadsticks. My mom, Melani, and Jamie decided to join me.

'So Kerri, now that you're 21, do you feel any different?' asked my nana.

'You know, I thought I might, but I don't. The best way to confirm it would be to pull out my driver's license and order a Mudslide.' I laughed.

'What's a Mudslide?' she asked.

'A Mudslide is a delicious alcoholic drink that's filled with vodka, Kahlua and Bailey's Irish Cream. Before it's poured, the glass is coated with Hershey's chocolate syrup.'

'Sounds too sweet for my taste,' said my aunt.

'How do you know what's in it, have you drunk it before?' asked my mom.

'No, I've never tasted it, but the girls at work have. Today we were talking about me turning 21 and my birthday plans. They highly recommended I order a Mudslide. '

'I've never tasted one of those either Kerri, but could I have a sip if you order one,' said Mel.

'When I get it, Mel, don't worry I'll share.'

The waitress came by with waters and breadsticks. We ordered our drinks and meals then tucked into the breadsticks.

'So how was your trip to England, did you have a great time?' asked my aunt.

'I did. Seeing Trevor again was amazing. We really enjoyed our time together, truly the best ten days of my life.' I smiled, thinking of Trevor.

'Really, why, what did you do there?'

'Trevor and his family were extremely welcoming and made plans while I was there. Trevor and I had day trips to surrounding towns. He showed me beautiful parts of England. We went to a town called Cheltenham, and like most towns there is a lot of history, and I enjoyed seeing the original stores like barbers, butchers, and bakeries. It was fun to walk along the old cobblestone streets. We also visited Oxford with his family, and the landscaped gardens were alluring. I had never seen so many different types of plants and flowers. We also took several tours; to Cadbury's Chocolate factory, a mineshaft, and in York, we visited the York Dungeons, which was a gruesome place.'

'Wow, that sounds fun,' said my aunt.

'It was. I miss Trevor and our time together.'

'Kerri, show them your ring,' said my mom.

I held up my wedding finger that held my promise ring. I received 'oohs' and 'aahs'.

'What does the ring mean?' asked my nana.

'It means we are in love, and we plan on being together. The only problem is how. Trevor does plan on coming over and visiting me soon, though.'

'Like I always say if it's meant to be it's meant to be,' said my nana.

Some time later, our drinks and meals were brought to the table. Everyone was famished, so we all tucked in.

Overall, my dinner celebration was wonderful. It was low key compared to my dinner at TGIF's with Trevor and his family. I thoroughly enjoyed seeing my extended family and friends in one place. Working full-time and commuting made it hard for me to visit them as much as I'd like to, and it was nice having that time to catch up on each other's lives. I think we all had a great time eating together, telling stories, cracking jokes and laughing, but that still didn't keep me from thinking someone was missing. Trevor.

Mel and Jamie came back to my house afterwards, and we had some more drinks and got a bit silly, taking drunken pictures of us with weird facial expressions while wearing the crazy ensemble of my hat collection; baseball caps, fishing hats, Mexican hats and others.

Trevor called late that night as promised.

'How was your birthday? What did you get?' he asked.

'It was great, me, Melani, her boyfriend Jamie and my family went to The Olive Garden for dinner. I mostly received cards with money in them, which is never a bad thing. I had my first official alcoholic drink, a Mudslide, and I showed off my ring.'

'That sounds good. I look at the bracelet you bought me and your ring all the time. I cannot believe it's been two weeks since you've been here.'

'I know. I missed you terribly today. Of all days, the perfect birthday gift would have been you here celebrating with me. Any luck with the job hunting?

'No, but I am positive I'll find a job very soon. Then I can save, and we can come up with dates when I can visit you.'

'I am looking forward to that. It's late, and you sound really tired. What's it three in the morning your time?'

'Yeah, but don't worry it's Saturday, and I can sleep in.'

'I think you should go to bed. Thanks for calling me; I needed to hear your voice tonight.'

We said our goodbyes, and he promised me he'd call me the following weekend.

\* \* \*

Surprisingly, my week at work went by quickly because for once the phone was ringing off the hook, and I was kept busy booking flights. I was anxious to receive Trevor's call as promised. When he rang, it seemed as if I was losing the ability to understand his accent the less time I was around him. I couldn't recognize what he was saying. I had to keep asking him to repeat. At one point, I laughed, which, as it turned out, was the wrong thing to do.

'What was funny about that?' he asked, confused.

'Um, I … I … What did you say?' I fumbled.

'I said my mum and I were in a car accident on Tuesday. Completely totaled the car,' he said.

'Oh, my God, I am so sorry. I laughed thinking you were telling a joke. Are you okay?'

'I'm okay,' he said. 'My mum hurt her back, though; her seat was broken in half.'

'That's horrible; is she in the hospital?'

'No, thankfully she was told to go home, take painkillers and rest.'

'That's good. Hopefully, her back will heal quickly, and she will no longer be in pain.'

'She should be OK. How are you? How was your work week?'

'The job is becoming more and more boring. I am looking forward to the holiday season. I was told the phone rings off the hook then.'

'I am sorry to hear this. Have you thought of looking for another job since you are not happy there?' he asked.

'I have, the thing that's holding me back is I make pretty good money here in Boston. I've considered looking locally, although I am not sure I'd be paid as much ... Have you received any calls for interviews?'

'No, but I was told by temping agencies there should be more job opportunities with the holidays coming up ...'

'I'm sorry it's taking so long for you.'

Then, the most unexpected thing happened. I ran out of things to say to Trevor and was skimming my brain to think of new topics to talk about.

'Anything else new?' I asked, trying to keep the conversation going.

'No, not really. I've been busy helping take care of Mum since the car crash.'

Because we were running out of things to say, we agreed to cut our two calls per month down to one. We also decided to write more letters and save the money from the extra call we'd make per month and use that money toward our travel expenses on our next planned visit.

It upset me that I ran out things to say on our last call. To ensure this wouldn't happen again, Trevor suggested we should write down what we wanted to say before our calls so that we could cover everything during our conversation.

* * *

A few weeks passed, and I received my first letter from Trevor since our time in England together. He had acquired two temping jobs at the same company; an administrative position during the day and a data entry shift in the evening. He was working eighty hours a week from 9 a.m. until 1 a.m. the following morning, Monday through Friday. He had also sent me a gift: a double cassette tape collection. He had made the tape cassettes even more special by taking the time to create case inserts with pictures, track listings, and notes on the music. He recorded himself on the tapes as well. I played them constantly on my small cassette player, often rewinding the tape just so I could hear his voice.

Towards the end of October, I started shopping for Christmas presents. I went a little overboard for Trevor and his family. I bought him some colorful fleece shirts, stocking stuffers, and a thick hooded sweatshirt. Nigel and Ben received some flannel shirts, and I found an artist selling unique teapots in Faneuil Hall, so I bought one for Claire's collection. I packaged them up early as I wanted to get them there on time. On our next call, Trevor asked me what I wanted for Christmas.

I told him I wanted just one thing. 'Baby, it's simple. I want you wrapped up in a fantastic shiny Christmas paper. You'd be lying comfortably under the Christmas tree with a big red bow and message that would read 'open me.' Of course, I wouldn't wait until Christmas to open my gift.'

Trevor laughed. 'I wish for that too! Seriously, though, what do you want for Christmas?'

I thought about it for a while. 'Could you please buy me a beautiful locket that can hold two pictures? I have a lot of photos of you now. I'd love to have your mum place a baby photo of you on one side, and I'll find one of me and put it on the other side.'

'OK, I'll see what I can do.'

* * *

When my Christmas parcel came, I ripped open the package immediately. The gold locket was heart shaped. I opened it, and there he was. A very tiny two-year-old Trevor, with hazel eyes, full lips and wisps of blond hair covering his chubby-cheeked face. I searched through several photo albums and found a picture I liked of me at the age of two. My hair was quite long, and I was smiling with big brown sparkling eyes. The joy radiating from that childhood photo mimicked how I was feeling now at 21. I found scissors and placed that happy little girl to the other side of the locket next to my childhood sweetheart who was the reason for my present happiness. I put on my gorgeous locket and admired it in the mirror. I never felt happier and yet more completely alone at the same time.

Christmas was the same as it was every year. My family and I got up and made cups of tea. We sat in our PJs around the tree and handed out gifts. Later that day, like we had done for years, we drove to our grandparents' house where we'd be joined by the rest of my mother's family. One of my favorite traditions was to eat the clementine my nana always stuffed in our stockings as we opened our gifts around her tree. The New Year replenished my vacation time, so Trevor and I discussed the next trip on our phone call. Since he started his new job as a temporary employee, he was not entitled to any vacation time yet. He had to work several more months before full-time employment would be a possibility. We decided I would use a week's vacation time to visit him in March, and he would visit me for three weeks in May, assuming he'd be hired full time by then. Although he'd have to work during my visit, I wanted to experience once again the normal couple activities like going to bed with him, waking up in each other's arms and sharing a meal or two while having a face-to-face conversation. This would be a welcomed break from the 3000 miles distance between us.

* * *

I felt better knowing we had plans to see each other. Weeks passed by, and I was busy with my usual Monday to Friday routine, getting up to workout at home in the wee hours before I had to get ready and catch my train. I joined my local gym to get out of the house on the weekends, and hopefully, meet some new friends and stay fit. Each Saturday afternoon I looked forward to step class, and afterwards I'd swim laps in the heated pool. Sundays were a day that was reserved for my mom and me. We'd get up late and enjoy making breakfast together, and I'd make us some tea while my mom grabbed the potatoes and onions. This was our main day when we'd catch up with one another after a long week at work. Having promised to always be truthful after my attempted suicide, I found that complete honesty became a habit, so it was never an issue for me to tell my mother anything that was on my mind. I knew she'd listen and give me advice if needed.

My mom made the best potato pancakes just like my grandpa, who taught her. We'd peel, cut and shred potatoes and onions, mix it all up with an egg and add it to a hot sizzling pan. While she was cooking our pancakes, I'd typically make *Jiffy* blueberry muffins from the box. By the time we finished our breakfast, the muffins would be ready. Hours later, we'd get in the car and drive to Blockbuster. It was our Sunday tradition to select way too many movies that were an assortment of comedies and chick flicks. Once home, we'd change back into a fresh pair of PJs and veg out in front of the TV for a good eight hours, or until it was time for bed.

On this particular Saturday afternoon in February, I had decided to ride my bike to the gym. It was a clear sunny day and a little warmer than usual. I worked out for an hour, spent some time in the pool and the steam room before cycling the five-mile trek home. I daydreamed a little while riding, not paying too much attention to the road when my front wheel hit a thick patch of gravel, and I lost control of the bike. I flew over the handlebars and hurtled toward the ground, skimming across the tarmac like a rock skipped across a pond. I finally came to a halt on the grassy median, narrowly missing the thorny ditch.

I lay there for a moment, disoriented. After realizing what had happened, I started to check over my body for any broken bones or gashes that might need stitches. My hands all the way up to my elbows and my shins to my knees were a mangled mess of scraped skin and blood. Thankfully, I didn't need any stitches. It appeared that almost every joint had somehow managed to hit the road, but from what I could tell, there were no broken bones. My knees were dripping blood down my legs. It hurt to move my elbows, and the palms of my hands stung. Not wearing a helmet, I banged up my head a bit. Sitting there, holding my throbbing head in my hands, I felt a headache coming on. As soon as the shock subsided, the pain started to course through my entire body. I was wondering how I was going to get back home when a car pulled up.

A woman called out, 'Are you okay, dear?'

I looked up to see a little old lady getting out of her car. She was small in height, maybe five feet at the most. Gray, short curly hair, and glasses framed her round, concerned face. She was dressed like your typical grandmother; red cardigan, white frilly blouse and black polyester pants.

'I think so,' I answered.

'That was a very bad fall, dear. I watched the whole thing happen from the other side of the road. I had to turn around to make sure you were okay. Are you sure you're all right?'

'Yes, I think I'll be okay; thank you so much. Not a lot of people would have done that.'

I slowly eased myself onto my feet; just moving to a standing position stretched and contracted my skin, which irritated the multiple cuts. Finally able to stand and balance myself, I felt the pain shoot all over my body. I limped over to my bike.

'Oh, you look pretty bad, in fact; let me give you a ride home.'

'I'll be fine; thank you.'

'You're in no condition to ride your bike. You're lucky you didn't break any bones. Look, I can put your bike in the back and drive you home,' she insisted.

I was a bit apprehensive, taught never to trust strangers, but because I was in so much pain and she was kind, I decided to let her help me.

'Thank you.'

I helped put my bike in her trunk and got into her car to give her directions home. Within five minutes, we arrived at my house. She helped me get my bike out. I thanked her for her kindness and watched her drive away, waving goodbye.

Not hearing from Trevor in weeks, feeling more and more like our relationship was slowly slipping away, I kept thinking how this crash was symbolic of my life spinning out of control.

I limped over to the front steps of my house and held onto the black wrought iron railing for support, feeling ready to pass out at any moment.

'Mom?' I called, opening the front door.

'Joe, are you home?' I called out again.

No answer. No one was home. I had no idea how many cuts and bruises were under my clothes. I could really have used somebody's help here. I slowly made my way to my mom's room and passed out.

* * *

The sound of the phone ringing woke me up. I opened my eyes to find myself in complete darkness. I had been asleep for quite some time. I continued to let the phone ring, hoping whoever it was would give up, but they didn't. Out of pure frustration, I got up and then sat right down again as pain ripped through my head.

*Why didn't we have phones in each bedroom?*

'Hello,' I said, picking up the receiver.

'Hello, Kerri.'

It was Trevor. His call shocked me. We hadn't scheduled a call. I was so pleased to hear his voice ... The pain seemed to magically disappear.

'Trevor, I am so glad to hear your voice.'

'I needed to hear yours,' he said, his voice slurring.

I looked at the clock on the wall; it was eight o'clock.

'Are you okay? Isn't it, like, one in the morning there?' I asked.

'Yeah, I just got home. I've been out with some friends from work.'

His slurring got worse. He had obviously had ten pints too many.

'Hold on,' he said.

There were the sounds of bangs and crashes followed by what must have been the toilet lid flipping up because his tinkle into the bowl was unmistakable. Charming!

'Ah, that's better,' he came back on the line, 'sorry 'bout that, um ... how are you?'

'I'm not doing too well. I ...'

'Hold on,' he said again.

Once again, the toilet lid crashed, followed by a vomiting sound.

I felt bad for Trevor, and my first thought was if I were there I'd help him, but I was also very annoyed as I was hurt and in pain and wanted his undivided attention.

I heard his dad's voice in the background. 'He's on the bloody phone to his girlfriend in America and throwing up in the toilet!'

A door closed, and Trevor came back on the line. 'Sorry. What were you saying?'

'I was about to say that I was thrown off my bike riding home from the gym, and I cut myself up pretty badly.'

'Oh, my God, are you okay?'

'Yeah, I think I am. My knees are all cut up. My hands sting, and I think I may have a concussion because I passed out when I got home. Actually, your phone call is what woke me up, but I think I'll be okay.'

I heard him sobbing on the phone; he was so upset from what I had been through.

'I wish I were there to bandage you up and take care of you,' he said.

'I do too.'

I couldn't stand there any longer. Blood was dripping from my knee again, and my head hurt so much I thought I might pass out once more.

'I need to lie down, and you should go to bed,' I told him.

'I wish you were going to bed with me; it hasn't felt the same since you left.'

'I know; I feel the same way.'

'Only a month left; I cannot wait.'

'Me neither. I gotta go my head really hurts. Thank you for calling, Trevor. It was a wonderful surprise, especially tonight.'

'I love you, Kerri.'

'I love you too.'

I hung up ... Holding onto the walls for support, I slowly maneuvered my way back to my mom's room. The minute I laid my head on the pillow, I blacked out.

# CHAPTER 13 – I CAN PROMISE YOU MAY BUT NOT FOREVER

The weeks leading up to the end of March seemed to drag. It was becoming more and more difficult for Trevor and me to keep up with each other, especially with his overwhelming work schedule. We wrote regularly and talked on the phone as often as we could, but I often felt that we were losing touch. That started to scare me because we were hardly engaged in each other's lives. The saying 'long-distance relationships rarely last' never bothered me, but after six months, I could feel the distance between us growing, and I didn't know if our love was strong enough to survive more time apart.

My travel agent job at Filene's Basement Vacation Outlet was excessively boring. Other agents were being sent out by the company to try out and report on popular vacation spots. I had asked to go, but my trip to England had interfered with the required training, which kept me from going. And so, I was left to man the phones, book flights and vacations for people escaping the cold New England winter.

The day finally came, and my mom dropped me off at the airport. I had booked the same red-eye flight with Virgin Atlantic. I arrived early Saturday morning at Gatwick International Airport. Just through customs, I scanned the area looking for Trevor, and that's when I saw him coming towards me. I immediately noticed how much he had changed in the last six months. His body looked leaner, and his shoulders broader. I was reminded of the first time we saw each other and again thought he belonged on the cover of *GQ*.

After exchanging hellos, I dropped my bag, threw my arms around his neck, and we kissed.

'How was your flight?' he asked as he picked up my suitcase.

'It was uneventful,' I said. 'I slept most of the way.'

Trevor put some music on as we drove out of the airport. I never heard this band before; I asked what it was.

'It's Marillion, you don't like it?' he asked.

'Not really,' I said.

'Sorry,' he said, and immediately turned off the music.

We sat uncomfortably in silence for about ten minutes until I spoke.

'I'd much rather talk to you all the way home anyway,' I said quietly. 'We have a lot to catch up on.'

We chose music we both liked, and the cold atmosphere lifted. We talked easily all the way home. Still, it didn't feel like the first time he picked me up and drove us to his home. There didn't seem to be that spark between us anymore. Here we were with only a gearbox and a handbrake between us, yet it seemed we were still an ocean away from each other. Why was this so difficult? I wondered if he felt the same way.

Most people date someone in their town or at least in the same state. Our relationship was definitely out of the ordinary.

Growing up and talking about relationships with my mom and nana, they would answer my questions with different scenarios on dating. The consensus was a couple might go on a few dates before mutually deciding to spend more time together. Those first few dates may start to become more regular, and lead to some more intimate moments. Say after a year or two of monogamy, they decide to move in with each other. Over time, they would find out about each other's quirks and habits and learn to compromise. Maybe a year later, he proposes marriage with a one to two-year engagement. After getting married, the couple would decide how many children, if any, and where to buy their first house.

Our relationship lived in another universe to the 'norm'. We not only had the distance against us but because he was five hours ahead, it made scheduling phone calls difficult. When we did get to speak to one another, it was typically every two to three weeks, and we only spoke for 30 to 60 minutes due to the expense. On a positive note, we got to know each other better than most people did through our continued letter writing. As much as I looked forward to our letters, they didn't compensate for our lack of time together. In our first year of dating, it had been crammed into a ten-day whirlwind romance followed by a six-month period of separation. I could see that this next stage in our relationship was going to be more difficult.

Once we arrived at Trevor's house, I found that his parents and brother seemed more excited to have me than Trevor. They welcomed me with big smiles and tight hugs. It was wonderful to see they had missed me as much as I did them, but I wanted to feel that from Trevor. I kept thinking of the phone call only a month earlier and how desperate he was to talk to me and tell me he loved me. What had changed? I was finally standing next to him in his house, and I didn't feel that connection. Looking over at Trevor while I was being greeted by his family, I could see the stress on his face. I wasn't sure if that was because of me or something else? At that moment, I felt like it was a mistake to have come.

Just like last time, Trevor had made space for me in his wardrobe. I got unpacked, and we decided to head out to The Castle, his local pub. It was nice being back in his town, seeing all the familiar places we had walked to before. A major difference this time was we walked around holding hands in silence, and every now and again, Trevor would talk about his job.

'I'm exhausted, I'm learning a lot, and I am grateful for the jobs. Unfortunately, the 80 hours are really getting to me now.'

'I work 40 hours a week, commute two hours round trip each day on the train, and that doesn't include the drive to the station or the walk to work.'

'By Friday, I am beat. I don't know how you do it,' I said.

'A 40-hour working week would be a nice change.'

'Any news on when these two temporary jobs will become one full-time?'

'My manager told me to hang in there; she believes the position will be available in the next month.'

'You have such a crazy schedule. Would looking for another job in another town be better than what you are doing now?'

'I think about quitting and finding another job all the time, but it took so long to acquire this one that I don't see the point, especially when I want to accumulate enough vacation time and money to come and visit you in May.'

Hearing Trevor mention he still wanted to visit me in May gave me hope we still had a future together.

We enjoyed a couple of hours at the pub ordering drinks and munching on a basket of chips. Trevor started to relax, and our time together started to feel less stressed.

\* \* \*

Sunday was an eventful day, preparing for Trevor's family Sunday tradition; roasted dinner, drinks and playing live concerts. Hanging out with his brother and parents was wonderful; I had missed this time with them. Nothing had changed between us; in fact, I felt closer to them than I did with Trevor. I made it a point to confide in his father how I'd been feeling and asked what he would do?

'I know it's been tough on you two. I can see the distance has become a problem. However, I still believe Trevor is crazy about you and feel you should not give up on him,' said Nigel.

I decided to relax, and thought of the saying 'actions speak louder than words' and found some contentment in the fact Trevor was busting his ass for me.

The weekend blew by too fast and, unfortunately, that meant Trevor was back at work on Monday.

* * *

During the day, I had a lot of time on my own. Claire was happy to have company, although I could tell I was in the way of her daily routine. When she wasn't busy with chores, she would curl up on the couch and sew. She loved to cross-stitch and was always working on a project. If you didn't find Claire around the house cleaning or out shopping, she would probably be in the living room stitching away.

When I wasn't with Trevor's mum, I spent the rest of my time with their dog Roxy, who had the sweetest face. His face, like the rest of his body, was covered in black fur with white specks here and there. He had long floppy ears and big brown eyes that always looked as if he was putting on a sad face for the chance of an extra treat. Roxy weighed at most 10 pounds and could be carried around like a baby—it was impossible not to fall instantly in love with him. I'd take him out at least once, sometimes twice a day for a long walk through the neighborhood. Trevor's neighborhood was wonderful to explore; I loved the uniqueness of each home compared to the cookie cutter homes in the States. There was so much daily activity going on it was fun to be a part of it. Walking past each home, I would look out for differences. Typically, our mailboxes are in the front of the yard facing the road; in England, they are built into the front door as a slot, and the homeowner could purchase a basket attached to the inside the of door or the mail would collect on the floor. Without fail, each home I passed had beautifully landscaped front and back gardens with brightly-colored flowers. It was so picturesque; I could have been looking at a *Home & Garden* magazine. The homes were mostly two stories, had skirt roofs and were so close together you could stand in between them and stretch out your arms and easily touch them. They all reminded me of magical cottages that I had seen while watching movies as a kid; *Oliver Twist, The Secret Garden, and Bedknobs and Broomsticks.*

On one outing, I decided to use my rollerblades I packed and to walk Roxy at the same time. We did well for a mile, and then turning a corner, we hit a hill. And that was it; Roxy was super excited and surprisingly strong and pulled me down the hill at such a fast speed I was caught off guard.

'Roxy stop, slow down, boy!'

Unfortunately, my words fell on deaf ears; he was enjoying himself too much. We began to pick up speed, and I could see the main road approaching.

The only thing for me to do was throw myself into a yard. As we passed a home without a picket fence, I threw myself on the grass and pulled on Roxy's leash to finally stop him.

A homeowner had seen the whole thing. She was in her late 20s, petite, around 5'2" with beautiful hazel eyes and long blonde wavy hair. 'Are you alright?' she asked.

'Yes.' I laughed. 'I didn't know if that idea would work, but it was worth a shot.'

'Oh, you're American?'

'Yes, I'm here for a week visiting my boyfriend.'

'That's nice. May I suggest taking your skates off and walking the rest of the way?'

'I agree. Roxy is full of surprises.'

The nice lady helped me up. After taking off my rollerblades, I carried them in one arm and Roxy in the other and walked us home.

Trevor's job allowed him three weeks' vacation; he was saving that time to visit me in May. Trevor had no other time off, making our time limited. Every morning, he drove his mum's car to work, so that he could come home and have lunch with me, and then we had the evenings together before going to bed. I, of course, had the pleasure of sharing his bed again, something I had missed terribly.

After three days there, though, I started to feel frustrated with our limited reunion. I had envisioned every minute spent together being a Hallmark moment, and the reality was sorely disappointing. Unfortunately, our mornings were a wash since he got up with only enough time to take a shower, get dressed and grab a cup of tea on his way out of the door to make it to work on time.

'I'm off, but I'll be home for lunch,' Trevor said each day.

It was disappointing; I was on vacation, yet it didn't feel like a vacation at all. I started to feel like a housewife having to wait hours until I got to see him again. When he came home for lunch, he seemed preoccupied and not able to relax properly. He'd speak maybe two words to me, and then we'd eat our lunch in silence. After an hour, he had to rush back to work for the afternoon. We had more time together when he got home in the evening. Unfortunately, our evenings weren't as exciting as the last time I was here. Each night, we'd eat at home with his parents before heading out to meet his friends at the pub, returning home to bed at closing time. Alone together in bed was the only me-and-him time we had the entire week.

* * *

On Wednesday, Trevor left for work a little earlier than usual since he had to walk. Claire wanted to take me shopping, and so we needed the car.

I was looking forward to us spending time together and getting to know her better without the boys being around.

'So what did you want to go shopping for, anything in particular?' I asked.

'Well, Trevor mentioned how he's never seen you in a full-length dress. I thought it would be nice to buy you one so you and Trevor could go out to dinner all dressed up this weekend.'

It was very nice of her to want to buy me a dress. I knew her days were busy, so I was very appreciative of the time she wanted to spend with me.

'Well, I'm not one for wearing dresses, but if it's something he'd like to see me in, I don't see why not,' I said, feeling completely uncomfortable at the prospect.

We drove into Birmingham and looked through every dress store we could find. I felt bad I didn't like anything she picked out for me. We had been to over half a dozen stores by the time I found something I felt comfortable wearing. The dress was soft pink, had a fitted waist with a row of buttons starting in the middle of the dress from the V- shaped neckline and finished an inch from the bottom. It was long and stopped at my ankles. I thought Trevor would like it. Claire was obviously thrilled; although I wasn't so sure it was a style she had envisioned based on all the previous dresses she had picked out.

'Wonderful,' she said with a big smile. 'I knew we'd find something eventually.'

We made our way over to the cashier's desk to pay.

'Now we need to find you some new panties and bra,' she said as she paid the cashier.

Going shopping with my boyfriend's mum for a dress I didn't particularly want was uncomfortable enough. Now we were going underwear shopping?

Once again, Claire's ideas were radically different from mine. I envisioned us buying a nice pair of white cotton bra and matching panties. Instead, we walked into a lingerie store, and I was shocked. I've never been in a store like this. My idea of a lingerie store is a small section of lacy bras, panties and some silk slips next to the women's section in a Bradlees department store. When she picked out a full matching black lace bra, lace thong panties, suspender belt and stockings for me, I was horrified. At that moment, I envisioned a sales lady coming over to ask me if I'd like to pair my ensemble with a selection of feathered whips and some flavored lotions and potions.

'You really don't have to buy me any underwear. I am more than happy to wear what I have brought.'

'Don't be ridiculous,' Claire said.

This was my worst nightmare.

If I had been out shopping with any of my girlfriends, then I might have tried something different, something a little more risqué like the stockings and suspenders get up. But no, here I was with my boyfriend's mother, shopping for lingerie, she would know only too well what would be on under my dress. All I could think was there was no way I could wear it and enjoy it with her son knowing she picked it out. I was way outside of my comfort zone. Every set she put together for me seemed to be more risqué than the last. I respectfully turned down each one, finally convincing her that a cotton bra, matching panties and a pair of pantyhose would suit me just fine. She gave in, obviously thankful as I was that our shopping ordeal had come to an end.

'Well, we got what we came out for. I think you'll look beautiful in your new dress. Trevor should be really pleased.' She seemed pleased with herself. 'Would you like to get lunch? I think we've earned it. Plus, it's my treat. No exceptions.'

How could I refuse? 'I'd love to go, but only on the condition that I treat you.'

'Nice try,' she smiled, 'but no, I'm paying. I insist. All I ask is that you wear the dress this weekend. That would make Nigel and me very happy.'

'It's a deal,' I replied.

Living with Trevor's family again for a week, but without the scheduled sightseeing excursions, gave me quite an insight into their lives and routine. Catching up with Claire, I asked her if she knew how Trevor was feeling about our relationship.

'Trevor is still in love with you and has been missing you very much. Believe me, we have never seen him so besotted. Hugging and kissing you in front of us has never happened with other girls. Let alone have them stay with us. He's at a point in his life when he wants a serious commitment. Unfortunately, for the last six months, you both haven't had the chance to date each other properly like other people, because of that he isn't completely sure if he wants to spend the rest of his life with you,' Claire said.

I was happy to hear he wanted to fully commit to me and saddened he wasn't yet sure. For me, I felt a hundred percent certain of my love and commitment to Trevor. I completely understood where he was coming from and wished we had been able to have a normal courtship. As much as I knew he loved me, it still hurt to hear, and now confirm, what I had feared for the last six months. I wasn't going to be discouraged and give up. I knew with all my heart that he was the man for me.

* * *

By the end of the week, I had started to wonder yet again if I should have come at all. We had spent every night in the same bed, shared breakfast, lunch and dinner and watched TV or hung out with friends at the local pub. No matter how much I tried, it didn't feel as though the distance gap between us was closing. It was no good. I finally realized that I couldn't hold our relationship together no matter how hard I tried. We'd be in the same room, and yet I'd feel like I was very much alone.

'Kerri, Trevor,' Nigel called to us from downstairs.

Trevor and I came downstairs to the living room.

'Trevor, your mum and I have made special plans for you and Kerri this weekend. As an extra-special gift for your twenty-third birthday, we booked you a two night's hotel stay in Croydon. We figured you two would appreciate some alone time.'

'Thanks, Dad, it's just what Kerri and I need.'

'Wow, thank you both so much.'

I walked over to Nigel and Claire and gave them hugs.

'You're both very welcome, now go plan what you'd both like to do while there,' he said.

We would be on our own for the weekend. It would be great to see if we got on better. Maybe this was our second chance.

* * *

Friday, after Trevor finished work, we arrived at the hotel at 8:30 p.m. It was different than what I was expecting to see in England of all places. The hotel was modern; the walls were constructed of glass with a matching covered canopy as the grand entryway. It stood three stories tall and was brightly lit. It reminded me more of a corporate building than a hotel. After unpacking, we changed and went out for dinner. Right away, I could tell Trevor was feeling more relaxed. I was relieved and thrilled we'd have the entire weekend to reconnect before I had to leave on Sunday.

We caught the train to London the next day, arriving at London Bridge Station. It was such a gorgeous day, we walked hand-in-hand over to Tower Bridge, stopping at an ice cream stand for a couple of Flake 99's – a vanilla ice cream atop a cone with a Cadbury's Flake – a stick of chocolate.

Licking our ice creams, we headed down to the *HMS Belfast* located on the dock between London Bridge and Tower Bridge. After buying our two tickets, we wandered off to explore the nine decks of the battleship. The museum was fascinating. We couldn't imagine sleeping in one of the tightly packed hammocks during duties in Arctic waters, or being stationed deep in the bowels of the ship when she opened fire on D-Day.

'I'm really hungry. Do you want to order some tea and sandwiches?' Trevor asked as we passed the onboard café.

'You read my mind. Let's sit outside.'

'That sounds brilliant. You get the table, and I'll get the food and drinks.'

It felt like we were working our way back to each other.

'Do you want to check out Tower Bridge? I've never been there before,' asked Trevor.

'Yes, that would be great. I enjoy England's history.'

'Why do you love history, is it just England or the world?' he asked.

'Social Studies was one of my favorite classes in school. It's not just England. I love seeing how our world has evolved over time. It fascinates me.'

Leaving the *HMS Belfast*, we walked across Tower Bridge and visited the Tower of London. As suspected, Trevor and I enjoyed the exhibition. We then took the tube to Trafalgar Square. I was impressed with the way Trevor navigated the train system. I've never been great with maps or directions. We walked holding hands down The Mall to Buckingham Palace, back up to Trafalgar Square again and on to Piccadilly Circus. We wandered across town past Leicester Square to Covent Garden, stopping at the various street vendors along the way. It was so wonderful to feel Trevor completely at ease with me again; it felt like the day I arrived six months ago. There were no awkward silences; we talked nonstop, flirted with each other, and the kisses were continuous throughout the day … As we approached Drury Lane, I saw a sign advertising *Miss Saigon* tickets on sale.

'Do you want to see Miss Saigon tonight?' I asked Trevor.

'That would be nice as I've never been to a Broadway musical. How about we go out to dinner first and then go to the musical?'

'Okay. Is that the time? We'd better head back to the hotel now and get ready if we want to make it back in time for the play.'

I bought the tickets for us, and then we caught the train back to Croydon to get changed for the evening.

As I ran myself a bath in the hotel room, Trevor went down to the bar to get us some drinks. Relaxing in the soapy, running bathwater, I thought how amazing our day had been. We had got on so well the whole time that I didn't feel the stress between us as I had all week. I was so engrossed in my thoughts, I didn't notice Trevor entering the bathroom with my drink.

'Why do you look so sad?' he asked.

Startled, I splashed water over the tub wall onto the bathroom floor. I didn't realize I was exposing every feeling I was having in that moment on my face.

'I was thinking about our wonderful day today and relishing in it. Tomorrow, I'll have to leave you once again, and I don't want to go… I was also wondering if you've made up your mind as to what your plans are with me and the future?' I asked.

He sat on the toilet seat and leaned over to kiss me.

'I can definitely promise you May when I come over and visit for three weeks, but I cannot promise you the future. You need to understand I am under a lot of pressure from you and my parents. I love you, Kerri, there is no denying that, and you make me very happy, yet we have not had a normal relationship. We have only had those ten days that were the most unforgettable days of my life, and these last six months have been terribly hard on both of us. I don't think it's fair for either one of us to expect to get married on that alone. I need to see you in your environment with your family and see if I fit in with all of that. Please don't ask me to promise you a future because right now, I don't think I can.'

He got up and walked back into the bedroom, and I sat there taking it all in. I knew in my heart he would say this. I just didn't want to believe it. All my dreams, all my hopes seemed to be fading away. Everything had told me that he was the one, and we were meant to be together. I had never been surer of anything in my life. I was convinced I would marry him.

Getting out of the bath, I wiped away the tears and tried to put on a convincing smile as I walked out. I got dressed while Trevor took a quick shower. We were not officially over; we still had a chance. He told me he loved me and wanted to visit me in May. Turning to the mirror, I put on my new dress. It was a great way to pull myself together again after what had just been said. I felt re-energized. Scanning through the stations, I found a song I liked from the radio/alarm clock and started to fix my hair and makeup. Looking in the mirror, I saw a strong woman who had overcome so much in her life. I wasn't about to quit now on my dreams. I felt happier and thought I hadn't done too bad a job.

'Wow, that's nice. You look beautiful.' He smiled.

'Thank you. I have to be honest; I don't like to wear dresses. In fact, I didn't want to go dress shopping with your mum. I was uncomfortable the entire time. Now, looking in the mirror, I am glad we did. I feel beautiful.'

'Good, are you ready to go?' he asked.

'Yup, I'm super hungry; I could devour a whole chicken.' I laughed.

With only so many hours left to this day, I was determined to have a fabulous evening with Trevor before tomorrow.

We took the train back into London, making our way down to the tube to get out at Covent Garden. We had dinner at TGI Fridays and then walked around the square to the theater.

*Miss Saigon* was outstanding. It was getting late, so we decided to make our way back to the Tube station and then take the train back to Croydon.

Regardless of our laid-back dinner and enjoyable time at the play, I started to feel the stress build again between us.

We sat quietly on the train until Trevor broke the silence.

'Did you have a good time tonight?'

'Yes, what did you think of the play?'

'I thought it was brilliant. The only part I didn't like was the main character Kim killing herself at the end of it.'

'Can you imagine what she was feeling deciding to give up her son and ensure he would be raised in the States?'

'No, I can't. I felt the entire play was intense. Should we head back to the hotel when we get off the train?'

'Yes. My feet are killing me; I don't wear heels anymore. They complete the dress. Unfortunately, they do a number on my toes.'

There was a party going on at the hotel, and since we were dressed up, we figured we'd slip into the party and enjoy some dancing. It was there on the dance floor I felt Trevor stiffen up against me. I was becoming frustrated. One minute it felt like we were getting on really well, and then the next minute it was as if he was building a wall between us.

The DJ took a break, and we got some drinks and headed to our table.

'What's wrong now?' I asked, impatient.

'What do you mean?'

'We seemed to be having a great time, and then there's dead silence. Like just now when I was rubbing your back on the dance floor, and you literally stiffened.'

'I am sorry. I'm dreading the next eight weeks of us being apart and going through the motions until we see each other again.'

'Finally, you're telling me the truth. How do you think I've felt all week? You've been so distant; I feel like I have been alone even when you're sitting in the same room. It's been just as hard on me as it has been for you. What's pissing me off is your constant silence! I need to know how you feel. I don't think I am asking too much when I am flying back tomorrow, and we won't see each other until May. Or should we even bother now? I snapped.

# CHAPTER 14 – HE'S NOT COMING

I didn't wait to hear Trevor's response. I grabbed the hotel key out of his jacket pocket and swiftly left the table. When I entered the hotel room, I quickly got undressed, not bothering to take off my make-up. I put on my PJs, shut off the lights and got into bed.

Moments later, Trevor entered the room turning on the lights.

'Kerri, please don't go to bed like this. I think we had our first fight, and we need to talk about it.'

'Talk about what? I think it's quite obvious you are not happy with me, and this whole week has been a waste of time. Why didn't we break it off before I came over? Why did you still want me to come and not really bother when I was here?'

'Because I still love you, and I wanted to see you. I am sorry I haven't been honest about my feelings. Now we both know how we are feeling. And I still want to come over. Can we just accept how we both feel and look forward to May?' he said.

I laid there listening to what he had to say. His words didn't take my anger away, yet I was grateful for him explaining himself.

'I am so mad right now Trevor. I had envisioned our time together for months since I booked the ticket. This is not how I wanted to spend my week, let alone my last night.'

'I know, and again I am sorry for my behavior. Can we make up?'

Trevor walked over to my side of the bed and sat waiting for my response.

'Okay, but promise me from this point onward, you'll be honest and share your feelings?'

'I promise. Can I come to bed now?' he asked apprehensively.

I pulled the duvet back as my answer. He quickly got into his PJs, got into bed and extended his arm, waiting for me to slide up to him. The minute I did, he pulled my chin up and kissed me.

'I'm sorry we've had a fight. I don't like fighting with you.'

'Me neither.'

I wasn't pleased we had our first fight, but I was glad it happened. We were finally being honest with one another. I didn't know what to expect when he came to visit, but I was happy he still wanted to make our relationship work, and that was enough for me.

After our first fight, I realized it was a good opportunity to come home and focus on me. It was devastating to even consider this option, but what if we had a disastrous three weeks together when he came to visit? I knew we'd have to accept the fact that we might break up and we would be nothing more than friends and would need to move on with our lives. I needed to think of a plan B without him. Did I want to stay at NLG and commute to Boston, or did I want to start looking locally and make plans to move out? I also started to make more frequent plans to hang out with girlfriends after work and on the weekends. Instead of staying in as I had for the last six months, I would go to parties in town or pack my bag and enjoy a weekend with Robin in Boston. It was great to venture out, socialize again and meet new friends in the process.

The day of Trevor's visit finally arrived, and I stood in the airport terminal with my mom, George, my grandparents and aunt waiting for the Arrivals door to open. His plane had landed, and the first wave of passengers started to wander out. As the numbers crested, and then inevitably broke, there was still no sign of Trevor. Thirty minutes ticked by and a couple of hundred non-Trevor's walked past. I was becoming increasingly emotional watching the passengers being greeted by their waiting loved ones. Finally, the crowd began to die down, and I remembered our conversation in the bathroom of the Croydon Hotel just two months ago.

'I can definitely promise you May, but I cannot promise you the future,' he had said.

I started to panic, felt the tears building, and turned around to face my mom.

'He's not coming. I think he changed his mind,' I said, defeated.

'Don't be ridiculous! Of course, he's coming. His seat must have been in the very back. It's a 747. You know how big these planes are, you book flights on these every day. Don't worry, he'll be out in just a bit, you'll see.'

George walked over. 'I checked the Arrivals board,' he said. 'It looks like three big planes landed around the same time.'

'I'm sure you're right. I'm being impatient as usual and need to calm down.'

My mom put her arm around me, and we continued to stare at the Arrivals door waiting for Trevor.

I feared that maybe he decided to end our relationship this way. That maybe the last time I saw him truly was the end. I was going to look like a fool, stood up at the airport in front of my family. Not only that, I quit my job at NLG so I could be with Trevor the entire three weeks.

Then, I spotted a familiar green and brown leather pattern. My eyes traveled up the sleeve of the jacket, and our eyes met. There was my Trevor. He was really here. He had kept his promise. Grinning ear to ear, I ran over to him as fast as my legs could carry me and threw myself into his arms, nearly knocking him over.

'Hey,' he whispered as he drew his head back and kissed me.

'Hey,' I replied, struggling to find balance in my knees.

'I thought that maybe you weren't coming,' I told him.

He looked at me like I had three heads.

'What? Why would you say that? I told you I would be here. Customs was a zoo.'

Hand-in-hand, I introduced my family again to the man they had heard so much about.

My family were as excited as I was to finally meet Trevor. George was the first to say hello and shake his hand. My grandfather shook Trevor's hand as well and then proceeded to introduce my grandmother. It was awesome to see this welcoming exchange. My nana, mom, and aunt all greeted Trevor with warm hugs one after the other.

'Can I take your bags?' George offered.

'Cheers.' Trevor handed George his carry-on and duty-free.

After stopping over at baggage claim, we held each other in the car and headed straight to dinner at Uno's Chicago Bar and Grill.

It was a Friday night; the music was loud, and the bar was crowded with the locals coming off of work. We fought our way to the booth and quickly read through the menus. I chose Uno's because they didn't exist in England and were famous for their deep dish pizzas. I was hoping Trevor would enjoy the pizzas as much as my family and I did. It was amusing to watch Trevor and my family interact with each other. As we waited for the waitress to return, I sat listening to my nana and aunt ask him question after question about anything and everything just so they could hear him talk. His accent was so thick that he stuck out like a beautiful British sore thumb in a restaurant full of Americans. Everyone appeared spellbound by his accent and wanted him to keep talking. Even the waitress seemed besotted by him and asked him to repeat his order a few times. Maybe that was because she couldn't understand what he was saying, but I knew better.

After Trevor ordered a pepperoni pizza and a glass of Sam Adams, my aunt started to ask Trevor more questions...

'So Trevor, how was your flight, did you experience a lot of turbulence?' she asked.

'Every now and again there was some, but overall the eight hours was uneventful.'

'I'm glad to hear it,' she replied.

'Did they serve you anything? A lunch or dinner?' my nana asked.

'I enjoyed the chicken dinner with mixed veg. It's not home-cooked, still it tasted better than I expected.'

'Trevor, Kerri and I have thought of many fun things to do while you are here. I wanted to know if there was any place, in particular, you wanted to go?' asked my mother.

'I really don't know much about Boston. Whatever you have planned, I am sure will be brilliant.'

George and my grandfather were too engrossed in their meals to make small talk.

We spent a couple of hours at the restaurant and had quite a bit to drink by the time we called it a night and headed home.

Once home, we unpacked Trevor's suitcase into the drawers I had cleaned out for him and got ready for bed. My mom had, unfortunately, stuck to her guns about the sleeping arrangements and had made up the pull-out couch in the living room for him to sleep on. I had argued with her that we were old enough to share a room. I had explained that his parents hadn't had any problem with us sleeping together in their house, regardless my words fell on deaf ears. She made it quite clear that this was her house and her rules.

My mom and George retired to bed while Trevor and I stayed up to watch TV in the living room. We made out while the TV flickered in the background. After thirty minutes, I got up.

'You're going to bed?' he asked.

'No,' I whispered, 'wait here a minute.'

I tiptoed halfway down the hallway toward mine and my parents' bedroom, and I heard my mom snoring, confirming both her and George were asleep. I crept back to the living room and settled down once again on the couch to resume our kissing.

'Coast is clear,' I whispered as I nibbled on his ear and moved my hand down his body.

Kissing, we playfully undressed. With my parents sleeping only two rooms away, we knew we had to be quick and quiet for fear of waking them up. To his surprise, I climbed on top of him. Gripping the back of the couch as I picked up the rhythm, I silently brought us both to a long awaited climax.

Satisfied, we laid back and cuddled for a bit before I gathered my clothes, kissed him goodnight, and crept back to my bedroom.

\* \* \*

Everyone slept in the next day. I woke up to my mom making tea.

'You want any?' she asked.

'Yes, please,' I answered.

'And Trevor?'

'Yes, he takes milk and two sugars,' I strolled into the living room to see if Trevor was awake.

'Good morning,' I said, seeing his swollen eyes squinting at me. 'How did you sleep?'

'Not so great,' he said, struggling to keep his eyes open.

My mom came in with the tea, and he sat up to take the cup from her, wincing as he stretched out arching his back.

'Good morning,' my mom said brightly, 'did you sleep okay?'

'Good, thanks,' he lied.

She went back to the kitchen to get her tea and returned to her room.

'There is a lump jutting out somewhere in this couch,' he said quietly after she had left. 'I think I got some of it in my back.' He arched his back again, his body cracking as he stretched.

The front door opened, and my brother Joe walked in with his girlfriend, Sarah. He had spent the night at Sarah's house and had come home for some clean clothes.

'Hey, Joe, this is Trevor,' I said, introducing them.

'Hi, nice to meet you again,' Joe said as they shook hands.

It was surreal seeing them together in the same room again. The last time I had seen them both together was in the Jacuzzi eight years ago when we all first met, and my brother was so tiny back then. Now, Joe was six feet tall, like Trevor.

'Sarah and I were thinking of going to the movies to see *Toy Story*. You guys wanna go?'

I was surprised by his invitation. He never invited me to anything.

'What time are we leaving?'

'It starts at six forty-five, and Sarah and I wanted to go out to dinner afterwards.'

'That sounds good; where did you want to go to eat?' I asked.

'No, we were only inviting you to the movies,' he talked down to me like I was the younger sibling.

'Oh, so what you are saying is we should take separate cars. Is that correct?' I said, controlling my temper.

This was typical of Joe's attitude; cocky and selfish. I think after years of not having a true father figure he could count on, he became bitter, especially of my relationship with our mother. 'Yes, that's right.'

'Fine, we'll show up for the movie in separate cars. See you tonight,' I said.

He scoffed and took Sarah to his room, slamming the door shut behind them.

'Wow, your brother's something else, isn't he?' Trevor commented.

'As much as I wish we could have a better relationship, he always acts this way, which reminds me why we don't. I remember when we used to get on well when we were younger. It was much better between us then. Unfortunately, those days are gone, and I've given up on being the only one who cares.'

I took a deep breath. 'Are you okay with going tonight? If not, we can tell them we changed our minds ...' I said to Trevor, aggravated.

'It's fine, let's just go and have a good time. We can do dinner on our own,' Trevor said.

After a leisurely afternoon, we all arrived at the movie theater on time. Trevor and I decided to share a large soda and popcorn. We followed behind Joe and Sarah to find some decent seats. *Toy Story* was the first computer-animated film anyone had ever seen. The movie was magical; we both loved how lifelike the characters Woody and Buzz were, and overall I think we all thoroughly enjoyed it. Unfortunately, hanging out with Joe and his girlfriend was pointless. They were engrossed with one another the entire time, only acknowledging our existence when it was time to leave.

Later, we ate dinner at Applebee's and then made our way home, stopping at the liquor store on the way to pick up some beer and wine coolers.

My mom and George were watching TV in the living room.

'Hey Mom, hey George, anything good on?' I asked as we entered.

'We are watching the Discovery Channel,' George said.

'What are they showing?' Trevor asked.

'Sharks and deep sea fishing,' George replied.

'I love to fish, but I do not like sharks. I couldn't watch it,' I said.

'Did you have a good time at the movies?' my mom asked.

'Yes, you would love *Toy Story*, the story line was awesome.'

'I thought it was impressive, it's amazing what they can do with computers,' added Trevor.

'That's good, where are Joe and Sarah?' she asked.

'They ditched us after the movie to have dinner on their own.'

'Typical,' she said.

We left my parents and headed to the kitchen. I cracked open a drink each, put the remainder in the fridge and led Trevor to my room. We sat on my bed listening to music while we made out, drank and talked.

After an hour, my mom came in. 'We are heading into our room. George's back is bothering him, so he needs to lie down. You're both welcome to watch TV in the living room.'

'OK, thanks,' I said.

I explained to Trevor that George had worked in construction for most of his life, and the resulting arthritis made it difficult for him to sit in one position for long, and after fifteen to twenty minutes he preferred to lie down.

We got changed into our PJs and made up Trevor's bed in the living room before getting some more drinks from the fridge and settling down to watch a movie.

That night, just like every other night, we retired to the living room to watch TV, waiting until my mom and George were asleep before we satisfied the longing we had for each other.

* * *

Several days later, just before Trevor and I were getting ready to head out for the day, my mom pulled me aside in the kitchen.

'What's the matter?' I asked.

My mother had been watching Trevor for days; I could tell she had been trying to get a feel for him. More than anything, I wanted my family to fall in love with Trevor as I had with him and his family. I knew my mom was apprehensive because I was her only daughter. I don't think she understood this was the real deal for me. Trevor was the man I planned on marrying. Now, she motioned me aside. She had a problem with Trevor, and I was about to find out what it was.

'Why does he always roam from one room to the other and stare at us?' She asked.

'What do you mean?'

'He's been here almost a week. When you're both home, he doesn't stay in your room, he'll walk to each room and stare. He doesn't say anything; he just stares. I don't like it, and I'm not sure I like him.'

There IT was. I was waiting for the first complaint about Trevor.

'Mom, he's shy; it's not like he has any place to go. We live in a small ranch home with only three rooms on one floor. We don't have a den or even an inviting patio to lounge in compared to his home. He's getting a feel for all of us. Think of it this way, you're Trevor and just flew to your girlfriend's family's house and didn't know anyone but her. How would you feel? You need to give him a chance. Can you please do that for me?'

She sighed. 'Yes, I can.'

* * *

The next day, I drove forty minutes to my grandparents' home so Trevor could meet the rest of my family. It was quite convenient that they all lived in the same house.

We arrived at my grandparents' house and let ourselves in through the front door.

'Hi, Nana,' I called.

We walked through the living room to the kitchen where we found my nana standing in front of the sink.

'Hi, Nana,' I said again, making her jump.

'Oh, I thought I heard something,' she flustered, 'but I wasn't sure. How are you dear?'

She came over and hugged and kissed me on the cheek.

'I'm good,' I said. 'You remember Trevor?'

'Yes,' she smiled and gave Trevor a hug too. 'Come in and have a seat,' she beckoned.

'I'll put the kettle on,' my nana said, 'does he want some tea?' she asked turning to me.

'He's right here, Nana ... Why don't you ask him?' I said to her.

'Tea would be great.' He grinned at her.

'Nana, where's Grandpa?'

'He's out food shopping,' she answered.

'Well, hello again,' said my aunt as she walked into the kitchen coming from her apartment upstairs. My aunt leaned against the kitchen wall, looking really nice in her red short sleeve blouse, jean pants and I noticed, sporting a new haircut, which I liked very much.  I preferred her brown hair cut short; it accentuated her pretty face styled that way.

'Hi, it's nice to see you again,' Trevor said.

She pulled out a chair and joined us at the table while my nana was making our tea.

Just then my grandpa came in the back door.

'Hi, Grandpa!' I practically yelled at him.

He walked in wearing his favorite baseball cap and black spring jacket, arms loaded with plastic grocery bags.  Grandpa nodded at us, put the plastic bags down on the kitchen counter, walked over to shake Trevor's hand without saying a single word then proceeded to put the food away. I loved my grandpa to pieces, but throughout my entire life, I've had very limited conversations with him. My nana had always complained that he never talked to her much or anyone for that matter.

'Do you need any help,' asked Trevor to my grandpa.

'No, I got it thanks,' he replied.

Nana busied herself – setting up each cup of tea using her special porcelain tea cups with matching saucers while trying to stay out of my grandpa's way in their small kitchen.

My grandpa's almost six-foot frame towered over my nana by a good foot. He was a bit overweight compared to my nana's petite size.

'So, are you enjoying your time here?' asked my aunt.

'It's been great so far. We've been hanging out at the house, and Kerri's been driving me around showing me her town and where she went to school,' he answered.

'While Nana finishes up making tea, shall I give you the grand tour?' she asked.

'Sure,' he said.

Meeting my family only days before, Trevor was no longer nervous anymore and looked happy to take the tour with my aunt.

She showed Trevor her house upstairs while I followed behind. A decade earlier, my grandparents had converted their attic into a full apartment for my aunt and her family. The apartment had two good sized bedrooms, full bath, kitchen, living room and an attic big enough for a small third bedroom and some storage space. My aunt took pride in her home; the walls were painted with a bright yellow color that reminded me of a sunflower. She adorned long white curtains to each window, and most of the walls were decorated with pictures of my cousins growing up. Each room was well organized for the limited space that she had. After the quick tour through the rooms upstairs, Trevor and I then walked downstairs through my grandparents' living room back into the kitchen. The kettle was whistling as we passed the kitchen, and I opened the first door on the right leading downstairs to my uncle's basement apartment.

During college, I lived at my grandparents' house for two years to save costs on living in a dorm. While I was there, my uncle converted the dark, damp basement into a one-bedroom apartment. I got to watch how my uncle built out the basement to include a very small full bathroom, kitchen and living room. My uncle wasn't home, so we quickly took a tour. As we passed the bedroom and bathroom on the left, we entered the kitchen to our right. It was considered a kitchenette and had limited cabinet space. The kitchen was fitted with a compact standing fridge and stove. There was just enough space to accommodate a two-seater table. The living room was right off the kitchen that completed the apartment. My uncle did a great job decorating by keeping it simple. He painted the walls bright white and sporadically hung pictures my nana had painted over the years. Each window hung white share curtains. Once the tour was over, we went back upstairs to find hot cups of tea and some gingersnap biscuits waiting.

We sat down to enjoy our cups of tea, and I talked with my nana. My aunt returned downstairs to join us.

'Does he want another cup of tea?' my nana asked me.

'Nana, he's right there!' I said indignantly.

'Yes, please, I'll have another,' Trevor grinned.

She put the kettle back on.

'Do they have electricity in England?' she asked him.

'No, we use candles,' he said with a straight face.

'Oh,' she said and pondered this for a moment.

I laughed. 'Of course they do, Nana. In case you have forgotten, it is the twentieth century.'

'Oh,' she said again and poured water into the cups.

She handed the cups of tea back to us.

'Do they have microwaves in England?' she asked, sitting back down at the table.

'No, we cook by fire.' Trevor gave his best caveman impression, beating his fist against his chest.

My aunt and I burst out laughing. My nana suddenly realized he was joking.

'Yes, they have microwaves in England, Nana. They have everything we have here in America,' I explained.

'Yes, England is not much different from here,' Trevor said.

I marveled at the way Trevor was interacting with my family. He was polite, courteous and kind, and ever so playful.

'What did you think of my family?' I asked as we got in the car.

'I liked them; they were all very nice, very funny,' he answered.

'I'm so happy to hear that.'

And we drove home.

* * *

The following weekend, we drove up to New Hampshire. My mom and George had booked four days in a three bedroom cabin on Lake Winnipesaukee, and the remainder of the week was to be spent at Yogi's Jellystone Park. George's family lived near the lake, so we were going to spend some time with them, and I was eager to introduce everyone to Trevor. I hadn't seen his family since I was eighteen when we drove up to hang out over the Fourth of July weekend.

The night before our trip, we packed our suitcases and coolers. In the morning, they'd be loaded into my mom's blue Ford minivan with the six of us; Mom, George, Joe, Sarah, me and Trevor. En route of our two and a half-hour drive, we stopped at the outdoor Premium Outlets in Tilton to have some lunch and wander around the shops. Trevor bought several pairs of jeans and a black jean jacket at the Levi store.

Trevor was wearing a big grin as he began loading up his hand basket with multiple pairs of Levi jeans. 'Kerri, I could shop here all day. The amount of money I am saving buying brand name Levi jeans and the jacket here is brilliant! There is no way I could buy this in England. I would have had to save money for another month or more to buy all of this at one go!'

'If there is anything else you'd like to get while you are here, please let me know. I've saved quite a bit over this past year, and I'd love to treat you,' I said, happily.

Trevor walked over and gave me a lingering kiss.

'No, thank you, I've purchased enough for the day.'

'Well, you do have several weeks left here. You probably want to stretch out your money?'

'I do, and there's another reason why I want to save my money.'

'What's that?' I asked.

'I want to buy you something special while I am here,' he said.

'Oh, and what would that be?' I asked curiously.

'Well, I thought after my three weeks here, we could get an idea of what you may really want or need, and then have a shopping spree. Does that sound good?'

'It does. I'd love to do that.'

We continued, looking through other shops after we exited the Levi store. After wandering around the outlet stores for another hour, we met up with my parents, along with Joe and Sarah at our designated rendezvous: the food court. After quickly showing one another what we bought, we walked back to the minivan and made our way up to the lake.

We pulled up to a quaint little cottage on the lake. The front screened-in porch had the feel of a small beach cottage, with two sets of black, well-worn rocking chairs with brightly-colored floral pillows in each seat. In between each set stood matching, rickety-looking, square-topped tables, small enough for a couple of coffee mugs at the most.

The cottage walls were painted white throughout. The rooms were bright and inviting with an abundance of light pouring through each window. The small living room was equipped with two red-colored cotton fabric sofas with scattered mix and match pillows and an open fireplace. The kitchen was quite bare and basic, having only the standard essentials; a small round wooden table with four chairs, a small fridge, an electric stove and a microwave.

There was a charcoal barbecue grill on the deck outside, which led to the woods where the newly bloomed leaves blanketed the trees that encompassed the lake. Several feet away from the charcoal barbecue sat a cheap white plastic table that was weather worn with old mold stains and a few cigarette burn marks with four matching plastic chairs that conveniently fitted under the table for storage. Returning to the cottage, we wandered through the bedrooms. Each room was decorated exactly the same. Two small windows with white lace curtains were tied back with white ribbons, exactly like the kitchen curtains. Each queen-sized bed was made up with a thick multicolored quilted comforter with two matching pillow cases.

'This one is ours!' shouted Joe.

'Okay,' said George, 'we have this one … Kerri, that leaves you in the third bedroom, and Trevor can sleep on the couch.'

'WHAT? Joe and Sarah who are twenty and nineteen get to share a room, but Trevor and I can't? That is not fair!'

'It's perfectly fair,' George replied.

'MOM!'

My mom walked out of the bedroom she and George had chosen, and confronted me. 'George and I discussed the arrangements before we left the house, and our decision is final,' she said, firmly.

## CHAPTER 15 – QUAINT LITTLE COTTAGE

An argument was brewing in the quaint little cottage we had just arrived at. My parents and brother on one side and me and Trevor on the other. This was more than about desire; it was a matter of principle.

What annoyed me was that my mother and George and younger brother had all colluded on the living 'arrangements' for this vacation and had not thought to include me in the discussion.

'You have got to be kidding me,' I complained, 'what are you afraid of, us having sex? Well, big newsflash here, Mom, we've already done it, and you already know that. What kills me is so have Joe and Sarah, yet you seem to turn a blind eye. Have you forgotten I am older and more responsible than Joe is? I've also been paying you both rent for the past year, and Joe just comes and goes as he pleases. Is it because I don't have a penis? Why do he and Sarah get to sleep together? Do Sarah's parents know, or is it okay because you said so? Nope, no way, I will not put up with this; if that is the way you're going to play it, then I think Joe should take the other couch.'

'What? That's not fair! Mom, we discussed this, you promised.'

'Oh, so the cat's out of the bag, you already agreed to this arrangement with him?' I was livid.

'That's it, so much for a family vacation. Nice impression you are all making with Trevor by the way. Mom, give me your keys, please; we're going to go find a hotel if you're going to insist he sleeps on the couch.'

'Okay, I give in; you can share the third bedroom together.' My mom sighed.

'Good, thank you.' I looked over at Trevor, flashing a victory smile.

We brought our suitcases in from the car and unpacked.

Afterwards, we got back into the car to go grocery shopping at the local Shop n'Save. When we got back, we went out on the small wooden back deck with a couple of drinks. George insisted on cooking on the grill; he grilled some chicken, corn on the cob, and steamed chopped carrots, broccoli, and cauliflower wrapped in aluminum for dinner. Since we didn't have to cook, it was nice to sit and relax while taking in the view of the lake, watching the boaters go by. The water was less than a ten-minute walk from the house.

* * *

The next day, when I woke up, I immediately felt the chill in the air. I rolled over onto my right side while pulling the blankets over my shoulder and looked out the window. A thick fog covered the lake, spread towards the cottages and beyond. I knew it would disappear when the heat from the afternoon sun burned it away. Turning back to soak up Trevor's peaceful face, as he lay sleeping beside me, I relished the fact that we didn't have to sneak around anymore. I knew we were on vacation, but getting along as well as we did, I could picture us living together as we had so often talked about and looked forward to more mornings like this. I slid over and gave him a light kiss on his lips before getting out of bed.

Quietly closing our bedroom door, I was desperate for a hot shower. I jumped into the shower only to find there was no hot water. I came out of the bathroom freezing and quickly wrapped myself in the first towel I could find. I had to jump back into bed with Trevor to warm up again.

The guys took quick showers, and the cold water didn't seem to bother them so much, but I really wanted to wash my hair. My mom boiled some water on the stove and mixing it with some cold water, washed my hair for me over the kitchen sink. It had been years since she had washed my hair for me. I thoroughly enjoyed her massaging the shampoo into my scalp. She took care not to get the shampoo into my eyes or water into my ears as she rinsed the suds away. While my eyes were closed, I remembered the days when Joe and I shared a tub when we were very little, and my dad was no longer living with us, and it was peaceful with just me, Joe, and Mom. Mom made our bath time fun and enjoyable. Once she was done toweling my hair dry, I noticed Sarah staring at us. She asked if my mom could wash her hair over the sink too.

It was nice to have everyone getting along after our argument the day before. It wasn't perfect by any means; nevertheless, I appreciated everyone making an effort with Trevor. We deserved to have our own room, and my parents weren't holding a grudge, which I felt allowed all of us to enjoy our time together.

We all had a quick cereal breakfast and headed out to George's sister's home. We were spending the day there. As we pulled up, everyone was busy outside preparing for the cookout. I quickly introduced Trevor to George's side of the family. His sister Jackie was shorter in height than George, but had the same fair skin, dirty blonde hair and matching blue eyes. Her husband Tom was a big guy and stood over six feet tall with jet-black hair, brown eyes, and a goatee. They had three kids Emily, Elizabeth, and David. Emily was the oldest and was Trevor's age. Elizabeth was taller than Emily despite being two years younger in age. I hadn't seen David in three years, and he had grown a foot or more over that time. He was no longer a teenager and had lost his baby face. He now looked a lot like his father and was almost as tall. Once again, Trevor's easy personality was a hit with everyone.

When the introductions were over, we all were asked to start preparing for the cookout. Jackie had invited neighbors too, and we needed to make sure the food was prepared before everyone was expected to arrive in the afternoon.

We typically visited George's family during our summer vacations and sometimes for New Year's Eve. Usually, it was just Joe, my parents, and me when we visited, and we all slept in their house. I would share a room with one of the girls; Joe would bunk with David, and my parents always used their pull-out sofa. Visiting George's family didn't make my relationship with him any stronger. He acted exactly the same at his sister's as he did at our home. He and his sister and brother-in-law were raised in a time when children were meant to be seen not heard. Thankfully for all us kids, those days were over. We were no longer children and finally able to add our opinions and hang out with the adults. This year was the first time my parents rented a lake house, which was nice because the four of us had our own rooms and some privacy. When there was a big cookout or special occasion like a birthday, graduation, etc., there were only four main activities you were expected to partake in; playing horseshoes, talking, eating and consuming as much alcohol as physically possible. Of course, if you were under the age of 21, you could only drink soda. This rule no longer applied to Trevor or me.

There was a lot of fun going on, but after a couple of hours, Trevor and I grabbed some plastic patio chairs so we could find a quiet spot in the yard away from everyone to spend some alone time together.

'Are you OK with being surrounded by so many people you don't know?' I asked.

'I am feeling a bit overwhelmed; it's nothing I can't handle. It's been interesting; they keep asking me to say the British version of American words like boot for trunk or trainers for sneakers. It was fun at first, but after two hours, I don't wish to play anymore.'

'I noticed that, and I don't blame you. I appreciate you getting on with everyone. It's really nice to see,' I said.

We sat quietly for a bit watching everyone else having fun playing horseshoes, water balloons, or squirting each other with water guns. I loved the fact that we could feel comfortable not feeling forced to talk. Ten minutes went by, and Trevor broke the silence.

'What are you thinking about?' asked Trevor.

'I was thinking that being here with you and sharing a bed again has been wonderful. I know we are on vacation, but this routine is something I want to continue full-time. The more time you're here, the better we get along; I cannot picture my life going back to the way it was.'

'I was thinking that too. We've had such a great week. I am dreading leaving at the end of the month.'

'Me too. What do you want to do about it?'

'I want to live with you full-time,' Trevor said, sounding determined.

'You must know how much I've wanted to hear you say that.'

'I know, and I am sorry it's taken me this long, but I needed to be sure. I've also decided I need to move out of my parents' home. The problem is I was recently hired full-time and saved to come here. I need more time to save for a first and last month's rent on a flat. That's going to take several months.'

'I'm in the same boat. I saved all year knowing you were coming; now I am unemployed, and all my savings will be used while you are here. What do you suggest we do?'

'Right now, we should enjoy our time together. I'm sure by the end of the month we'll have come up with a plan.'

'Okay,' I said.

I was thrilled to hear Trevor's was ready to be together full-time. Everything I always wanted with him seemed to be falling into place.

George and Tom came looking for Trevor; they wanted to teach him horseshoes. I went looking for coolers. It was the first summer where I could take alcohol out of the cooler without having to ask, and I relished in gloating at Joe and Sarah, having to grudgingly be settling for soda. The grill was loaded up with ribs, steaks, and chicken, which were cooking on low and would be ready to eat later that afternoon.

Trevor and I helped set up the tables outside for the food and condiments. Throughout the day, we had fun playing badminton and horseshoes. Most of our time was spent around the fire eating, drinking, and making s'mores. It grew chilly after the sun went down and Jackie's neighbors left. The girls and David with Joe and Sarah decided to stay and enjoy the fire. The rest of us; my parents, Jackie, Tom, Trevor and I decided to go in.

'Trevor, do you play any card games?' asked Tom.

'I do, I am pretty good at poker and blackjack.'

'Really, do you want to join in? We typically play many card games to finish the night,' said George.

'We get pretty rowdy, but I am sure you'll have a lot of fun,' said my mom.

'Okay, sounds good,' said Trevor.

'Trevor, there is room here.' Jackie pointed to an open space on the bench seat.

I wasn't in the mood for cards; I wanted to watch instead.

Trevor showed them all how efficient he was in shuffling not one, but two decks of cards and proceeded to deal them out.

I thoroughly enjoyed watching all of them drink more, get louder than usual and playfully argue until everyone was hysterically laughing.

After several hours, the six of us helped clean up and then headed back to the cottage around midnight.

\* \* \*

We met up with George's family three days that week. Our time was spent between hanging out at their house and swimming at the lake. Lake Winnipesaukee is one of my favorite lakes to visit. It's 21 miles long and almost nine miles wide containing 258 islands and is the largest lake in New Hampshire. The scenery was breathtaking; surrounded by a kaleidoscope of multicolored blossomed trees and a multitude of cottage communities. On our last day, we were invited to attend Elizabeth's graduation from College. Her graduation ceremony was in the morning, followed by another cookout with friends and family in the afternoon. Jackie had rented a place out in the woods near her college, and I could tell she went above and beyond to provide a beautiful celebration for Elizabeth. A large tent was erected in the clearing over rows of tables and chairs. A wooden dance floor was laid with a stage at one end for the band she had booked. It was a big to do. The guest list was long, and it looked like they had invited every single person they knew. I introduced Trevor to everyone I knew, which I think was too much for him.

'How are you doing? I know there is a lot going on; are you overwhelmed at all?

'It's a bit much meeting all these people I don't know; still I'm having a good time,' he said.

'Do you want to find a quiet place, which at the moment seems impossible? I'm sure we could try?'

'No, it's okay. I'll be fine; I need a moment outside of this tent.'

'Okay, let's grab some drinks and get some fresh air,' I said.

Trevor and I grabbed some drinks from the cooler and walked outside the tent. A moment turned into 30 minutes, and we decided it was best to rejoin the party. When we walked back in, Elizabeth was having a great time on the dance floor with Joe, Sarah, her friends and most of her family. It was nice to see Joe making an effort with Sarah, introducing her when needed. Overall, the day was a success; we all had a great time eating, drinking and dancing the afternoon away, and when it was all over, we helped pack up and headed back to Tom and Jackie's house where we were staying the night. We opened more drinks and food when we got back to the house and sat in the kitchen playing cards until the early hours of the morning.

* * *

The next day, late in the afternoon, we all drove out to Fun Spot; the local Family Entertainment Center. Founded in 1952, it held every video arcade imaginable. Ever since the age of 12 when George's family moved up to New Hampshire, we'd been coming to Fun Spot trying out all the classic arcades and several rounds of bowling. I learned how to play Centipede at Fun Spot; one of my favorite arcades games. The adults teamed up against us 'kids' for two highly competitive games of bowling. Of course, we didn't stand a chance; most of the adults had been in local bowling leagues at some point and were well practiced. After conceding defeat in both games, we wandered around the arcades for a few hours on our own.

The day was a blast, and afterward, we all said our goodbyes to Jackie and her family. The six of us needed to clean up the cottage because we were checking out in the morning.

After checking out of the cottage, we drove to the cabin we rented for two days in Yogi's Jellystone Park. Previously, I had told my mom how Trevor's family enjoyed camping every year in France. So she thought it would be fun for Trevor to experience camping at the Park. For years, my family and I would travel to the park with our pop-up tent camper for a week. The park had a ton of activities, and we always had a great time. For the first time, my parents rented a cabin. There was no way we would have all comfortably fit in the pop-up tent camper. The cabin was a similar set up to the lake cottage, except it was a little smaller, and there wasn't a screened-in porch. There, we swam in the river and hung out by the pool for the first day and sat around the campfire drinking beer and roasting marshmallows for most of the evening.

* * *

On our second day, it rained nonstop, so my mom, Trevor and I headed down to the clubhouse to play bingo. Entering the clubhouse, it was as if we entered into a Bingo Troll Shrine bordering on a cult. The tables were decorated with 100s of multi-fluorescent hair colored Bingo Trolls ranging in colors from pink, purple, blue, green, orange and yellow. They had pictures of these little characters on everything; T-shirts, purses, fluorescent colored ink dabbers, and placemats. Trevor and I felt out of place. We didn't know if we were going to upset the Bingo Troll gods by not honoring their presence and decorating our section of the table with dolls of our own. The three of us got our cards and sat down at a table to play. Looking around the small hall, we could see that the crowd was mostly made up of old-ladies with varying multi-colored hairstyles. Their hairstyles I imagined were actually inspired by their love of the dolls.

'Mom, Trevor, I keep wondering if the ladies meet up before the game and bend their heads over, spray their multi-colored locks with hairspray and then blow-dry them into a cone position,' I whispered.

'I swear we are the only ones in the building with natural hair color,' my mom said laughing.

'Their hair almost seems to match the color of those little plastic figures they're holding,' Trevor commented. 'What are those things?'

'Lucky Bingo Trolls dolls,' my mom answered, 'they're supposed to bring you good luck in Bingo.'

'Oh, um, OK,' he said, not convinced.

The action was fast, and we had a hard time keeping up with the numbers being drawn and checking them off on the six cards that we each held. I glanced over at Trevor's cards as ball I-19 was called.

'Ninedeeeeeen,' shouted the crowd of old aged biddies in unison.

'I have one left on this one,' said Trevor as he dabbed at the number with his ink blotter.

He was managing to keep up with the numbers to some extent.

'Two little ducks,' announced the caller.

'Quack, quack,' rattled the ladies at our table.

'What the hell does that mean?' Trevor asked, confused.

'22,' my mom answered.

'BINGO!' shouted an old lady as she jumped up and started waving her bingo card in the air, her blue hair with pink highlights flapping wildly in the breeze from the overhead fans.

'Arrrghh,' he sighed, 'I was so close.'

We didn't win at Bingo, but it was fun, and it passed a few hours away. Since it was still raining when we got back to the cabin, we ordered and picked up Chinese takeout. We stopped by the convenience store on our way back to the campground for more beer and wine coolers. After dinner, the six of us sat in the cabin while the rain poured and played cards until we turned in for the night.

\* \* \*

The following day, we packed up to go home just before lunchtime. Then, we stopped off in Meredith, New Hampshire, for lunch at the Harts Turkey Farm restaurant, which had an all-turkey menu: turkey nuggets, turkey pie, turkey meatloaf, turkey sandwiches.

Trevor and I thought it was hysterical. Thankfully, we both loved turkey, so it wasn't going to be a problem.

The tall yet skinny teenage waiter, with an abundance of short curly red hair and glasses, came by, eager to take our order.

Trevor ummed and aahed at the menu and then asked, 'Do you have chicken?'

'I'm sorry, no we don't,' replied the waiter looking confused and annoyed at the same time.

'Any beef or pork perhaps?'

I knew Trevor was kidding, and I was wondering how long the waiter would take to get it. After a few seconds ticked by, Trevor started to laugh as well as the rest of us, including the waiter.

'I was just messing with you mate; it had to be asked with a menu dedicated only to turkey.'

The waiter relaxed and took our orders.

Trevor was happy to eat turkey since it's not a regular food choice in England. The rest of us loved turkey dinners, especially when we only ate them once a year for Thanksgiving, so this felt like a treat. The waiter returned with our drinks, followed by our turkey meals and we all tucked in.

'That was good,' said George about fifteen minutes later as he mopped up the last of the gravy on his plate with some bread.

I looked over and saw that he had indeed finished. The rest of us were only halfway through our meals. George drained his glass, picked up his keys and left the restaurant.

'Did he just leave?' I asked my mom, mortified. 'You have got to be kidding me. We're only halfway through our meals.'

'He's gone to the car,' she said as if it was nothing out of the ordinary for her.

'That's rude and embarrassing,' I pointed out.

'I know. He's set in his ways. If he's done and wants to go, then he will,' she defended him.

'That's not acceptable,' I argued. 'It's not only rude to us; it's disrespectful to you. Aren't you upset by it at all?'

'Of course, I am,' she said, 'but it is what it is. Let's just finish our meals and head out.'

I was so embarrassed. I could see that Trevor and Sarah looked uncomfortable. Joe seemed unfazed. We were used to this behavior. George always did exactly what he wanted to do.

I leaned over to Trevor.

'I'm sorry for George's actions,' I said. 'I would love to say this never happens. Unfortunately, it's been this way for as long as I can remember. If George is done, then it doesn't matter to him what everyone else is doing, he just ups and leaves,' I explained.

'It's okay, don't worry about it. We're having a good time.' Trevor put his arm around me for a reassuring hug.

We quickly finished our meals, stopping by the gift shop on the way out. I wanted to spend more time in the gift shop if only to make George wait. Unfortunately, my mom ushered us out after a few minutes.

'He probably left so he could have a cigarette in the parking lot,' Joe said as we exited the restaurant.

'No, George doesn't smoke anymore. He gave it up,' my mom said, in clear denial.

Joe and I rolled our eyes at each other. There were many times when our mom wasn't home, where Joe and I caught George smoking without him knowing.

We got outside and scanned the parking lot for the minivan, finding it perched on the edge of the restaurant exit with its engine revving.

'This is ridiculous,' I said.

My mom ignored me. We wandered over to the waiting van, opened up and climbed in. Already set in drive, the car was on the road by the time the sliding door had closed, and we hurriedly put on our seat belts. George drove like he was on a mission, and we got home in record time by late afternoon.

Not long after we got home, my best friend Mel called and asked if we wanted to go out clubbing with her and her boyfriend Jamie ... Mel lived not far from the club. She shared a second-floor two-bedroom apartment with her boyfriend, Jamie and her younger sister Naomi. She asked if we wanted to spend the night after clubbing, and we thought that would be a wonderful opportunity to get time on our own. Mel and Jamie arrived to pick us up at seven thirty, and after a short introduction, we left.

'Do you like Bud?' Jamie asked Trevor as we made our way out to the car.

'I guess,' Trevor answered.

'I got us one each for the road,' said Jamie as he pulled out two huge bottles of Budweiser, popped the caps on both and thrust one into Trevor's hand.

'Oh, thanks,' said Trevor.

'You guys should sit in the back with those,' said Mel, 'I'll drive.'

I got in the passenger seat.

'Wow, this thing is bigger than a Newky Brown,' said Trevor as he took a big swig from his bottle.

'Good?' asked Jamie.

'All right,' Trevor lied.

I thought it was sweet Trevor lying to show appreciation for Jamie's kind gesture. You can take the British man out the country, but you cannot take the country out of the British man; he preferred British ales.

The club was packed, but we managed to find an open table in a corner and settled down with some drinks. We chatted loudly for a while over a few more drinks and then got up to dance. It was great all of us getting on so well. It didn't feel like it was the first time we all hung out. At one point, we were tired from dancing and headed back to the table.

'Do any of you like to play pool? I know Kerri can play sort of. How about a couple's game?' asked Trevor.

'Yeah, that sounds fun. I am pretty good at pool actually,' said Jamie.

'This should be interesting,' said Mel.

Trevor picked a table and set up the balls. We all chose pool sticks and rubbed chalk onto the tips.

'You look like a professional, how long have you played pool?' asked Mel.

'I had a snooker table at home and have been playing since I was twelve,' said Trevor.

'Were you on a team or did you play for fun?' asked Jamie.

'Only for fun with my brothers and occasionally we'd team up with our dad.'

'Well, sounds like you're going to kick our asses.' Mel was laughing, enjoying the fact she and I both sucked at pool.

We played a good game. I completely sucked as expected, but I was quite pleased to see Jamie and Mel hold their own against Trevor.

It was a good game. To celebrate all our efforts, we ordered more drinks and baskets of fries.

Intoxicated, we danced and drank the evening away, leaving the club in the early hours of the morning in a drunken stupor to stagger our way back to Mel's car.

Mel didn't have much to drink and drove us to her place.

'I set out the blow-up mattress on the floor in the living room for you guys,' said Mel.

She opened the door, and we walked into her apartment. She had pushed the couches to one side of the small living room to put down the single blow-up mattress for us. A tiny kitchen was on the other side of the apartment. A narrow hallway ran from the living room which led to the two bedrooms and a bathroom. In the corner of the living room, a small scuttling sound emanated from a large cage covered over with a blanket.

'What's that?' asked Trevor.

'Oh, that's my sister's ferrets,' said Mel as she pulled back the blanket for a moment so we could see the skinny ugly creatures.

With the blanket drawn back, the ferrets seemed to wake up, and they rammed the cage together. Mel pulled the blanket back down. 'They won't bother you,' she said.

'Well, it's late, and I need my bed. If you need anything else, just knock on the door okay?' said Mel.

'Okay, thanks for asking us out guys; we had a great time,' I said.

'No problem, see you in the morning,' remarked Jamie.

'Night,' said Trevor.

Mel and Jamie retired to their room while Trevor and I snuggled up under the blankets over the narrow inflatable mattress.

We lay there making out for a while but were distracted by the ferrets.

'Slam, scratch, bang!

'What the hell is that?' asked Trevor.

'It sounds like the ferrets are slamming into the cage; do you think they might break free?' I replied.

'No, let's ignore them, where were we?' said Trevor.

'Bang, screech, hiss!!

'OK, now they are really freaking me out, they are starting to sound like snakes,' said Trevor.

'Let's try and not pay any attention to them. Where were you again?'

'I was right here at your neck.' Trevor started to nibble at my neck.

Bang! Hissss! Screeech!

'I think they are going to burst through; they sound so angry!' said Trevor nervously.

'Agh! Seriously, these ugly ferrets are a mood kill,' I complained.

'Look there, what is that?' asked Trevor.

We both looked over and noticed from that back corner of the cage two sets of yellow eyes looking at us; it was totally creepy.

'No wonder they are acting up, their blanket has been pulled back at that corner. Maybe that's upsetting them. I'll put the blanket back, and hopefully, we can have some peace and quiet,' I said.

The minute I lay back down and started kissing Trevor again they started.

Hisss!! Screeeech! Bang!

'I'm going to kill those ferrets,' I whispered to Trevor.

'No, I am,' he replied.

'I cannot believe Naomi loves these animals. They're rodents and not exactly the cuddly kind,' I grumbled.

'Well, we are here for the night, and really there's not much we can do. Let's just forget them. Where were we again?' Trevor asked, gently grabbing my chin and tilting my face toward his.

'Oh yes, I remember,' he said and bent down for a passionate kiss.

# CHAPTER 16 – BOSTON

My mom took a few days off from work to spend some time with me and Trevor. We got up early, packed snacks and filled up water bottles for our full day out. We drove and caught the train into Boston and, getting off at Back Bay Station, we walked to the beginning of the Freedom Trail in Boston Commons.

We could not have picked a better day to explore Boston. At seventy-five degrees and not a cloud in the sky, it was an unusually cool day for the end of May. The three of us meandered across the Commons, stopping as we were excited to view the State House with its gleaming gold dome before walking down Park Street to the Granary Burial Ground where we spent half an hour wandering the tombstones looking for famous people. Continuing, my mom took photos of us together at the Benjamin Franklin statue. We explored the trail to the Old South Meeting House and then the Old State House, stopping at both to browse the museum exhibits. The three of us had worked up an appetite and stopped for drinks and lunch at the Green Dragon Tavern, one of the many restaurants at Faneuil Hall before perusing the shops at Quincy Market. Faneuil Hall has always reminded me of the scene in *Bedknobs and Broomsticks* when the kids and the older couple are walking around the various vendor carts in Portobello Road. We spent a good hour moseying around the markets and saw several street artists and decided to get a caricature done.

'I like to ask my customers where they met as a couple. It helps me in what I create. So, where did you both meet?' asked the artist.

'We met in a Jacuzzi on holiday at the Marriot Hotel in Orland Florida,' Trevor said.

Thirty minutes later, we got to see our finished caricature. The artist drew the two of us with extremely large heads, grinning from ear to ear. An abundance of foam was building upwards, surrounding us and pouring over the sides of the large wooden Jacuzzi. We loved it. The artist did such a great job; there was no denying it was us, and we paid extra for a picture frame. We stopped at a small fruit stand to buy some cherries and then headed off to find the red painted line to continue our Freedom Trail walk.

My mom and I munched on the bag of cherries as we walked, spitting out the cherry pits on the roadside. Trevor walked a few yards ahead of us, and I thought it amusing to try out some target practice. Every so often, I hit the back of Trevor's head with the pips. As a result, he had developed a slight twitch, his hand spasmodically reaching up to protect his head after each pit that hit him. I knew Trevor knew what I was doing and was being a good sport; this only made it funnier. I burst out laughing, and my mom joined me as he turned around with a disgruntled look.

'Kerri, stop it. It was funny at first, but enough is enough now,' he said.

'Trevor's right, you should leave his head alone now,' my mom said and continued laughing.

He looked so funny trying to be upset with me that we couldn't stop laughing. Poor Trevor, he was outnumbered.

'Sorry, baby, I couldn't help myself,' I said, hugging him.

We continued the trail, passing the Paul Revere House and the Old North Church where Robert Newman had lit the two lanterns in the tower signaling that the British were arriving by sea and made our way across the Charlestown Bridge. The temperature had increased since morning, and the tiny breath of wind coming from the Charles River offered a slight relief from the hot afternoon sun. We followed the red line, stopping briefly at the USS Constitution; it is a grand ship, named by George

Washington and was built in the North End of Boston, at Edmund Hartt's shipyard. We didn't take a full tour of the ship; instead, we took pictures of it and in front of it. Carrying on the red line, we finally arrived at the Bunker Hill Monument at the end of the trail, where we sat for a while to rest with our water bottles.

'I find it kind of ironic that we walked past the Paul Revere House, famous for him riding horseback and screaming at the top of his lungs, 'THE BRITISH ARE COMING, THE BRITISH ARE COMING!' And here I am crazy in love with a Brit.'

'I was just thinking that,' my mom said with a chuckle.

I started to laugh, and then Trevor and my mom joined in with me. It had been over an hours walk, and we were tired but determined to continue with the trail. It seemed that the end of the trail was in the middle of nowhere, and it took a lot of effort to pick ourselves up to make the trek back to the city.

'I could use a real drink; do you both want to find a pub, and I'll buy you a wine or cocktail?' asked Trevor.

'That sounds nice,' said my mom.

'How about we get a drink in Faneuil Hall and order some fries, I am hungry,' I suggested.

'Let's stop at The Black Rose; I noticed some lagers on their outside menu I'd like to try,' said Trevor.

'Sounds like a plan,' I agreed.

We enjoyed a yummy basket of fries and a round of refreshing drinks. After an hour, we all decided it was getting on, and we should make our way back to Back Bay Station and head home.

The following day, we ventured back into Boston to take Trevor to see his first baseball game at Fenway Park.

My mom drove her minivan because Joe had invited two friends to the game too. The drive took about 45 minutes, and the afternoon traffic wasn't bad at all.

I made sure to grab the two back seats in the minivan so we could have time to ourselves.

'I'm looking forward to seeing the game. I've only watched Cricket and Rugby,' said Trevor.

'Baseball is one of my favorite sports; I've been excited to see the game with you since we booked the tickets. I am curious to see what you think.'

My mom found cheap parking several blocks away from Fenway Park. It was a beautiful day, and I enjoyed the walk to the stadium.

There was quite a crowd for a weekday game, and we waited twenty minutes in line at the drink stand before finding our seats. My mom was thrilled with the seats she had purchased behind the home plate, even if the seats were right behind the designated walkway. We certainly got a good view of the baseball field surrounded by bleachers. It was great to see all the players out on the field warming up.

'Did you play baseball at school?' my mom asked Trevor.

'No, the main batting sport in England is cricket,' he answered, 'although I think we did play softball a few times in the summer.'

'Cricket? Hmm, I don't really understand that game,' she said.

'It's simple enough. It's a very long game, longer than baseball because you have to get the entire team out and not just three batters.'

'Oh,' my mom said.

'Yes, cricket,' he said satirically, 'ten minutes of excitement dragged out over several hours, or even days in some cases.'

'Really?' I asked.

'Yeah, I expect baseball to be a bit more exciting. You played baseball at school, didn't you?' he asked me.

'Yes,' I said. (I could visualize our team picture vividly. I was proudly kneeling beside my teammates wearing my orange baseball cap, orange jersey with number 10 on the back of my shirt and white baseball pants. The kids standing held their gloves and the ones kneeling like myself had to rest their glove against their bent knees. I was in front because I was the tallest kid and only girl on the team.)

We turned our attention to the field as the players ran on, and the game started. The first few innings went by without much action. In the middle of the next innings, Trevor turned and looked at me, confused, then got up and walked over to the railing and stood staring out at the field as if looking for something. He returned still looking puzzled.

'What's the matter?' I asked.

'I don't understand,' he said, 'they keep stopping at weird intervals of play. They seem to play for five minutes or so and then when you think they're going to throw the next pitch they stop and hang around for five minutes. I don't get it.'

'Oh, that'll be the commercial breaks,' said my mom.

'What do you mean?' he asked.

'They stop playing for the commercial breaks on TV.'

'You're kidding?' He looked like it was the most ridiculous thing he had ever heard.

'No, the game is televised,' she explained.

'Oh.' He didn't look convinced.

'They don't do that in England?' I asked.

'No,' he said, 'can you imagine it?' He put on a commentator's voice, 'Gazza's moving up the pitch, he passes to Lineker, Lineker's in perfect position and ... wait! Hold everything! Everyone stay where you are! We'll be right back after these important announcements!'

'Well, when you put it like that ...' I chuckled.

'I'm going to get another drink,' he said. 'Does anyone else want anything?'

'You want to get some hot dogs?' asked my mom. 'Here, I have some money.'

'Can you get us some beers?' asked my underage brother.

'Uh, sure,' he answered, 'although I'm not sure they'll let me get that many. They seem to be pretty strict on the alcohol laws here.'

'I'll help carry,' I offered.

We left to get the food and drinks. Trevor was right; the concession stand would only allow him to bring back two beers, so he bought himself one. We got the hot dogs and returned to our seats.

'Sorry, they wouldn't let me buy more than this. Your mom, Kerri and I would have to go and purchase drinks separately to get drinks for you three, and I don't think your mom would approve,' he said.

'No problem,' said Joe.

The game was longer than we all would have liked because of the commercial breaks; we enjoyed ourselves anyway. It was late when we exited the stadium.

\* \* \*

Later in the week, I took Trevor to meet my old workmates at National Leisure Group. Robin met us as we exited the elevator on the fourth floor and agreed to come out to lunch with us. I introduced Trevor to everyone.

They all knew what Trevor looked like having plastered my cube with pictures of him, but when you added that thick sexy British accent, like me, they all became mesmerized.

'Are you enjoying yourself in Boston Trevor?' asked the new girl Joan.

I didn't know her at all; I was told she had filled my position three weeks ago.

'Yes, areas of Boston remind me of London.'

'What else have you been up to?' said Robin.

'Kerri's family has planned a lot of outings; we spent time at a Lake House and campground for a week in New Hampshire and several activities here in Boston. This week, we went to see a Redsox game.'

'Sounds like you've been busy,' said Joan.

'My time here has been brilliant,' answered Trevor.

We stayed about half an hour and then left with Robin for lunch, the girls giving me the 'thumbs up' as we headed for the elevators. Looking at Trevor, he was becoming more and more uncomfortable with all the attention.

I laughed and pulled him and Robin into the elevators. 'Trevor, you really need to get used to girls falling for you. It still blows my mind that you do not know how gorgeous you are with an equally charming personality.'

'Please stop it,' Trevor said, turning a new shade of red.

'It's quite refreshing,' piped Robin, 'we're used to good looking guys who know they're good looking and turn out to be complete assholes who only love themselves.'

We arrived at the Cheers pub on Beacon Street and took pictures together in front of the Cheers sign. Although the décor was authentic, and the warm ambiance in the pub was welcoming, Trevor and I were a little disappointed that the layout of the pub inside was different from the TV show. In the TV show, the bar sits in the center of the room with counters on all four sides. The actual pub is a lot smaller, and the bar backs onto a wall and only two sides have counters. Robin and I ordered Mudslides while Trevor got a Boston Lager. We sat at the bar and drank, and Robin started talking about how she wished we had more time in Boston so we could have an official pub crawl.

'We should have planned our time together better before Trevor got here. I would have taken you guys to The Pour House, followed by The House of Blues, and lastly we would have finished the night going to an Irish Pub called McGreevy's. They have this amazing band called The Dropkick Murphy's.'

'Sounds like we would have a brilliant time,' said Trevor.

'I don't know why we didn't think of that, Robin. All we have is today; we have plans later,' I said.

Two hours and three rounds had gone by when Robin noticed that she was an hour late getting back to work.

'I don't really feel like going back to work this afternoon. I am having way too much fun with you two. Plus, it's Friday,' Robin pointed out.

She carefully got up and walked over to the pay phone. She was on the phone for a minute or two before coming back wearing a huge grin.

'I called and told my boss I wasn't feeling too well,' she said, 'so I'm free to hang out with you two all afternoon.'

'Cool! Let's get another round!' I offered.

We stayed two more hours until we couldn't possibly drink anymore. Trevor and I had plans later, and so did Robin, so we called it quits.

'Thanks for meeting us, Robin. I am so glad you got to meet Trevor.'

'I had a blast. I wish you could stay longer Trevor, we would have fun on that pub crawl,' said Robin.

'When I come back to visit Kerri, I'd love for us to pick up where we left off.'

* * *

On our last day together, we decided to go and visit my dad and my two younger brothers, his wife was out. It was a hot sunny Sunday afternoon. We chased my brothers around the backyard for a while, picking them up and turning them upside down or twirling them around by the arms. We played for about an hour until we got tired. They had so much energy and begged us to play longer.

'Kerri, want to play catch?' asked Zach, who was adorable and five.

How could you ever say no to two sweet, beautiful boys with blond locks and hazel eyes? I loved them to pieces. I was sixteen when Zach was born and twenty when Peter was born, regardless of the age differences we all got on so well. It was a privilege to be their big sister.

'Of course, Zach; go get the ball and gloves.'

'I got Peter. We are going to have piggy back rides. Or I should say I'll be the one giving the ride. I don't think Peter could carry my weight,' Trevor said laughing.

'Yeah, there will be none of that unless you've seen other almost-two-year olds lift 170-pounds of weight?' I giggled.

'Pick me up, Treasure,' asked Peter, holding his adorable arms up to Trevor.

'No problem.'

'I love that Peter cannot pronounce your name,' I said.

'Ironically, this is what I called myself when I was his age not being able to pronounce my name either.'

'Trevor when you're done giving Peter a piggy back ride, do you want a beer?' asked my dad.

'Sure,' replied Trevor.

Trevor and I were having a great afternoon playing with my brothers. Zach and I caught several pop-ups and grounders. After a while, Trevor and I made teams; me with Zach, and Trevor with Peter running around the yard in competitive piggy back races. I loved watching Trevor interact with my brothers; it only solidified the fact I knew he'd make a great father one day. I didn't need my father's approval, still it was nice to see him and the boys getting on with Trevor. We played for another hour until we got tired. The boys had so much energy and begged us to play longer.

'I'm going to sit down for a while,' Trevor said, out of breath.

He sat on the deck, and my dad passed him a Keystone light beer.

'Thanks,' he said, cracking it open.

Trevor wouldn't normally be seen dead drinking a light beer, but he drank it anyway just to be polite. They made chit-chat while I sat at the kitchen table drawing spaceships, Toy Story characters and anything that came to our imagination with the boys. We had been there for three hours. After Trevor's beer, we headed out to the car to leave. I gave my brothers big hugs and kisses, and my dad surprised me with a longer than usual hug.

'You've picked a good one there,' he said softly.

'I know,' I said and got into the car.

I grew up with my dad being mostly out of my life. When we were together, he never really showed too much emotion with Joe or me. When he did it always surprised me. I wished he was like this while we were growing up. I could have said something more than 'I know,' but after all these years I still didn't trust him with my heart.

It suddenly dawned on me as we waved goodbye that Trevor was going home tomorrow, and I felt both a nauseous sensation deep in my stomach and then heat spread up my back. I wasn't sure, but I think I was having an anxiety attack.

'You all right?' Trevor asked.

I didn't want Trevor to see me like this. I wanted this feeling to pass so we could enjoy the rest of the day.

'Uh-huh,' I answered, looking straight ahead.

'Your dad seemed nice,' he said.

'Hmm,' I said pre-occupied with the thought of him leaving me. It was no use; my heart was feeling like it was literally being torn apart.

I'd had the best three weeks of my life with Trevor. His time here only confirmed how much we loved each other and should be together. I couldn't believe I wouldn't be waking up to him in my bed after tomorrow. It just wasn't fair.

'Do you want to stop at that pizza place we saw on the way here?'

'Sure,' I said, tight-lipped.

'What's the matter?'

'Nothing,' I lied.

I was a terrible liar. He sighed and turned his head towards the window. We spent most of the car ride in silence. I knew he was frustrated with me for not telling him the truth.

We got a booth by the window and ordered some sodas, a small pizza each and some wings to share.

'You're pissed off with me. What did I do?' Trevor asked.

I didn't answer.

'I must have done something,' he said. 'Tell me, please, I don't want to spend my last night here with you like this.'

My eyes welled up, and I broke down. 'You're leaving me tomorrow, and I don't know what we're going to do,' I sobbed. 'I can't handle the distance anymore. I mean, where is this going? What do we do next? Do we save enough money to visit each other God knows when? I can't go on like this,' I said.

I stared out of the window as the waitress set our drinks down.

'Don't say that,' he said as the waitress left, 'I love you, and I want us to be together all the time; I just don't know how to do that right now. It's not like I could get a job here and stay, is it?'

'I don't know. I'm sure there would be a lot of red tape,' I said.

'We'll figure it out and make it work. We just need a little more time.'

We ate our food, and arriving home; we locked ourselves in my bedroom to make love for the last time.

\* \* \*

We got up early the next morning so that Trevor could say goodbye to my mom and George before they headed off to work.

He checked in for his Virgin Atlantic flight, and we stood in the terminal together waiting for the flight to be called.

'I hope you had a good time here,' I said.

'I had a great time with you,' he said. 'Tell your mum again thanks for having me.'

'I will,' I said, fighting back my tears. 'I wish you didn't have to go.'

'I don't want to go,' he said, holding me tight. 'I love you.'

'I love you too. Call me and let me know you got home, okay?'

'I will.'

He kissed me one last time, then turned and was gone.

# CHAPTER 17 – INDEPENDENCE DAY

The trip home from the airport was quite stressful. After I watched the plane take off, I must not have been paying attention to where I was going because I suddenly found myself outside the terminal. There were parked airplanes, ground staff wandering around and baggage carts whooshing by. I tried to backtrack, but I became even more lost. I ended up on the other side of the terminal and had to walk the length of the terminal to get inside once again. I asked security where the parking lot was, and they helped me back to where my car was parked.

I got into my car and started home, running into traffic by the Ted Williams tunnel. I missed the 93 South Exit and got stuck on the Massachusetts Turnpike with no clue where I was going. Tears streaming down my face, I thought about how the day could not get any worse. The love of my life had just left to go home, I got lost in the airport, and now I was on some endless highway heading to nowhere.

Thankfully, I saw the signs for 95 South and finally got back to familiar territory. My mom was waiting up for me when I got home.

'What the hell happened? I was worried. It's really late. Was his flight delayed?'

'No, I got lost. Lost in the airport and then in Boston.'

'What were you doing in Boston?' she asked.

'I took a wrong turn outside the tunnel and ended up on the Turnpike.'

'Oh, that's horrible.'

'Tell me about it. I was practically hyperventilating in the car. After an hour of being lost, I thought I was going to have an anxiety attack,' I said.

'I'm glad you got yourself home safe,' she said.

'Trevor said thanks again for having him,' I said, sitting down on the couch next to her.

'Oh, he's welcome. I liked him in the end.'

'I could tell. I wasn't sure how long it was going to take you, but what's not to like? Do you really think it's all going to work out?' I asked.

'I'm sure it will honey. You both need to work out a plan. I am not sure what that is – coming from two different countries … What I do know is you are not the only two people who have had this problem and eventually worked it out to be together,' she said, encouragingly.

'You're right. I just know I cannot have a full life without him.' I leaned over to my mom, placing my head on her shoulder.

'It'll be okay,' she said, putting her arm around me and pulling me toward her to hold me, 'I'm sure you will both work it out. I know it's not your strong suit, but you just have to be patient.'

I spoke to Trevor on the phone after he had arrived home. His dad had picked him up from the airport that morning. He slept for most of the flight. I told him how I got lost in the airport and on the drive home.

'I am so sorry this happened to you, but I am so glad you got home safely.'

'Me too. We need to finalize a plan. I can't do this anymore, and I know you can't either. These last three weeks proved that there is no one else for me, Trev. It's always been you, and it's always going to be you.'

'I feel the same way about you, Kerri. I know we'll figure it out. Please give us a little more time. Let's schedule a call in two weeks.'

'Okay. In the meantime, I'll go through the phone book and make some calls. Hopefully, I'll be advised how it's possible to live and work in each other's country legally.'

I felt drained of hope when we hung up. I guess I must have been thinking that after our three weeks together, all of a sudden, our whole situation would simply solve itself, and we'd live happily ever after. Now, I found myself alone again with no job, and nothing to do except wait.

Over the next two weeks, I busied myself with cleaning and reorganizing my room. I helped my mom out around the house by cleaning, grocery shopping, and taking over laundry duty. The gym was a great distraction. I could spend hours there taking aerobic classes and laps in the pool. I met a new friend who showed me how to exercise with weights. Some days I'd drive to visit my father and grandparents.

No longer commuting to Boston and getting home late, I had more time at night to hang out with Mel when she got home from work. Our talks would focus on how it would be possible for me to move to England or for Trevor to move here.

'Have you figured out the logistics of how you two can live and work in each other's country?' asked Mel.

'I have made several calls, and the long and short of it is that without obtaining a Visa through a job or having a Fiancée Visa, I am pretty much shit out of luck.'

'There is one easy solution to that.'

'What's that?' I asked.

'Well, it's pretty obvious, isn't it? Get married.'

'You of all people know I would marry Trevor in a heartbeat. Of course, it would be nice to have a 'normal' relationship where we could live together, eventually get engaged and not feel rushed in planning our wedding.'

'I know, but what if that is the only way you two can be together in the same country?'

'If that were the only way, I would do it. I think Trevor would too.'

'When is he going to call you again?' asked Mel.

'This Saturday, it will be two weeks since we last spoke. I am hoping he'll have come up with a plan.'

* * *

Trevor called on Saturday as scheduled.

'You sound tired. You're still working nights?'

'Yes,' he groaned, 'eleven at night until eight in the morning, it sucks. It doesn't help that my dad calls every day at noon to ask my mum if I'm up yet. He doesn't seem to get it. He thinks I'm a lazy sod lying around in bed all day.'

'What's his problem? What does your mom say?' I asked.

'She just laughs. She tells him every time that I've only been in bed an hour or two; he still does the same thing each day.'

'I'm sorry, baby.'

'It's all right. I keep thinking I should call him up at two in the morning and ask him why he isn't up yet.'

'Yeah, you should.' I laughed. 'He might think differently about it then.'

'So, I was thinking, what do you think about moving over here and living here with me, or I could move over there and live with you?' I asked.

'Well, I don't think either one of us could work legally, and I want to try and get a proper IT job and acquire some experience before I try and make it in another country,' he said.

'I could move over to you,' I said hopefully, 'I don't see why I couldn't resume my travel agent career in England. Would your parents mind? I could help clean and do whatever else was required of me to pay my way.'

'I can ask,' he answered, but he sounded uncertain.

So I decided for us. I was moving over to England. I had two years' experience as a travel agent. If I wasn't legally allowed to get a job, I didn't doubt I'd be able to find a job working under the table cleaning hotel rooms and/or waitressing like I did in college. I was sure his parents wouldn't mind me living there temporarily while looking for a job. Trevor was not comfortable moving to the States without having any experience in IT, and we agreed we didn't want another year apart. Me moving to England seemed our only option.

Checking my bank balance, I found I had just enough money for a flight. I called my friends at NLG in Boston and booked a reasonably priced return flight to Gatwick leaving on the Fourth of July with a return date three months ahead. I figured I could change the return flight later if needed. I would bring only my clothes, and I'd leave everything else behind in my room. I knew my parents would understand, but I also knew my mom would be heartbroken that I would be leaving indefinitely. I wasn't a kid anymore, I was almost 22, and I had watched my friends date their boyfriends for years, and some were recently getting engaged. Why couldn't Trevor and I have the same opportunities?

With my decision made, I waited to call Trevor the next day to find out if he had spoken to his parents about me moving over.

* * *

'Trevor, please explain to your parents, it's not for good. My thoughts are that we save enough money to rent our first flat together. Also, if we found an affordable flat in the city, we wouldn't have to worry about buying a car anytime soon.'

'I didn't have a chance the other day to ask because I overslept and was running late for work, but I'll ask them after I get off the phone. I am sure they'll understand.'

'Please also let them know I'm happy to pay my way with food and rent.'

'I will. I am sure this plan will work. They see how unhappy I am without you, and I've told them I want to marry you. I don't want to lose you, Kerri.'

'I don't want to lose you either.'

Hearing us say we didn't want to lose one another confirmed I was making the right decision to be the one to move over.

'What day were you thinking of moving over?'

'Is today soon enough?' I said excitedly… 'Seriously, though, I was thinking July Fourth. That way, I would be able to have one last Fourth of July barbeque on the third with my family. I'll leave the Fourth and arrive to you on the fifth. I'll take the red-eye again.'

'That's two weeks away. I don't think that would be a problem at all. I know my parents will say yes. They love you, why wouldn't they?'

We agreed we'd speak in a couple of days.

* * *

I knew his parents loved me as I did them. They both had expressed their feelings often enough when I was there. They were not ignorant of the fact our first year of dating was extremely hard on both of us. I felt positive they would support our decision. Over the next two days, I started to sort through my closet and bureau. It was hard to be selective because I wanted to pack everything I owned. I started to sort through my clothes thinking of the seasons in England, date nights, possible interviews and everyday wear; this helped me to be choosier.

It was hard not to take all my special mementos, but I knew I had to be practical of what I packed with only being allowed one suitcase and carry-on on the plane. Most of my suitcase was packed with T-shirts, sweatshirts, jeans, socks, pajamas, toiletries, sneakers and some pumps. I also chose two blouses and skirts for interviewing and our date nights. Thinking of our future flat together, I made sure to pack some framed photos of us taken at Tower Bridge, Oxford, Boston, Fenway Park and New Hampshire.

A couple of days later, Trevor called me back with the good news! I got the okay to move over!

Later that night, I prepared myself to break the news to my mom. She was lying on her bed watching TV. George was out with buddies. After I told her my decision to move over to England, her eyes widened, yet within minutes her expression changed to acceptance. After all, it wasn't as though she hadn't overheard all my planning with Trevor on the phone over these past few weeks. I waited for the arguments to follow. In my house, screaming is our normal way to respond when we have a disagreement with one another. So it was a pleasant surprise when I only received concerned questions from my mother.

'Is there no way Trevor can move here to the States? I am sure he could get a job doing something?'

'Trevor could, but not in IT. That's the problem; he's set on gaining more experience in IT in England and feels he'd be overlooked by an agency with him being young and inexperienced.'

'I am okay with him moving here, and you both could live here in your room. You could get another job, and he could work under the table until he found something,' she pleaded.

'Trevor and I did talk about that. He's only had an admin job these last seven months. I can see his point with IT on the rise, and it's a high paying career. He feels he'll have more luck finding an entry level job in IT in England.

'I don't like it one bit,' she said.

'I know, but you have to understand he's not confident he'll find anything and doesn't wish to be a burden. I feel I'd have better chances in England because I've worked two years in travel and tourism. Overall, it's not a perfect solution because no matter what we do, one of our families will be upset.'

'You're my only daughter; you're supposed to stay here, meet a nice guy, date for a while, move in, and then plan your wedding. I didn't plan this for you; I didn't expect this at all.'

I always knew what my mom wanted for Joe and me. She had told us enough times while growing up. That was her plan for us, not mine. I never dreamed of staying in our hometown and raising a family there.

Since I was 17 and traveled to England, I fell in love with the country. I had wanted to see more of the world and pictured a life of traveling abroad. For once, I needed to worry about my happiness, not the happiness of everyone else.

'I know what you want for me, but I always knew it was him. He's the only person I want to be with, and I need to try to make this work. If it doesn't, at least, I tried.'

* * *

The weeks that followed flew by. I was busy. I canceled magazine subscriptions, canceled my car insurance, and my parents said they'd deal with my car. I visited my grandparents, my father and brothers and made plans to hang out with my friends one last time before I left. I selected cards for my parents, Joe, Nana, and Grandpa, my aunt, and Melani. I wrote a letter in each card letting them all know how much I loved them and would miss them greatly. My only request was for them not to read it until I left.

Several days before I left, George surprised me. 'I thought we could have some time together before you leave. I was thinking a nice morning ride on the bike out to Cape Cod. We could grab lunch and walk around. Would you like to do that?'

My mother always said George cared for both Joe and me, unfortunately for us, he wasn't one for words. He would use action instead. That action was shown with fixing our cars mostly. The easy conversations I witnessed over the years with my friends and their dad was something I envied with both my dad and George. As kids, the sum total of our interaction with George was being told what to do, or else. Now that Joe and I were young adults, our relationship with George didn't change.

Since this was the first and only time George ever wanted to spend time with me, I agreed. 'That sounds really nice, but you should know I am a little nervous, never have ridden on a motorcycle before.'

'You'll be fine.'

Riding on the back of George's bike was exciting and terrifying at the same time. I made sure to hold on tight to his waist. I was paranoid if we hit a bump I'd fly off the back of it.

'Make sure when we make turns you turn your body with the bike. If you don't, we could tip it!' George yelled over his shoulder at me.

'Oh, OK!' I yelled back over the overwhelming noise of the bike's engine.

We pulled up near the Cape Cod waterfront an hour later. 'In the mood for burgers?' George asked.

'Sure, they smell great from here.'

After entering the nearest burger joint, we placed our orders and sat in silence. George and I never really talked a lot on our own, it was always the four of us, or Joe and I would retort one worded answers to his questions. We never spent any one on one time together, and I am sure he was just as stuck for words as I was.

'So do you have everything packed and ready for your trip?' George said, finally breaking the silence.

'Yes, I can only take so much unless I want to pay more, of course. After Trevor being here, I only had enough money left for a round trip ticket.'

'I'm sure you're all set, and if you need anything from your room, your mom will send it no problem.'

'Yeah, I thought Mom would be OK with that.'

After we finished our meals less than an hour later, we walked to the waterfront. What a gorgeous view. I enjoyed smelling the sea salt in the air and watching the many boats coming in from the ocean and docking in Cape Cod Bay. After the stress of travel preparation, it was a breath of fresh air to come to this seaside town.

'You ready to go?' asked George.

That was quick; I think we had less than a 30-minute walk and ten minutes of enjoying the view. But as I was with George, I should have known that our time would not be the entire day as I had assumed.

'Sure.' I was grateful for the outing, but I was also feeling quite annoyed by the abruptness of it all.

\* \* \*

Two days later Joe, Mom, George and I drove to my nana's town with our pre-purchased tickets for the VFW – Veterans of Foreign Wars, Fourth of July cookout, which is held every year on the third of July. It was something we did as a family every year.

There was a DJ blasting music from inside the VFW that also could be heard over the outdoor speakers. Each year, we chose a table outside. I always enjoyed the aromas when walking past the grills loaded with marinated chicken pieces, beef burgers, hot dogs, and sausages. The side dishes were the same each year; coleslaw, macaroni and potato salad, chips, fries, and corn on the cob. Desert was typically cake, pastries, ice creams and watermelon.

We got our table and waited for my grandparents and aunt to arrive.

'Hi, Kerri!' shouted my nana as she walked toward us with Grandpa and my aunt following behind.

'Hi, Nana and Grandpa, how are you both doing?'

'I am good, Grandpa's doing well too.'

'So are you all packed up and ready? You're leaving us tomorrow right? I really don't want you to go,' said Nana.

'Yes, all packed up; I am sad to leave but excited to go.'

'How long do you think you'll live there?' asked my aunt.

'I don't know exactly. I booked a round trip ticket to return in three months 'time. If all goes well, I'll change the return date. If not I'll be back in October.'

'Well, I'm gonna miss you, and I wish you the best of luck,' said my aunt.

'Thank you, I'll miss you all too. I need to do this; we cannot stomach the idea of seeing each other once every six months again. Right now, this seems like the only way to be together.'

'Let's get our meals and sit down and have a nice dinner together,' said my mom.

After enjoying our meals, the seven of us walked up to the main street with our chairs to pick a spot and get settled for the Fourth of July parade. It was a blast as always. The clowns were hysterical throwing candy out to the kiddies. I enjoyed watching the many handmade floats passing by. It was awesome to see all the uniformed men and woman receive applause for their time in service. The big bands from nearby high schools sounded amazing, and each of their choreographed performances was timed perfectly to the music they played.

The day was bittersweet. I was surrounded by my family enjoying the parade. For the first time in my life, my family tradition didn't feel the same. I felt a part of me was already gone. The colorful, noisy parade marched by me, but my heart and mind were already in England.

You knew the parade was over each year when the fire trucks were followed by several rounds of gunshots. It's an exciting, loud event.

After the fireworks, everyone came over to me for one last hug, to wish me well and say goodbye. There was not a dry eye among us, apart from my brother who didn't seem even mildly affected. He stood there looking uncomfortable. I wasn't sure if he wanted to say goodbye to me or not. We hugged nevertheless, and I kissed him.

'I'll miss you, Joe, please watch out for Mom and George. I'll call as often as I can. Know I love you very much and want only the best for you.'

'I know,' was all he said.

\* \* \*

The next day flew by … Before I knew it, it was time for me to be picked up by Mel for my two-hour check-in at the airport. I had asked her to drive me to the airport because my mother said driving me would be too hard for her.

'It's that time, isn't it?' she said while I lugged my suitcase and duffle bag out on the drive getting ready for Mel. My parents followed me outside, my mom holding my carry-on.

'Yes, I'm going to miss you so much, but I know I've made the right decision.'

'I'd drive you, but I just can't,' said my mom.

'I know.'

Melani pulled up just then. 'It's not every day you drive your best friend to the airport knowing she'll be moving to another country. I am so happy and sad right now.'

'I know, Mel. Please don't get me started. I am doing all I can to hold it together,' my mom said, clearly holding back her tears.

I walked over to my mom and hugged her. I was feeling a lot of emotions. I loved her. She was always there for us growing up, always trying to protect us from our dad. She was our provider for all we had; giving us love and support. Frankly, it was weird saying goodbye, especially not knowing when I would return. I was also feeling very sad and guilty for leaving, and at the same time feeling extremely happy for the future I had dreamt of having over the last year with Trevor. This would be a huge transition for all of us, but I knew over time she'd eventually be OK. I didn't feel I needed to worry too much because she had George and Joe, her career and our family was only 40 minutes away. We wouldn't lose touch because we'd make the time to talk each month. Me moving out and flying across the Atlantic may not have been what either of us had envisioned for my future, but it was definitely time, and I was ready.

'I love you, Mom. I'll call as soon as I can. Don't forget the five-hour difference, and I won't be there officially until the fifth.'

'I love you too. I'm going to think of it as if you are off to college. I cannot think of it as you leaving me.'

What do you say to this? I felt stomped by this response. It actually took me by surprise. For me, it was a chance of a lifetime to follow my heart and my dreams. For her, I felt me moving out was more a form of betrayal. We were so close, but she needed to figure out how to get on with her life without me at home. I hugged her again, and, this time, a little tighter.

George walked over and hugged me. 'Take care of yourself. Have a safe flight.'

'I will. I'll call you both in a couple of days.'

I put my luggage in the trunk. It was four o'clock, and we really needed to go; traffic was always horrific at this hour driving into Boston. We loaded my suitcase and duffel bag into her car.

'It was nice seeing you two. I'll take good care of Kerri. She'll make it to the airport on time,' said Mel.

'Thank you for driving her, Mel, I really appreciate it,' said my mom.

'You're welcome.'

We got into the car and drove off.

An hour later, we arrived at the Departures curbside, and Mel helped me get my bags out.

'You're sure about this?' she said, pulling me close.

'Yes, I think so.'

'Call me when you get there so that I know you're okay.'

'I will. Thank you for driving me.'

'No problem, Kerri. It will all work out. I really believe so. Say 'Hi' to Trevor for me, and good luck.'

She got into her car and drove off. I turned, picked up my bags and headed into the terminal. I checked in, got through security and hurried through the gate.

I quickly found my seat on the plane by the window and stowed my carry-on. I sat down and watched the other passengers boarding.

Sitting there, I started to picture the moment I would finally be reunited with Trevor. It wasn't a six-month separation this time; it had only been a month.

Did he change in a month's time? Were his parents really okay with me living with them?

I wanted this transition to be as easy on everyone as possible. I knew me moving in with them wouldn't be uncomplicated by any means, but I hoped they knew I was grateful and excited for the opportunity.

The seatbelt sign came on, and the captain announced that they were preparing for takeoff. I fastened my seatbelt and opened up the window shade. My stomach churned, and I realized how nervous I was. I was really doing this. There was no turning back now. I was leaving everything behind. This was it.

I didn't sleep at all during the eight-hour flight. I relished the fact that I was free and about to start my life over and begin anew. My life before consisted of only work and some fun on the weekends. It was boring, I had the same routine day after day, and I felt completely alone. Moving to England and living with Trevor full-time, I felt together the possibilities were endless.

We landed early, and I was impatient as we taxied to the gate and waited for the passengers before me to disembark. At last, I grabbed my carry-on and fought my way out of the terminal. I felt a twinge of déjà vu as I tidied myself up in the same bathroom as I had done the year before, and headed off to baggage claim.

I wandered out of the Arrivals door; I couldn't believe I was here in England and officially living here now. I stopped abruptly to look around at the direction boards, and a rushing passenger behind almost tripped over me, knocking my carry-on off my shoulder.

'Sorry,' he gasped. 'I didn't see you there.'

'Yeah, sorry,' I said and bent down to pick up my bag.

It was then, as I stood back up that I thought I caught a glimpse of my name; a flash of black marker on a blank white sheet of paper. I looked again, but it was gone. I continued along the chained out corridor searching the crowd, hopefully.

'Kerri!' I heard that familiar voice.

I turned to my right, and there he was, in his favorite leather jacket, T-shirt, and jeans; all smiles and gorgeous as ever. He was holding a poster board and had penned big black letters spelling out my name.

It was euphoric seeing him. I kept thinking *we did it! We really did it!* I sprinted to him, clumsily banging my bags against my legs as I ran.

'Trevor!' I dropped my bags and threw my arms around him, almost knocking him over.

Trevor was laughing excitedly by my reaction.

'I'm glad this is finally happening,' I said to him.

'Me too, you ready to go home?'

I nodded.

He picked up my luggage, and we walked out of the airport together and into our new life.

# CHAPTER 18 – ALWAYS

It was our first Christmas Eve together. After three months of living with his parents, Trevor and I decided it was time to find a place of our own. For the last two months, we lived on the third floor in our two-bedroom flat in a beautiful town called Cheltenham. Though I had lost my job as a travel agent two weeks before Christmas and didn't have money in my pocket, I was still extremely happy with how everything turned out.

That night, Trevor did his magic in the kitchen like he always does. He knew how to cook so well because he was taught at a young age by his grandmother. It was wonderful helping him prepare dinner. We peeled and cut carrots and potatoes and filled two additional pots with peas and corn. For the first time in my life, I got to stuff a chicken and cover it with strips of bacon. While dinner was cooking, we set the table, and Trevor opened a bottle of wine.

'It's been brilliant living on our own these last two months. I'm so glad you made the decision to move here. It was what we needed.'

'It was, and I'm still in shock that I live here with you. I am so grateful to wake up to you every day knowing we are building a life together.'

Sixteen months before when I first visited Trevor, we were enjoying drinks and concerts on the T.V. His family and I were sitting on the couch looking through their photo albums in the living room when Phil Collins started to sing '*Always*'. I was mesmerized by the lyrics. This song hit a chord with me. I felt Phil Collins was seriously singing his song for Trevor and me.

Trevor leaned over and asked me to dance right then and there.

'This is our song; this is it!

He nodded, pulling me from the couch and held me as we started to dance. He held me closer to him so he could whisper the lyrics to me as we danced.

*'Dreams will all come true being here with you*
*And time will fly*
*Caring each day more than the day before*
*Till spring rolls by*

*And when the springtime has gone*
*Will my love linger on?*

*I'll be loving you, always*
*With a love that's true, always*
*When the things that you plan need a helping hand*
*I will understand, always, always*

*Days may not be fair, always*
*But that's when I'll be there, always*
*Not for just an hour, no, no, not for just a day*
*No not for just a year but always*

*Until forever is through*
*Until there's just me and you, always'*

Written by Kenny Gorelick and Walter N Afanasieff.

Looking back over the last 16 months, it's ironic how the lyrics to our song were true. We have been through so much this past year, and we never gave up on one another. I knew we'd be together always.

What a wonderful first Christmas Eve this was turning out to be. We had just eaten a gorgeous roasted dinner with yummy red wine and now we were enjoying listening to a Sting CD Trevor had put on earlier.

Trevor got up from the table and walked over to the CD player. I wasn't sure what he was going to put on next, and then I heard Phil Collins, and I knew. He was playing our song.

He came over to me still seated at the table. 'May I have this dance?'

I took his hand.

As we were dancing, I couldn't believe how much my life had changed in five short months. I looked around and felt so blessed. Dancing with Trevor was reminding me of how much our relationship was like a 'dance' that we had been doing throughout the years. We had fallen in love all those years ago, had to be separated, then fell in love again, were separated yet again, but still working to be together. And here we were now living together in our first apartment.

These last two months had flown by; I had experienced working full-time as a travel agent illegally, and Trevor was fully employed in a first line IT support position. With our combined salaries, we had saved enough money to purchase our first car, a couch, an IKEA build it yourself full-size bed and an IKEA kitchen table with four matching chairs. Our kitchen came with the basics; tiny four-burner gas stove, microwave, and dorm size fridge/freezer. Next to the fridge stood our two in one washer/dryer machine; I'd never used appliances this small nor had I ever seen or used a two in one washer dryer before. We lucked out when his parents gave us their orange Denby cookware set; some dishes, cutlery, and glasses. As far as I was concerned, we could have lived in a cardboard box, and it wouldn't have mattered. I was so happy and thought this night couldn't get any better.

As our song finished, Trevor lifted my chin and kissed me. He then got down on one knee.

'What are you doing?'

'If you let me, I am going to propose to you.' Trevor looked nervous.

'Oh, my God, are you serious?'

'Kerri, you were my first love, and I know you'll be my last. You are my life; my past, my present, and future. Will you marry me?'

Trevor then slipped on my engagement ring. I was shocked again to see it was the original ring I had picked out 16 months ago for my twenty-first birthday present. A solid gold band adorned with emeralds and diamonds. I never got to have that ring because when the jeweler sized it to fit my finger, all the jewels fell out, and we had to choose another ring.

'You always manage to surprise me … Wait, did you really go to the jeweler this week with Matt from work or was that bag actually meant for me?'

'I thought you were going to find out; you are so good at finding things out. I had a feeling you'd want to put my coat away when I got home because you've been doing that every night since you lost your job. As you took it off me, I slipped out the box and put it in my suit jacket, then went to the bathroom to hide the ring. You almost ruined my surprise.'

'Wow, you're good.'

'Kerri, you haven't answered my question, is it a yes?' he asked, looking worried.

'YES! Of course, yes!'

We sealed the deal with a passionate kiss.

* * *

*Today was the day!*

On February 24th 1996 by the Justice of the Peace on a rainy Saturday afternoon, we were ready to be married.

I was told rain on your wedding day is a sign of 'good luck'. Our ceremony was quick but beautiful.

We had a small wedding; only nine people in attendance. Our guest list included: Trevor's parents, both sets of his grandparents and his brother. We couldn't afford the proper attire; Trevor always wanted to wear a top hat, waistcoat and have tails on his suit jacket. For me, I always imagined a white or ivory form-fitting dress, my hair up in a bun with a gorgeous bouquet of autumn-colored flowers. Instead, we bought a new two-piece suit for Trevor, and I settled on a beautiful form-fitting black dinner dress with a red blazer. His parents provided the flowers; a wrist corsage for me, which I pinned to the left collar of my red blazer, and a matching boutonniere for Trev. The most expensive item we splurged on was two 28 carat thick gold wedding bands that we had engraved '24 Feb 1996' inside each one.

Our best man was Chris, Trevor's best friend. Chris brought his girlfriend, Rachael. I didn't have a maid of honor or bridesmaids, and Trevor's dad gave me away since none of my family could afford to travel to England.

At 12 noon sharp, we stood there in front of the Justice of the Peace surrounded by Trevor's family and friends and said our vows. Trevor being nervous started stuttering. This didn't happen once, but twice when he had to say 'I know not of any lawful impediment.' Trevor kept saying, 'I know not of any unlawful impediment.' By the third time, he said it correctly, and we all had a good laugh because of it. I didn't really care if he screwed up on our vows, all I wanted to hear was 'I do' and 'I pronounce you husband and wife.' It was the quickest wedding I ever attended, and it was mine. In less than thirty minutes, we were pronounced husband and wife and kissed each other solemnly.

After we signed our wedding certificate, we all headed back to our flat for the reception. The stuffed mushrooms, chicken wings, sausage rolls, salad and champagne we had prepared the previous night were a hit. Trevor's grandmother made our decorative wedding cake. It was a small two layered fruit cake covered in yellow marzipan beautifully decorated with yellow marzipan roses on top of the cake, accented by white icing that looked like pieces of lace on all four sides of the cake. Trevor and I were extremely grateful for her kind gesture. Unfortunately, most Americans grew up with a dislike for fruit cake, and I was one of them. When it came time to cut our cake, it was quite an eventful moment. No matter how hard Trevor and I tried to cut through the icing, we found it very difficult to say the least. After three attempts proceeded with hysterical laughter including ours, his grandmother did the honors. Not wanting to disappoint his grandmother, I made sure to eat a full slice of fruitcake.

After we got married, we lived in England for an additional 20 months, before moving back to the States in November 1997 after enjoying a 30-day cruise from England to the Dominic Republic. We then flew to Boston where my family was excited to have us both back in the States. We moved because we wanted to start a family eventually and felt we'd be able to afford a good size home with a backyard and have better-paying jobs than we could in England.

I cannot believe almost 20 years have gone by so quickly. This February 24th, 2016 will be our 20th anniversary. I feel blessed to have a wonderful supportive husband and three lovely children.

A special note: Trevor will always be my Davy Jones. After I heard the sad news of Davy Jones passing on February 29th 2012, I wanted to know more about him and looked him up on the internet. I was shocked and found it a bit symbolic to read Davy Jones shared Trevor's birthday. They were born 26 years apart, on the same day, December 30th. I wish Davy Jones was still alive. I would have loved to meet and thank him in person. He'll never know how much he influenced me to want to marry a British man.

## KERRI'S LETTER TO YOU

Dear Reader,

By now you and I are truly friends. You have seen my downs and my ups, and you've stuck with me through my life. My wish for you reading this book, my true life memoir, is to see all I have gone through, all I have witnessed and had to deal with.

Over the last twenty-one years, I can honestly say I've grown and learned a lot about myself. I have learned I'll always be a suicide survivor and what that means to me is I will always have dark thoughts, regardless that it's been 29 years since I attempted to take my life. I find I have my dark thoughts or demons as I sometimes call them when I am extremely stressed and feeling out of control. My mind will immediately bring up the thoughts that I am not good enough; I am a burden, and everyone would be better off without me. Of course, those thoughts are further from the truth. I used to think I would never feel that hopelessness ever again, especially when I am truly happily married, and we produced three great kids. But that's my reality. Over the last twenty-one years, Trevor has always been my rock and has encouraged me to talk about whatever I am feeling, no matter how bad. This has helped me grow as a person and become better at dealing with those thoughts. I finally love myself for who I am, imperfections and all, and I know I am loved beyond measure by my husband and our children, and that's what LIFE is all about.

My further wish is that you learn the life lessons that I had to learn the hard way:

I would always suggest being honest and open to a trusted confidant, such as your mother, best friend or partner. For me, I've had the opportunity to always feel comfortable talking to

Trevor and Melani for the last twenty-one years, especially during the time I had a miscarriage in 2003. This was my first miscarriage after carrying two healthy pregnancies and dealing with the death of our child. Trevor and I had to talk honestly and openly because it didn't only affect me; it affected him and our girls, who at the time were four and two and a half and didn't understand why Mommy had a baby in her belly one day and didn't the next. I found it healthy to deal with the loss of our baby by speaking to a psychiatrist. I knew I was falling into another depression over the loss of our baby, and I wanted to be proactive in my healing mentally as well as physically. Having not isolated myself with my grief, I made sure to speak to my husband, my close friends, and spent a month visiting a trained professional. After some time, and given the 'OK' from our doctor, I felt ready to focus on the hope of having another baby. I love that help is one letter away from hope and talking when in such pain is one of the best forms of healing. After four months, I became pregnant again, and in the summer of 2004, Trevor and I welcomed our son, Luke.

Another way I have coped with depression and bullying, even at my current age has been to use practical steps such as reflecting on positive thoughts to alter the pattern of depressive thinking. I truly believe your inner world reflects your outer world. By setting small goals and celebrating your successes and achievements, you will help create self-worth. I was inspired by watching the movie The Secret. The purpose of the film The Secret is to convey this very message that our 'thoughts become things' and we are all 'living magnets'. We all need to always be mindful of what we are thinking today, throughout the day because that's how we create our tomorrows. When I was writing this book, I didn't have all the funds necessary to publish it. So I decided to create a GoFundMe account. Now it was really hard for me to ask my friends online, in person or over the phone to help me raise money for my book. I kept thinking of 'WHY' I wanted to write my book and what I wanted to accomplish by writing it. And my 'WHY' which was to hopefully save a life, to prevent further suicides and to stop bullying, was bigger than my negative thoughts of what my friends might think of me for asking. During the four months it took me to raise the funds needed to publish my book, I received 95% positive feedback. Most of the comments were very dear and personal, and I was very touched and sometimes cried from all the love and encouraging messages I was receiving. The remaining 5% was negativity toward my GoFundMe campaign not from close friends, but from acquaintances. They said in PMs on Facebook that I should 'kill myself'. That I was 'stealing people's hard earned money' and that I was a 'sinner' and should have 'died.' These hateful bullying messages hurt me. I am not going to lie, but they also inspired me to continue to reach my goal and pursue my dream of writing my book. It blew my mind that at the age of 42, I was still being bullied, but I laughed it off and used any anger I felt in receiving those messages and turned it into positivity, fueling the fire to continue. I also would wish them well and forgive each person who said those horrible words. Because in my mind, those people are hurting inside for whatever reason, and my invitation to help me raise money brought those feelings out. So I wish them healing.

A great way to fight off depression is in taking practical steps in establishing a workout regime to increase endorphins, which are natural fighters of depression and choosing a healthy diet. I have worked out since I was little with my mom to Jane Fonda tapes, and this built a great foundation on the importance of exercise. For the last twenty-one years, I have committed to working out at least an hour five days per week. I am very proud of myself and enjoy the sweat and the burn after a workout. I enjoy cardio workouts, kickboxing, and made two athletic goals over the last eight years. The first one was to participate in a marathon and a half. I signed up to walk in the Avon - The Walk To End Breast Cancer in 2007. I trained for nine months and joined a team of amazing women, and over two days in Charlotte, NC I walked a total of 39.3 miles and raised $2000. My second goal was to run a 5K when I turned 40. I trained for four months with the C25K app program and ran my first 5K within 30 minutes. Over the last five years, my family and I have taken a closer look at our diet and have opted for a meat free lifestyle. Trevor and I are vegan's and our children are vegetarians. It wasn't an easy transition, we are still learning, and we've never felt healthier. I would also suggest that if you have a dream, something good you really want to achieve in your life, to tell others about it and find people to support your dream to make it come true. For example, if I didn't ask Sophie to give Trevor the bracelet and letter explaining how I felt when she did, would things have worked out differently? Sophie was a key element in empowering my dream to be with my Davy Jones. There is great power when you collaborate with your friends, colleagues, and family. This collaboration builds a wonderful support in networking, and it all starts with communication.

Overall, the power of gratitude is something I take very seriously because of what I have been through and witnessed growing up. I make it a point to be thankful for ALL I have each and every day the minute I wake up. Before I get out of bed, I think about my 10 things I am most grateful for. I came by this idea by reading *The Ultimate Gift by Jim Stovall,* a book I highly recommend reading. My list changes weekly, overall I am grateful for EVERYTHING. For the past year, I have been a part of a Dream Builder group, and it's been wonderful reading other's posts upon posts of what they are thankful for and being a part of that too. Taking the time each day to see what you have and are grateful for, instead of what you don't have is an important tool to truly live a happier life. Giving thanks is enormous, and I suggest you write down what you are grateful for each and every day. Once you make gratitude a daily routine, you'll notice your life will change for the better. After Mary's suicide and the counseling provided at Sky's school, I made sure Sky was comforted and knew both Trevor and I were here for her any time she wanted to talk about Mary and how she was feeling and dealing with her death. The journal has been a huge help for Sky. She felt comfortable to write down her thoughts and share them with us when she wanted to. We also wanted Sky to understand that over time the pain of losing Mary will subside, but how she felt about her will always stay with her. It was OK if she was mad at Mary, but she also needed to forgive her and never forget her. Trevor and I sat down with our kids as a family to instill the best form of healing is communication and to never hold in their thoughts. No matter how they were feeling, we wanted them to feel comfortable talking to us about any and all situations they needed to deal with. We taught them to deal with a problem like I have; finding out the facts and breaking down the problem one piece at a time to find the best solution. This is always easier said than done, but after our discussions, we always manage to work the problem out, and life doesn't seem in despair as it had by sharing their feelings.

Life is hard; it's also very beautiful and rewarding. My biggest wish is after reading my book you will find you do not have to find a permanent solution to a temporary problem. Life is truly short, and those years in school are where I feel we find most of our pain, but, in reality, these problems are short.

There is a whole world waiting for you to show how truly extraordinary you are and are meant to be here.

You are worth it.

You, like me, are meant to be here and to create your best life now.

With Love, Kerri

# Pictures

Left Page: a selection of pictures 1994 - 1995 inc. Trevor and Kerri dancing in Trevor's parents living room; Caricature, Faneuil Hall, Boston, MA May 1995.

Top of this page: Trevor and Kerri making silly faces in Oxford, August 1994; Trevor age 15, 1987; Kerri age 20, journaling her memories of England; Wedding Day - "trying to cut our cake", February 24th 1996.

# Acknowledgements

They say: "It takes a village to raise a child." I can honestly say this memoir, gestated over the last three years, is my fourth child. It would not have come to fruition without the help of my village, made up of wonderful people both near to me and all over the world. As a first time author, I had no idea how much time, commitment and help I would need. Thankfully, that help has been forthcoming. My husband, Trevor, our children, Sky, Britain and Luke, and others in my village (you know who you are) have provided continual support and encouragement. My heartfelt thanks go out to all of you who have helped me make the dream of telling this story a reality. I am very blessed to know all of you and feel forever grateful.

If it were not for Teresa Haskins (a.k.a.TT), I wouldn't be alive. TT you were my guiding angel. You entered into my dysfunctional life when I needed you. Your love and friendship enabled me to be a little "normal" when I first moved to town, thoroughly drugged and depressed over being such a burden. You took the "Alien" I thought I was and made me feel "accepted". Had you not called on the night of my attempted suicide, I would not have had the opportunity to meet Trevor and to have three beautiful babies. I will be forever grateful for your friendship during my darkest days and for saving my life. Thank you TT.

It is to my 'Dave Jones', my husband, Trevor Gardner, that I owe my deepest thank you. No matter what venture I choose to undertake, you always support me. When it came to writing my book, you encouraged me to never give up on my dreams, and to never stop writing, no matter how difficult it was at times. You have been my guiding light, my rock. Thankfully, you have put up with all of my craziness, going on 21 years now. I cannot picture my life without my best friend. You not only helped me write this book, you took several hours over several months to help edit the draft as well. I THANK YOU and will love you ALWAYS Trevor.

To our children Sky, Britain and Luke, who have endured almost three years of my continual writing and editing - if they needed me when I wasn't at home or at work, they came to know that they would find me in front of my computer, writing my book. They have been wonderful and supportive and have given me the time I needed to write and have understood WHY writing this account has such significance to me. I am very blessed and grateful to have three great kids. I hope I have instilled in them how important it is to follow through with your passion and never give up on your dreams. You three and Daddy are my daily WHY. The reason I wake up every day happy and excited, feeling fortunate to still be here and have a fulfilling life.

Thank you to my very cool, very unique and lifelong friends Melani and Robin. I am super grateful for the times I called each of you to pick your brains at moments when I couldn't quite remember details that you knew. It meant a lot to me to have both of you read through the very first drafts of this book. I appreciated when I asked and received your very honest opinions. Throughout the last three years, no matter if I was struggling with the book or thought I was done, you were both my personal cheerleaders - through phone calls, texts or PMs on Facebook, you encouraged me to never give up. Thank you, Melani and Robin from the bottom of my heart! I love you both, and I couldn't have completed my book without you two!

After 24 months of writing and two state moves that brought us back to Raleigh, I decided it was time to find an editor. I came across a familiar name; Alice Osborn. Alice and I had met during my first year in Raleigh, back in 2007. We met through BNI – Business Networking International - when I was a sales rep for SendOutCards. I called Alice and we set up a meeting. I hired her after that meeting and am grateful for all the support and hours we both put in, collaborating on my book and all of her endless edits.

Thank you Alice, you were an important part in my journey, and I will forever be grateful!

After completing my edits with Alice, I decided to publish on Amazon.com. That's when fate intervened and I met Susie Bencen of iAMO Marketing Agency at http://www.i-amo.com. Susie is a one-stop shop! She's brilliant, patient, funny, a perfectionist, my friend who has helped me publish my book on Amazon. Her main focus is helping business owners grow their business and she also helps authors build a marketing platform they deserve at www.bestbookbuzz.com!

It's been an adventurous almost six months working with Susie. Through her guidance, I have learned how to become a better writer. I have had my book edited yet again and found areas where I was missing vital information for character building that I didn't think necessary at the time. I also learned more about memoir writing and how to build the foundation of my new author/speaking business. Susie hired Jennifer FitzGerald who designed the Book Cover. The three of us have put our heads together and, using an idea suggested by Susie's husband, my book cover came together beautifully! I loved all the help she gave me, her listening ear through all my tears and frustrations. No matter what, she has provided unending support to me on my book creation journey. I highly recommend Susie for all of you wanting advice with book marketing or growing your business. I'd also recommend Jennifer FitzGerald for book covers!

My village wouldn't be complete without all the support and generous donations I've received from my friends during my GoFundMe campaign. I didn't want to create a book that would sit on a shelf or stay in a box. I wanted to positively impact others' lives through my personal story. I wanted all who read my book to really hear me, to know that they would never have to take the measures I did to get rid of their pain. I needed them to understand that no matter where they are in their lives, their pain is temporary. That finding a permanent solution to a temporary problem is not and will never be the answer. If it weren't for all those who contributed to my GoFundMe campaign, I wouldn't have had the opportunity to fulfill my dream of helping others of all ages.

I want to give a BIG SHOUT OUT AND SAY A BIG THANK YOU TO ALL WHO CONTRIBUTED TO MY BOOK FUND AND WROTE LOVELY MESSAGES OF ENCOURAGEMENT:

Justin Adams; Azniv Adamian; Bobby Anderson; Betty Antibus; Louise Armstrong; Rebecca Arthur; Rita Badaloni; Lola Bahri; Tony Baldassarro; David Barber; Chris Baumann; Alan Watts; Kari Berg; Gayle Berkeley; Lexi Bishop; Brett Blair; Timothy Blomstrom; Daniel Bratton; Terri Brown; Toni Bua; Mark Campbell; Jennifer Cann; Nadia Caouette; Tania Cooper;

Lynne Daniel; Brian Darby; Nick Davel; Bill Davis; Chanette Deans; Therese Demare; Tony DeRico; Amit Dhull; Allison Diego; Victoria Erfle; Loui Ebeling; Maggi Flett; Lucie Flowers; Sharon Flynn; Melissa Forziat; Justin Gambino; Liesl Ganes; Leticia Garcia; Ty Garibay; Tina Gilmore; Rich Gp; Robert Hancock; Melani Harmon; Jason Harrison; Natasha Harris; Phillip Henderson; Nukhet Hendricks; Jenny Homan; Linda Horn; Michael Hughes; Black Hulk; Cory Jones; Katalin Kerekes; Suzanne Kieper; Vlad Kiraly; Anna Kochenkova; Andrew Krieman; Evelyn Larson; Tracy Leonardi; Rebecca Lichtman; Valerie Lipstein; Dina Love; Sharon Luke; Isabel Martins; Ann Marie Meyers; Lynn Milsho; David Mooney; Nicolle Neely; Veronica Nieves; Justin Nimergood; Emily Northern; Elizabeth O'Connor; Alice Osborn; Lucie Hola Owens; Bob Paddock; Amy Palmer; Heather Parisi; Diane Parker; Patty Pauletto; Sherril Paul; Nadia Pauwels; Carolyn Peacock; Shannon Pearson; Mary Perez; Lisa Petr; Karolyn Pierce; Loren Pinkney; Martin Ponce; Shawn Precourt; Vincent A. Preziotti; Marisa Garra-Punshon; Kristen and John Purcell; Andres Quintana; Teri Ranger; James Reilly; Evangelina Reynoso; Sonia Richardson; Angela Ritchie; Katherine Roberts; Chari Badua-Robinson; Naomi Rodrigues; Landa Ruweha; Nadya Saltykova; Becky Schaefer; Patrick Schuppe; Amazawa Sha; Laura Shortridge; Victory LeRoi Smith;

Nathalie Sorensson; Jennifer Spencer; Clari Stella; James Stewart; Mark Stone; Ric & Nic Swiner; Jem Switajewski; Filomena Tavares; Pamela Tetreault; Baloo Thomassen; Petra Thomas; Venetia Troop; Danii Turnbull; Debbie Turner; Chris & Rachael Twiner; Maria Unger; Martha Navarro Villarreal; Adelina Visentin; Karlene Walters; Susan Warner; Shelley Whizin; Shannon Wiggins; Tom Wiggins; Catriona Wright.

## About the Author

Kerri Gardner is a wife, mother, author, blogger, motivational speaker and suicide survivor.

Kerri graduated High School in 1992. She attended and graduated from Bay State College in Back Bay Boston in 1994. She considers herself a JILL of All TRADES.

Unlike other authors, Kerri didn't go to school for writing. Instead, for years after her attempted suicide, she started writing and collecting journals. She excelled in Literature class in both High School and College. Writing was always a true passion; she never believed it could be a career choice for her.

After years of "trying out several careers," including Travel Agent, Admin Assistant, IT Help Desk Support, Sales for 15 years through a home based business, Real Estate Agent and Dental Assistant. Finally, Kerri realized her true passion was to follow her heart and write that book that she had longed to write for years, yet was afraid to try. Being ashamed of her attempted suicide for 25 years, it took an email from her daughter's school explaining that a friend of her daughter killed herself over the weekend. While Kerri realized that the school would be taking whatever measures it could to ensure each student had help in dealing with the loss of their classmate and friend, the email was the catalyst that enabled Kerri to stop being ashamed of her suicide attempt and use her story to help others dealing with depression, bullying, and suicidal thoughts.

Kerri is an optimist, a true leader, and a believer that we all can have our "BEST LIVES NOW," regardless of the pain from the past or current circumstances. Kerri believes we live in an abundant world full of exciting new opportunities. She feels that with positive consistent action toward your dreams, you can produce a happier, more fulfilling life of your own design. Kerri lives with her husband Trevor and their three children in Raleigh, North Carolina.

Kerri Gardner is available for select speaking engagements. To inquire, please contact Kerri through her websites www.authorkerrigardner.com and www.kerriscrazylife.com

68459198R00177

Made in the USA
Charleston, SC
10 March 2017